People Management and Performance

D0141315

Do human resource management practices actually work? Debate has raged among practitioners and academics as to the validity of HRM theory in improving organisational performance. Indeed, while the rise of the knowledge-based economy means there is a greater reliance on getting the right people for the right jobs, increasing outsourcing has seen the HRM function itself come under serious threat. In this context, this ground-breaking study exploring the real-life effects of HRM policies is both fascinating and timely.

Sponsored by the Chartered Institute of Personnel and Development in the UK, John Purcell and his team from the University of Bath directly examine the experiences of a range of employees, both line managers and front-line staff, working for high profile organisations, including Tesco, Nationwide and Selfridges. Using empirical data from over 1000 in-depth interviews, research projects conducted between 1999 and 2007 create a new theoretical model which answers two very important questions:

- What are the links between strategic HR and business performance?
- How and why are HR practices linked to performance?

Moving away from the rhetoric of so much HRM debate and research, *People Management and Performance* explores what actually creates organisational commitment for different occupational groups, as well as the particular needs of professional knowledge workers. These are then linked to different HR practices and to the performance and productivity of specific aspects of the different businesses.

This is a vital new contribution to this area of study. It will prove invaluable to all students of HRM and business and management, as well as practitioners working in the field.

Professor John Purcell is currently Strategic Academic Adviser at Acas and Research Professor at the Industrial Relations Research Unit, Warwick Business School.

Dr Nicholas Kinnie is Reader in Human Resource Management in the School of Management, University of Bath.

Dr Juani Swart is a Senior Lecturer in Organisation Studies in the School of Management, University of Bath.

Dr Bruce Rayton lectures in Business Economics and Strategy in the School of Management, University of Bath.

Sue Hutchinson is Principal Lecturer in HRM at the University of West of England Business School.

People Management and Performance

John Purcell, Nicholas Kinnie,
Juani Swart, Bruce Rayton and
Sue Hutchinson

 Routledge
Taylor & Francis Group

LONDON AND NEW YORK

First published 2009
by Routledge
2 Park Square, Milton Park, Abingdon, Oxon, OX14 4RN

Simultaneously published in the USA and Canada
by Routledge
270 Madison Avenue, New York, NY 10016

Routledge is an imprint of the Taylor & Francis Group, an informa business

© 2009 John Purcell, Nicholas Kinnie, Juani Swart, Bruce Rayton
and Sue Hutchinson

Typeset in Times New Roman by
Bookcraft Ltd, Stroud, Gloucestershire
Printed and bound by
CPI Antony Rowe, Chippenham, Wiltshire

All rights reserved. No part of this book may be reprinted or
reproduced or utilised in any form or by any electronic, mechanical,
or other means, now known or hereafter invented, including
photocopying and recording, or in any information storage or
retrieval system, without permission in writing from the publishers.

British Library Cataloguing in Publication Data
A catalogue record for this book is available from the British Library

Library of Congress Cataloging in Publication Data
People management and performance / John Purcell ...
     p.cm.
     Includes bibliographical references
     1. Personnel management. 2. Performance. 3. Employee motivation.
     4. Employees—Social networks. 5. Corporate culture.
     I. Purcell, John, 1945–
HF5549.P4147 2007
658.3–dc22   2008001581

ISBN13: 978-0-415-42780-7 (pbk)
ISBN13: 978-0-415-42779-1 (hbk)

ISBN10: 0-415-42780-0 (pbk)
ISBN10: 0-415-42779-7 (hbk)

Contents

Figures

Tables

About the authors

Professor John Purcell is currently Strategic Academic Adviser at Acas and Research Professor at the Industrial Relations Research Unit, Warwick Business School. Between 1995 and 2007 he was Professor of Human Resource Management at the School of Management, University of Bath. For much of this period he was also Editor of the *Human Resource Management Journal*. He is also a Deputy Chairman of the Central Arbitration Committee.

Dr Nicholas Kinnie is Reader in Human Resource Management in the School of Management, University of Bath. He has conducted a range of research projects in the areas of people management and performance, the links between managing people and managing knowledge, and HR practices in telephone call centres. His work has been published widely in a range of academic and practitioner journals.

Dr Juani Swart is a Senior Lecturer in Organisation Studies in the School of Management, University of Bath. She specialises in Knowledge Management and the management of knowledge workers, building on her background as a Chartered Psychologist to develop both theory and practice perspectives on the knowledge-based view of the firm. Her recent research projects link the intellectual capital and HRM and performance debates. She has published widely in the areas of people management in knowledge-intensive firms, intellectual capital structures, systems approaches to knowledge management and network influences on strategic choice.

Dr Bruce Rayton lectures in Business Economics and Strategy in the School of Management, University of Bath. He is originally from the United States and has degrees from the University of Puget Sound and Washington University in St Louis. His work examines the impact of corporate social performance on employee commitment, as well as the nature of the psychological contracts between employees and their employers, and the extent to which employees share in the financial returns of their companies. Bruce's publications include articles in the *International Journal of Human Resource Management*, *Business Ethics: A European Review*, and the *Journal of Corporate Finance*.

Sue Hutchinson is Principal Lecturer in HRM at the University of West of England Business School. Prior to this she was involved in teaching and research at the University of Bath where she worked for the Work and Employment Research Centre. Before entering academic life she worked as a policy adviser for the Chartered Institute of Personnel and Development and as an adviser in industrial relations. Her current research interests include the link between people management and performance, the implementation of the Information and Consultation Regulations, the role of line managers, and alternative dispute resolution in small/medium-sized businesses.

Foreword

During the first decade of the twenty-first century it is clear that CEOs of organisations, private and public, have begun to focus on people issues as a key differentiator for competitive performance. This goes far beyond the traditional "people are our greatest asset" to a growing understanding that people make the real difference to performance. The focus for CEOs is on the talent and skills that people bring to and develop within organisations to enhance organisational performance. CEOs are concerned about skill gaps, emerging demographic trends, leadership competencies and the ability to capture and embrace the creativity and innovation of people within organisations. They consider finding solutions to these challenges as the key to competitive success or improved delivery of services.

This book helps to address the understanding and potential practical solutions required to improve performance through addressing people issues within organisations. It places the employee (people!) at the centre of the analysis and examines the tensions and dilemmas that need to be managed within complex organisations. It looks at the requirements, through practical case studies, to manage diverse groups of people in different ways in order to recognise varying needs. It recognises, as reflected in the growing focus of CEOs, the importance of line management and leadership in the successful implementation of people practices. Finally, and helpfully for practitioners, it creates the link between the important 'theoretical' models and how they can be implemented in practice.

Ron Collard
Partner, Pricewaterhouse Coopers
Visiting Professor
School of Management, University of Bath

Acknowledgements

We are deeply indebted to the employees, middle managers, HR managers, and executives in the organisations concerned in this research for their time, patience and enthusiasm.

Much of the research reported here has been supported by the Chartered Institute of Personnel and Development. In particular we record our thanks to Angela Baron, the policy adviser responsible for a number of projects, Ward Griffiths and Duncan Brown the Deputy Directors of the CIPD and Ron Collard the Vice President who commissioned the original research. Jon Parsons has also made very useful comments on various drafts. We thank them all.

We are grateful for permission to reproduce the following figures:

Figure 3.2: from Wright, P. and Boswell, W. (2002), 'Desegregating HRM: a review and synthesis of micro and macro human resource management research', *Journal of Management*, 28(3): 247–76; permission courtesy of Sage Journals.

Figure 6.3: from Lepak, D. and Snell, S. A. (1999), 'The human resource architecture: toward a theory of human capital allocation and development', *Academy of Management Review*, 24(1): 31–48; permission courtesy of the Academy of Management.

Introduction

Research into the links between strategic human resource management and business performance has dominated academic and practitioner debate in the field over the last 20 years. The claims made for the positive impact of HR practices on performance, especially in the mid-1990s, raised the profile of the issue for practitioners and policy makers. However, debate rages among academics over these claims and many practitioners remain attracted to, but sceptical of, the ideas put forward.

The appeal, indeed romance (Wall and Wood 2005), of the subject is not difficult to see for both academic and practitioner audiences. At a senior practitioner level an improved understanding of the effectiveness of various HR practices is important as markets become more global and competitive. The rise of the knowledge-based economy means that organisations are increasingly relying on their human capital for their success providing an opportunity for HR practitioners to demonstrate their value to the business more than they have in the past. The research offers HR academics the possibility of them being on a par with their colleagues from finance and marketing, rather than being the poor relations as has so often been the case (Legge 2001).

It is ironic, however, that this high level of interest, some would say pre-occupation, has taken place at a time when HR practitioners have found themselves under pressure from two sources to justify their contribution to the organisation. One threat to the very survival of the specialist HR function itself comes from outsourcing, e-enabled HRM and delegation to the line managers. A second derives from the move towards more flexible models of the firm where much smaller groups of staff are directly employed and a whole range of activities are provided by a variety of partners and subcontractors (Lepak and Snell 2007). Taken to its extreme this model would simply leave purchasing managers to coordinate the suppliers of labour. Why, in this context of increased externalisation of employment, should managers be concerned with the contribution of HR practices? Changes such as these have left HR professionals wondering what, exactly, the future holds for them (Caldwell 2003). Certainly, there has been no shortage of debate over the role of HR among practitioners in both the US (Losey *et al.* 2005) and the UK (CIPD 2007b; Pass 2006). These discussions also have a long history within the academic and popular press (Legge 1978; Skinner 1981; Tyson 1987; Ulrich 1997).

HRM has therefore been leading something of a 'double life' throughout the last two decades claiming to make a critical contribution in theory while being threatened with marginalisation in practice. This is hardly surprising since the very pressures which threaten to undermine HR also create the incentive to provide much-needed hard evidence of its contribution to organisational performance. Some authors (Legge 1995) have seen this as further evidence of the gap between the rhetoric of HRM's contribution to the bottom line and its rather more depressing reality of powerlessness, lack of a distinctive contribution and low levels of accountability.

It is against this controversial background that this book seeks to address the key issues linking strategic HR and performance. It draws on existing and recent research in order to examine the claims made for links between HR practices and organisational performance. We aim to address the key issues in the HR–performance field by looking beyond the rhetoric of the written HR strategy and practice to examine the reality of how HR practices are actually experienced by employees and their line managers. We seek not simply to review the existing research since there are already a number of excellent reviews (Becker and Gerhart 1996; Becker and Huselid 2006; Boselie *et al.* 2005; Combs *et al.* 2006; Delery and Doty 1996; Huselid and Becker 2000; Lepak *et al.* 2006; Purcell 1999; Purcell and Kinnie 2007; Wall and Wood 2005; Wright and Gardener 2004; Wright *et al.* 2005). Nor do we simply wish to add yet more data to the ever-increasing pile. Rather our aim, in addition, is to step back from the detail of the debate to develop a theoretical model which is underpinned by extensive empirical and previous research to analyse the people management–performance link. We use this model to guide our analysis of the data we have collected and to consider the implications of our findings for all parties.

There are two principal questions which we seek to address:

1   What are the links between strategic HR and business performance?
2   How and why are HR practices linked to performance?

Our aims are therefore relatively broad (see Figure 0.1):

1   discuss and evaluate existing research;
2   propose an analytical model – the HR causal chain;
3   elaborate on and illustrate this model drawing on extensive empirical data;
4   apply this model to explore the differences between occupations and the links between people management–performance for two groups – professional knowledge workers and those employed in the financial services sector;
5   consider the implications of our findings for theory and for practice.

We draw on a variety of sources of evidence:

•   data from previous research in the area;
•   our own empirical data – discussed in more detail below;

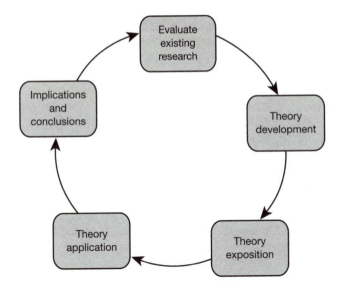

Figure 0.1 Thematic development

- data from the Workplace Employee Relations Surveys in 1998 and 2004 (see Kersley *et al.* 2006);
- surveys conducted by organisations where we believe the data collected are valid and reliable.

The empirical evidence on which we draw comes from a series of research projects, mostly sponsored by the CIPD in the UK, since 1997. Most, but not all, of these data are drawn from case studies which we have conducted during that period. These data are mostly qualitative, but also include some quantitative material. This methodology reflects much of our thinking regarding the principal shortcomings of previous research: it has simply failed to engage with the appropriate parties and levels in order to produce results which are truly useful. Ironically, this empirical shortcoming can be traced back to more fundamental theoretical shortcomings which we discuss. Further details of our research method and the case studies are given in the Appendix.

Our methodological and theoretical approach, and indeed our style of presentation, seeks to steer a course between the highly sophisticated analyses which are almost impenetrable to the layperson and the more journalistic accounts of 'how I made a success of this'. Indeed we are seeking to combine an approach which is: accessible, but closely based on theory; evidence-based but using data drawn from identifiable cases and analytical without recourse to too much jargon. We believe this book is particularly suited to the needs of students – especially final-year undergraduates, specialist postgraduates and those on MBA programmes – and to practitioners.

The book is therefore divided into four sections (see Figure 0.2):

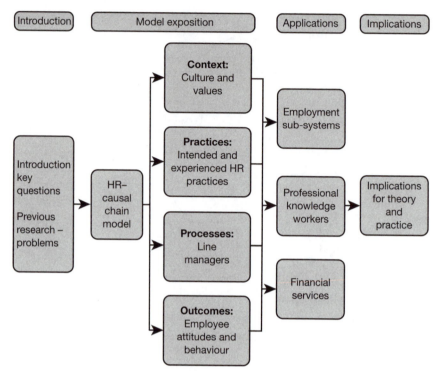

Figure 0.2 Structure of the book

- **Introduction**, evaluation of previous research and theory development – Chapter 1;
- **Model exposition** in four chapters examining culture (Chapter 2), HR practices (Chapter 3), the role of line managers (Chapter 4) and employee attitudes and behaviour (Chapter 5);
- **Application of the model** to study different employment sub-systems (Chapter 6), professional knowledge workers (Chapter 7) and the financial services sector (Chapter 8);
- **Consideration of the implications** for theory development and for practice (Chapter 9).

1 Understanding the link between people management and organisational performance

Introduction

The introduction to the book outlined our principal aim which is to examine the links between people management and performance drawing on relevant theory and empirical data. As we explained there are four sections to the book (previous research and model building, model exposition, model application and implications and conclusions). This chapter examines the previous research and puts forward the model which will form the backbone to the book. It has four specific aims:

1 to provide an overview of the previous research;
2 to identify particular problems which need to be addressed;
3 discuss the concept of Human Resource Advantage;
4 to put forward the HR causal chain model which we will use throughout the book (see Figure 1.1).

We begin the chapter therefore with an overview of previous research in the field.

Previous research into the links between strategic HRM and business performance

There has always been an intuitive feeling that the way employees are managed affects the performance of the organisation. This is an unstated assumption behind

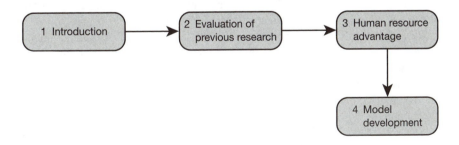

Figure 1.1 Structure of the chapter

much of the research stretching back to the theories of Scientific Management, the Hawthorne studies and the Total Quality Management movement. However, much of this early work lacked a strategic focus (Legge 1978; Golding 2004).

In the early to mid-1980s there were studies, mostly in the US, which looked in a more focused way at the possible links between HR and performance. The texts by Beer *et al.* (1985) and by Fombrun *et al.* (1984) were thought to be particularly influential and in some ways represented a major leap forward in the area. However, these studies were not based on empirical research and as Truss (2001: 1122) notes there were no attempts at this stage to measure performance in any well-defined or systematic way.

Since then we can identify two types of literature that have emerged in the field of HR and performance: the work aimed mostly at practitioners usually written in an accessible style and the more detailed work aimed at academic audiences which is sometimes opaque and difficult to interpret and apply.

Those in the first group include Jeffrey Pfeffer (1994, 1998), Dave Ulrich (1997) and Linda Gratton (2000). This work can itself be traced back to Peters and Waterman (1982). These books tend to use case studies to illustrate their main thesis of the positive impact of HR practices on business performance. Their impact on the practitioner community has been widespread through their adoption by professional associations such as the CIPD, consulting and conference activities and their use on undergraduate, MBA and executive programmes. This work is not without its critics such as Legge (1995) who drew attention to the gap between company rhetoric and reality and Paauwe (2004) who advocated a more critical approach especially in the measures of performance used and the attention given to institutional contexts.

The key academic research can be traced back to Mark Huselid's 1995 article in which he sought to measure the contribution of HR to performance in much more well-defined and precise ways than in the past. Huselid sought to consider the impact of High-Performance Work Systems on various measures of performance (principally financial performance but also including other measures such as employee retention and turnover) drawing on a survey of 968 US firms. He found that 'the magnitude of the returns for investments in High Performance Work Systems is substantial'. Indeed, 'A one standard deviation increase in such practices is associated with a relative 7.05 per cent decrease in (labour) turnover, and on a per employee basis, $27,044 more in sales and $18,641 and $3,814 more in market value and profits, respectively' (Huselid 1995: 667).

Research in the UK (Patterson *et al.* 1997) came up with similar findings. Using a sample of 67 UK manufacturing businesses studied over time they found that 18 per cent of the variation in productivity and 19 per cent of profitability could be attributed to people management practices. These were a better predictor of company performance than strategy, technology and research and development.

Since then there have been several hundred studies looking at the links between HR and performance and many of these have focused on the links between HR practices and performance – which are studied in detail in Chapter 3. Boselie *et al.*

(2005) report that there were 104 articles in the area in refereed journals between 1994 and 2003. Despite this extensive effort the goal of establishing a clear link between HR practices and performance still seems some way off. As Purcell and Kinnie (2007: 533) noted 'numerous review papers ... have found this field of research often wanting in terms of method, theory and the specification of HR practices to be used when establishing a relationship with performance outcomes'. Moreover, there has been an intense debate surrounding the very nature, purpose and outputs of the research (Keenoy 1997; Legge 1995; Hesketh and Fleetwood 2006).

Much of the research in the field has been criticised for its excessive emphasis on the quantitative analysis of data collected by the survey method and for its neglect of theory development. For example, Guest (1997: 264) commenting on the early research noted that 'While these studies represent encouraging signs of progress, statistical sophistication appears to have been emphasised at the expense of theoretical rigour. As a result the studies are non-additive, except in a very general way'. More precisely, Wood (1999: 408) argued that 'The empirical work ... has concentrated on assessing the link between practices and performance with increasing disregard for the mechanisms linking them'.

We will now consider these criticisms in more detail before putting forward our proposed framework for analysis. This is designed to answer the call from Guest (1997: 263) more than 10 years ago 'if we are to improve our understanding of the impact of HRM on performance, we need a theory about HRM, a theory about performance and a theory about how they are linked'.

Evaluation of this research: identifying problems

An extensive debate has emerged over the value of the HR and performance research. A series of important reviews referred to earlier have sought to evaluate the methods used and the results obtained.

Wright and Gardner (2004: 312) summarise these problems:

> While evidence mounts that HR practices are at least weakly related to firm performance, significant methodological and theoretical challenges exist ... Methodologically, there is no consensus regarding which practices constitute a theoretically complete set of HR practices; how to conceptually categorise these practices; the relevance of business strategy; the appropriate level of analysis; or how HR–performance and firm performance are to be measured ... Theoretically, no consensus exists regarding the mechanism by which HR practices might impact on firm outcomes.

We can recognise two kinds of critiques which have been made: those concerned with methodology and those dealing with issues of theory. We will examine the methodological issues first because these have taken up most of the attention and then turn to the more basic theoretical problems which ultimately are more important.

Methodological problems

The methodological problems have been concerned with data collection, measuring performance and the scope of HR practices.

Data collection

The data collection problems begin with the source of information. Many, if not most studies, have used postal surveys sent to single responders such as a senior HR manager (Wall and Wood 2005: 441). They are asked from a predetermined list of HR practices to indicate which are in use and often, but not always, to estimate the proportion of employees covered by each practice. Often the same respondent is asked to estimate the productivity, performance or profitability of their firm relative to others in their sector (Wall and Wood 2005: 442). Alternatively, published accounting data is used. Statistical techniques of varying degrees of sophistication are then used to explore the nature of the relationship between the two sets of variables. As we have already noted Huselid (1995) conducted one of the earliest studies and few subsequently have reached his level of sophistication. The general conclusion is that there is a clear observable relationship between the adoption of HR practices and performance outcomes with generally the greater the number of practices in place, the stronger the positive relationship. Gerhart (2005: 175) summarises some of the evidence:

> One standard deviation increase in HR system practices (relative to the mean) designed to enhance workforce ability, motivation and opportunity to contribute was associated with roughly 20% better firm financial performance. Consider that this finding means that firms one standard deviation above the mean are 120% of mean performance, while those one standard deviation below the mean are at 80% of mean performance, making for a 120/80 = 50% advantage of being +1 standard deviation versus −1 standard deviation. This is a large deviation.

Gerhart (2005: 177) goes on to spoil the story by suggesting that the 'effect size is so large as to perhaps not be credible'. Large-scale databases of multiple numbers of firms or branches of large organisations have been able to establish representative data showing the nature of this relationship. 'Sophisticated' HRM, often referred to as High-Performance Work Systems (HPWSs) or High-Commitment Management (HCM), has been associated with better performance.[1] What, of course, is not at all clear is the direction of the relationship. Cross-sectional research can only reveal associations, not causality, and it is equally plausible that excellent firms will both be able to afford sophisticated HR systems and wish to invest in them.

The methodological downside to this type of research, which some say is fatally flawed (Wall and Wood 2005), can be summarised in three ways. First, respondents may have incomplete knowledge, for example, of how many employees are covered by a particular practice, especially if the respondent is located at the corporate office of a firm with numerous business units. There is also the difficulty of assuming that HR practices are translated into actual practices, as discussed later. If multiple respondents are used to try and overcome this problem there is surprisingly little consensus between them (Gerhart *et al.* 2000). The overall reliability of HR practice measures is 'frighteningly low' (Wright and Gardner 2004: 316). There is also an attribution problem where the HR respondent in a successful firm may assume that a practice exists or how else could the firm be successful?

Second, one cannot rely on the same person to estimate HR practices and performance. This 'common method variance' is equally frightening. Third, no account is taken of the lag effect. How long does it take for an HR practice to impact on performance? Measuring HRM and performance in the same time period cannot possibly show that HRM drives performance (or the reverse that good performance drives better HRM). Wright *et al.* (2005: 412) are even harsher. They note that 'by far the most prevalent design [in the 66 studies they reviewed] is what we call "post-predictive" because it measures HR practices after the performance period resulting in actually predicting *past* performance [their emphasis]'. Thus, overall, 'the literature on the HRM–performance relationship has (a) universally reported significant relationships between HRM and performance, (b) almost exclusively used designs that do not logically allow one to draw causal conclusions, and (c) very seldom actually tested for a reverse causal order' (Wright *et al.* 2005: 416).

These same authors then argue that three criteria need to be used to establish cause. First, cause requires that the effect be present when the cause is present and be absent when the cause is absent. Second, the proposed cause must exist in time prior to the proposed outcome and, third, all other variables that might cause the outcome are controlled for (Wright *et al.* 2005: 411). These are tough criteria and, when used as far as possible by Guest *et al.* (2003) and by themselves, no unambiguous HR–performance effect is uncovered (but by the same token one cannot 'suggest that HR practices *do not* have a positive impact on performance') (Wright *et al.* 2005: 433, their emphasis). This leads Wright and his colleagues to argue that (Wright *et al.* 2005: 411) 'this body of work lacks sufficient methodological rigour to demonstrate that the relationship is actually causal in the sense that HR practices, when instituted, lead to higher performance'.

The problem of performance

Interestingly, Guest *et al.*'s study used both 'objective' (i.e. published) performance data and their respondents' subjective evaluation of their firms' performance relative to their competitors. Using this subjective test, HRM was associated with 'high comparative performance' (2003: 311). It is premature to write off such subjective evaluations and rely exclusively on objective performance or profit measures. In multi-sector studies, such as Guest *et al.* (2003), it is necessary to control for sectoral variances in profitability. Some sectors generate much higher returns than others. Informed respondents may have a better idea of sectoral conditions than revealed by simple published returns. It is also extraordinarily difficult to meet the third criterion for causal studies, that of controlling for all other potential causal influences. As Hitt *et al.* note in their study in professional service firms, 'firm performance is a function of many variables both inside and outside a firm ... Thus, for one set of variables (human capital in their study) to explain 3.6 per cent of the variance in firm performance may be significant' (2001: 25). Published corporate accounts are problematic since they cover different business units and perhaps countries where different HR systems are likely to be in place in part because of different regulatory or institutional regimes (Paauwe 2004).

There are two much more fundamental problems with the use of financial performance data (Boselie *et al.* 2005: 75). First, they are far removed from HRM influence – too distal. Second, it takes for granted that firms seek to structure their HR systems to maximise financial outcomes, often in the short-term sense of shareholder value.

The problem with published financial measures is that no convincing explanation can be provided as to why, or indeed how, HR practices have an influence. As such, the research is remarkably uninformative from a practitioner point of view beyond the knowledge that the 'more' HR practices the better (the so-called 'Huselid curve'). This has led many researchers to use, or at least call for the adoption of, more proximal measures of performance which seem more likely to be directly influenced by, or an outcome of, worker behaviour. Typical here would be employee turnover and absence, scrap rates, sales per employee and customer satisfaction. Harter *et al.* (2002: 273) found that there was a rank ordering in their correlations between overall employee satisfaction/engagement and measures of performance. The highest were with customer satisfaction, loyalty and employee turnover followed, in rank order, by safety, productivity and, lastly, profitability. Proximal measures are not without their difficulties. They too need to be adjusted for sectoral variants. Typical measures of labour management performance like turnover and absenteeism are highly variable between sectors with nursing and teaching, for example, exhibiting higher than average sickness rates. Retail firms and call centres have higher than average labour turnover, at least in the UK. Useful work in retail banking involving comparisons between large numbers of branches using identical HR practices has been done by Gelade and Ivery (2003) and Bartel (2004). This research is discussed in more detail in Chapter 8. An increasing number of large firms in sectors where staff are customer-related now collect their own data from surveys of employees and customers mixed with operational measures and financial performance to develop sophisticated models of HR and performance for their own purposes. The seminal work undertaken in Sears in the USA in the 1990s has been a major influence (Rucci *et al.* 1998).

The assumption that profitability and financial performance are (or should be) the end goal of HRM is a more profound issue. There are a number of reasons for questioning such a belief. First, as Jacoby (2005) had shown in his comparison of US and Japanese firms, there are major differences of emphasis with the former dominated by shareholder value and the latter using more of a stakeholder approach. The work of Paauwe (2004) lends credence to the view that we need to take account of 'varieties of capitalism', as noted too by Godard (2004). The focus almost exclusively on shareholder value may be a case of 'US exceptionalism'. Even if shareholder value were accepted as the dominant and legitimate end goal for HRM this use of short-term financial indicators may fail to satisfy shareholders in the longer term. Ostroff and Bowen (2000: 216) draw attention to 'the persistent finding that organisational effectiveness is multi-dimensional'. Emphasis on organisational agility and the search for sustained competitive advantage places different requirements on HRM in its contribution to organisational success (Wright and Snell 1998). Boxall and Purcell (2003) add a third fundamental goal for HRM – social legitimacy. This can be seeking to be 'an employer of choice' or meeting social expectations enshrined in law and social practice. While attempts are often made to justify certain HR practices in terms of their bottom line contributions, the ultimate purpose of some, like diversity policies, is the eradication of discrimination. This is not to deny the importance of HRM contributing to performance; merely to note that financial performance is only one dimension of effectiveness.

The problem of the scope of HR practices

Having dealt with problems concerning the dependent variable, performance, we now need to consider the input to the model of HRM: the HR practices used in analyses. Alas, many problems abound here too. There is no agreement on what constitutes 'HR practices' let alone a full set of them.[2] Behind these differences is the long-standing debate of whether HRM requires 'a distinctive approach to employment management' (Storey 1995: 5), sometimes referred to as 'developmental humanism' or 'soft' HR, or a generic term covering all aspects of the management of labour (Boxall and Purcell 2003: 4). The former tends to focus on 'innovative' HR practices while the latter takes a broader perspective to include, for example, collective work relations often excluded from American studies (Deery and Iverson 2005). Godard's (2004) review of the 'high performance paradigm' (HPP) finds little support for links with performance but notes increases in work stress (an outcome not usually included in studies). He observes that 'it is again possible that practices traditionally considered to yield positive outcomes for workers such as traditional group work or information sharing are as effective or even more effective than practices associated with HPP' (2004: 360). We need to find a list which does not assume positive outcomes and may reveal negative associations with performance, or no links at all.

Attempts to resolve this 'list' problem have led to a focus on 'HR architecture' (Becker and Gerhart 1996; Lepak and Snell 1999; Wright and Gardner 2004). This proposes that 'HR practices … be classified into four levels, including guiding principles, policy alternatives (different practices), products (competences and behaviours that practice promotes) and practice-process (the effectiveness of execution of the practice)' (Wright and Gardner 2004: 314). Researchers need to choose the level or levels of practice to investigate rather than rely on an undifferentiated list.[3]

The firm's overall approach to HRM is established in guiding principles. Wright and Boswell (2002: 253) suggest that 'a consensus is emerging around conceptual categories of employee skills, motivation and empowerment'. This allows for a broad conception of HR architecture to cover practices designed to build and retain human capital and to influence employee behaviour (motivation and empowerment). This is now usually referred to as 'ability, motivation and opportunity' (AMO) (Boxall and Purcell 2003).

AMO broadens the architecture dimensions to cover 'knowledge, skills, ability' (KSA) (e.g. Delery and Shaw 2001), motivationally based practices implied in intrinsic and extrinsic incentive structures and rewards, and opportunities to contribute and participate on and off the job. Once AMO is used as an analytical structure, the policy alternatives (second level) and 'products' (third level) can be specified. They will vary from firm to firm. No definitive list of 'best practices' suggested by those advocating a universalistic model of HRM can be predicted. Rather, a range of policy alternatives appropriate to the firm in its sector (or country) can be identified (Datta *et al.* 2005) and different mixes of practices may have the same performance outcome ('equifinality'). This neatly sidesteps the problem of 'horizontal fit' which requires the number, strength and combination of practices to be identified which is especially troublesome where the hypothesis is that the effect of combinations of practices is multiplicative. Bowen and Ostroff (2004: 206) note that 'different sets of practices may be equally effective so long as they allow a particular type of climate to develop (e.g. climates of innovation or service)'. Thus, the use of an analytical structure such as AMO helps us to deal with the problems of deciding which HR practices should be studied. This is especially so since the need is to focus on the combined impact of HR practices rather than the utility of each individual practice.

Our discussion has revealed a number of serious methodological problems with the research which has been conducted. However, in many ways these concerns are quite narrow and inward looking. A focus on these alone runs the risk, as Lepak *et al.* (2006: 220) said, of 'putting the cart before the horse'. We need to step back therefore to look at the broader theoretical concerns. Once we have done this we then consider the concept of Human Resource Advantage and our own organising framework.

The problem of theory

The use of AMO raises the question of how the choice of appropriate practices influences performance. This is the problem of theory which has two aspects: the nature of the relationship between HR and performance and the definition of HR itself.

Relationship between HR and performance: the black box

Even if robust causal correlations are found between the adoption of a certain mix of practices and performance we do not know why this occurs. We have no evidence on the nature of any intermediary processes that need to occur to produce such relationships. For this reason this is referred to as the 'HR black box'. Boselie *et al.* (2005: 77) confirm 'the impression that the "linking mechanism" between HRM and performance and the *mediating* effects of key variables are largely disregarded. Indeed, while we found plenty of acknowledgement of the existence of the "black box" and some speculation on its possible contents, few studies tried to look inside'.

Looking inside the black box requires specifying an HR causal chain. At the centre of the chain are employee attitudes and behaviour and it is this which raises the most vital question in the HR–performance debate. If 'the distinctive feature of HRM is its assumption that improved performance is achieved through people in the organisation' (Guest 1997: 269), why is it that so few researchers actually study the people: the employees and their attitudes and behaviour? While Delery and Shaw (2001: 190) argue that 'HRM practices and job design have the most significant direct influence on the skills, motivation and empowerment of the workforce', they go on to say that 'measuring the most important aspects of workforce character-istics may, however, be beyond our capabilities'. They do not say why. Only 3 out of 25 studies examined by Wall and Wood (2005) and 11 of the 104 reviewed by Boselie *et al.* (2005) used employee survey data. Edwards and Wright (2001: 570) correctly assert that 'it remains rare for studies to assess links in the chain, with effects on employee commitment being a particularly rarely studied issue'.

This absence is hard to understand, let alone justify, given the tradition of employee-centred research in organisational behaviour and industrial relations. It stems, almost certainly, from the use of multiple-firm data sets where single management respondents are only able to indicate the intended practices and their coverage. They cannot reliably report on employee perceptions of these practices as they experience them. Thus, the usual steps in research, of theory determining the research questions and thence the choice of method, have been reversed. Meth-odological considerations have determined what questions can be asked while factors beyond the reach of the chosen method, however important, have been ignored. As Guest (2001: 1095) candidly put it, 'almost inevitably, both for the sake of brevity and to increase the chances of publication, many published papers tend to play down a number of methodological and analytical concerns'.

Wright and Nishii (2004) address this issue by proposing an elaborated model of the HR causal chain which is divided into five steps, moving from intended, to actual, to perceived HR practices, followed by employee reactions, and then performance. This model provides an excellent basis for understanding the links between HRM and performance which we build on in the next section.

What is HRM?

If it is the overall effect of the HR system, or its 'strength', which employees respond to, then the parameters of such a system need to equate as closely as possible to the employees' experience of the world of work and the range of practices the employer uses to structure this. What are the features of organi-sational life which are likely to influence employee attitudes and behaviour? HR practices, as we have traditionally viewed them, will be a necessary, but never a sufficient, component. The role of line managers as agents enacting HR practices, and the transmission of organisational culture (sometimes referred to as 'climate') will need to be included. Both of these touch on questions of leadership and the nature of the relationship between manager(s) and employee(s). Critical features of the firm's operational system as it affects employees, seen in staffing levels, job design and the 'social relations of production' (Edwards and Wright 2001: 581), will be relevant since these determine how many employees are required, the interface with technology, skill levels required, and strongly influence what people actually do at work. Beyond these, factors such as organisational values and culture will be influential.

Scholars have only recently begun to apply these features of organisational behaviour to HRM and its effects on performance. Wright *et al.* (2005: 419) give examples of leadership, organisational culture and line-management enactment influencing performance. They argue that 'a "spurious" relationship might exist if there were an actual true co-variation between the measures of HR practice and performance yet, there was no direct causal relationship between the two variables'. HR practice measures may be acting as proxies for these wider variables of leadership, culture and manager behaviour. They conclude that 'studies that do not control for a full set of variables that might cause performance may lack the data necessary for making valid causal inferences' (Wright *et al.* 2005: 420). However, to be able to apply controls, the variables must be measured. The justification for collecting such data merely to control for variances, alongside the usual suspects of firm age, sector, size and certain workforce characteristics, can only be made if there is a clear, unambiguous, agreed definition of what HRM is. This is far from the case. From a practitioner perspective, questions of leadership, culture and managerial behaviour are commonly seen to fall within the HR manager's area of activity with growing roles in the management of change and organisational transformation. Thus, on grounds of theory, and from both employee and HR manager perspectives, it is argued that a wider definition of HRM is necessary. Some use the wider term 'people management' (Paul and Anantharaman 2003; Purcell *et al.* 2003). This has some merit since it signals a wider research agenda and avoids one of the pitfalls in HR–performance research where respondents erroneously believe the research is about the efficacy or the importance of the HR department. This is a very different question from that considered here.

To sum up our discussion so far we can see that the existing research has problems with both the methods of research and the underlying theory. We now move on to develop our framework for analysis which begins to overcome some of these problems. We begin by examining the work of Peter Boxall and his colleagues on Human Resource Advantage.

Human Resource Advantage

Boxall and his colleagues have been developing the concept of Human Resource Advantage for some time as a way of understanding the links between HR and performance (Boxall 1996, 1998; Boxall and Steeneveld 1999; Boxall and

Purcell 2003, 2008). This is the series of policies, practices and processes that together contribute to the competitive advantage of the organisation. Human Resource Advantage is composed of a Human Capital Advantage (HCA) and an Organisational Process Advantage (OPA). This framework is attractive to us because it creates a dual focus on the design and content of HR practices *and* the role of line managers and employees in putting these into action.

Although there are a variety of forms of capital which are critical to organisational performance (Swart 2006) our discussion focuses on the generation of HCA which involves developing superior practices in key areas such as recruitment, selection, training and team building designed to ensure the best people are employed and these staff develop high levels of skill. However, there is unlikely to be a competitive advantage in the practices themselves because they are easily copied (Mueller 1996). It is the processes and routines required to put these practices into operation as intended that are more difficult to replicate and form the OPA (Boxall 1996: 267). These processes, such as team-based learning and cross-functional cooperation, develop over time, are socially complex and causally ambiguous (Boxall and Purcell 2003: 86).

Both HCA and OPA can generate competitive advantage, but they are most effective when they are combined together. The form of HR Advantage is likely to change as the firm grows through the establishment, mature and renewal contexts (Boxall 1998). Thus 'While knowledge of individual HR policies is not rare, the knowledge of how to create a positively reinforcing blend of HR philosophy, process, practice and investment *within* a particular context is likely to be very rare' (Boxall and Purcell 2003: 86). This 'social architecture' is created and re-created at all levels in the firm and is therefore especially difficult to imitate (Mueller 1996: 177).

The key theme running throughout our discussion has been that the acquisition of HR Advantage depends on developing both a capital and a process advantage (Purcell 1999: 36; Boxall and Purcell 2003: 22). We therefore need to understand how HR practices are actually translated into operation before we can thoroughly begin to understand the links between HR and performance. It is important to look at the routines and processes, or using another language, both the formal and informal practices which make up the day-to-day realities of organisational life.

Studying OPA is much more difficult than looking at practices because these processes are often tacit and intangible and their dynamics are not adequately captured by research approaches which rely exclusively on data collection by postal questionnaire and analysis by sophisticated statistical packages. In fact OPA is only seen most clearly when it is absent, when things go wrong: there is infighting between departments, poor knowledge sharing within and between project teams, or people do not work to their full potential.

The concept of OPA is derived from research carried out into the resource-based view (RBV) of the firm.

Resource-based view

The resource-based view (RBV) is an economic perspective useful for assessing the strategic resources available to a firm. The RBV suggests that the basis for a sustained competitive advantage resides in the application of a bundle of valuable, rare and inimitable resources at the firm's disposal (Wernerfelt 1984: 172; Rumelt 1987: 557–8; Barney 1991: 105–6; Peteraf 1993: 180). The RBV draws attention to both tangible and intangible assets of the firm, as well as the set of 'capabilities' held by the firm. Capabilities are defined as the capacity of a firm to 'deploy resources, usually in combination, using organisational processes, to effect a desired end' (Amit and Schoemaker 1993: 35). The RBV perspective is useful in strategic HRM because it helps us understand how HR systems can function as 'capabilities' which allow firms to leverage human capital and other resources to achieve competitive advantage.

According to the RBV, HR can contribute to building a sustained competitive advantage by developing the following:

- Value – what resources of value does the firm have, and how can HR assist in the development and coordination of these resources in such a way that value is realised?
- Rarity – are the resources and capabilities of the firm different from those of its competitors?
- Inimitability – is imitation of the resources and capabilities of the firm by competitors difficult/costly/time-consuming?
- Organisation – Is the firm organised, ready, and able to exploit resources/ capabilities that are valuable, rare and inimitable?

Petra De Saá-Pérez and Juan Manuel García-Falcón (2002: 124–5) argue that human resource can be a source of competitive advantage by addressing each of the four points above directly:

> We can say that this resource adds value to an organisation because people differ in their capacities and abilities, and, therefore, in their contribution to the firm. Human resources are rare because it is difficult to find people who guarantee high performance levels in the organisation due to the labour market's heterogeneity. Their inimitability emerges from the difficulty in duplicating people's knowledge, abilities, experience and behaviour, at least in the short term. Moreover, the high transaction costs involved in people recruitment can be a significant obstacle to their mobility or acquisition. Finally, people are a resource difficult to replace because not everybody has the same capacity to adapt to the different environments and technologies, and those who are able to create value in one context may be unable to do so in others. (Wright *et al.* 1994)

Research into the resource-based view emphasises what is distinctive, as these are the potential sources of valuable differentiation for firms. However, we need to remember that firms also need to have the baseline characteristics right before developing distinctive characteristics. These are what Hamel and Prahalad (1994) and Boxall (1996) refer to as 'table stakes': the resources and skills needed simply to play the game. 'Table stakes', at least in HR terms, represent resources and capabilities which are imitable across firms, and while they are not capable of providing sustainable competitive advantage their presence is vital as their absence would result in a strategic disadvantage. Only once these 'table stakes' have been met should the strategic focus move on to the valuable, rare and inimitable differences between firms.

Truss (2001) notes one of the problems with the RBV is its emphasis on the importance of synergy and fit between the various elements of the HR system and asks how compatible a systems-based approach is with flexibility (Becker and Gerhart 1996: 789). Others have critiqued the RBV more generally for its reliance on a foundation of economic assumptions like efficient markets, rationality and equilibrium (e.g. Bromiley and Papenhausen 2003), and for weaknesses in its logical construction (e.g. Priem and Butler 2001). Despite these critiques, the RBV provides a series of useful testable hypotheses regarding the role resources and capabilities play in creating and maintaining competitive advantage (Barney 2001).

The RBV describes a role for tangible and intangible resources and capabilities in the creation of competitive advantage. If we are to understand this in the HR context we need to consider what has come to be known as the 'black box' research.

Application to HR: examining the 'black box'

The importance of examining the implementation of HR practices was noted by Becker and Gerhart (1996: 793) when they argued that 'future work on the strategic perspective must elaborate on the black box between a firm's HR systems and the firm's bottom line'. Moreover, 'more effort should be devolved to finding out what managers are thinking and why they make the decisions they do' (1996: 794). This emphasis suggests there is a need to understand how and why HR practices influence performance and to move away from the simple input–output models which have policy inputs on the left-hand side of the model and outcomes on the right-hand side.

When we begin to look inside the 'black box' we find that there are clearly differences between the espoused practices and the practices in use. For example, Truss (2001) draws on her research in Hewlett Packard to highlight the importance of the informal processes that exist alongside the formal practices. There were clear gaps between what the company claimed they were doing and what was actually experienced by employees 'in areas such as appraisals and training and development the results obtained were not uniformly excellent; in fact some were highly contradictory' (Truss 2001: 1143). Although the formal appraisal processes in HP rewarded employees' performance against targets related to the company's objectives, 'informally what counted was visibility and networking if people wanted to further their careers' (Truss 2001: 1144). Despite espousing the value of training, less than half said they got the training they needed to do their job, fewer than half felt the appraisal system was working well and less than one third felt their pay was fair. 'These are all examples of a strong disconnect between the "rhetoric" of human resource management as expressed by the human resource department, and the reality as experienced by employees' (Truss 2001: 1143). This 'highlights the importance of the informal organisation as mediator between policy and the individual' (Truss 2001: 1144).

Research into formal and informal practices has a long tradition in the industrial relations literature (Terry 1977; Brown 1972, 1973) and sheds important light on contemporary concerns about the processes that are actually important. This makes a focus solely on formal practices inappropriate, and in particular we need to consider the role of the 'individual manager as agent, choosing to focus his or her attention in varying ways' (Truss 2001: 1145). We examine this under the heading of discretionary behaviour. However, before we do this we need to consider the role of employees when engaging in discretionary behaviour.

Employee discretionary behaviour

Research in the US steel, clothing and medical equipment industries highlights the importance of employee discretionary behaviour (Appelbaum *et al.* 2000). Drawing evidence from managers and shop floor employees as well as a study of formal HR practices, they found that the willingness of employees to engage in discretionary behaviour depended on the creation of opportunities to participate, skill development, and motivation and incentives (Appelbaum *et al.* 2000: 118–20).

Their key finding was the positive effects of High-Performing Work Systems on plant performance most importantly through increased discretionary effort by employees and the increased rate of knowledge accumulation. Moreover, these practices had a different effect on performance in different industries (Appelbaum *et al.* 2000: 227). In steel there was evidence that quality and employment security raised 'up time' by 8 per cent, incentives by 13 per cent and work organisation by 14 per cent and HPWS as a whole by 17 per cent (Appelbaum *et al.* 2000: 108). In clothing modular production involving self-directed teams reduced sewing time by 94 per cent and led to substantial cost savings. In medical equipment the opportunity to participate is closely linked to value added per dollar and profits and quality (Appelbaum *et al.* 2000: 108). The likelihood of employees engaging in this discretionary behaviour is also influenced more generally by the role of line managers.

Role of line managers in bringing practices to life

Recent research has looked at the discretionary behaviour of managers, especially first line managers and their contribution towards the development, or absence, of an organisational process advantage.

Numerous studies have observed how, over the last decade, line managers have played a more prominent role in the delivery of HR practices such as performance management, team leadership and communications as an increasing number of people management activities have been devolved to them (Hutchinson and Wood 1995; Renwick 2003; Larsen and Brewster 2003). The importance of the role of line managers has been recognised by both recent research (Marchington and Wilkinson 2002: 232–7) and earlier work on the 'forgotten supervisor' (Thurley and Wirdenius 1973; Child and Partridge 1982) and the role of the line manager in the emergence of informal practices (Brown 1972, 1973; Terry 1977; Armstrong and Goodman 1979).

HR causal chain model

Our discussion above has revealed that there are a whole series of problems which need to be overcome before we can thoroughly analyse the links between HR and performance (Becker and Huselid 2006: 900). Perhaps most importantly we need to develop a theoretical model which can be applied in a range of contexts. In doing so we are adapting what has been referred to as 'analytical HRM' (Boxall *et al.* 2007b: 4). The primary task of this analytical approach is to 'build theory and gather empirical data in order to account for the way management actually behaves in organising work and managing people across different jobs, work-places, companies, industries and societies'. In particular, we adapt this analytical approach in an attempt to understand not only the 'what' and 'why' of HRM, but also the 'how' of HRM – that is 'the chain of processes that make models of HRM work well (and poorly)' (Boxall *et al.* 2007b: 7).

We believe that the work of Wright and Nishii (2004), discussed above, provides a good basis for this model and offers genuine insights into the links between HR practices and performance. The purpose of this model (Figure 1.2) is to iden-tify the key causal steps in the chain from intended HR practices to performance outcomes. It does not seek to show all interconnections, nor map in any accurate

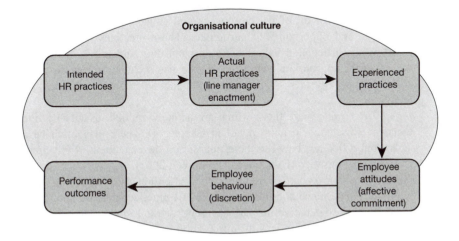

Figure 1.2 HR causal chain in the organisational context

way the HRM experience of a given firm and its employees. The model allows attention to be focused on critical steps that have to be taken if HRM is to have a performance outcome.

Our principal development of the Wright and Nishii model subdivides employee reactions into employees' attitudinal reactions and their subsequent behaviour. Three types of behaviour need to be specified, namely the competence needed to perform the job, discretionary behaviour, and turnover and absence (or retention and attendance). These types of employee behaviour are highly interrelated yet are logically and empirically distinct.

Second, we need to develop our causal chain model further if we are to capture these key additional features discussed in the most recent research. Figure 1.2 pays attention to the experience of HRM by employees, especially to the role of the line manager when implementing HR practices. As we will explain we believe it is essential to distinguish between the practices which are intended and those which are actually experienced by employees. The key stage here is the actions taken by line managers to put the intended practices into operation – what we refer to here as the actual HR practices.

The final modification is to set the causal chain model within its wider organisational context. The most important characteristic of this is the culture which exists within the organisation. As we will discuss, this culture can have a powerful effect in either supporting or undermining the impact of the HR practices. The model does not predict a particular research method. Indeed, as many review papers have noted, there is a need for qualitative and quantitative research at unit level, firm level, sector and country if we are to understand both the relationship between HR practices and performance outcomes and the dynamics of the interconnections.

These lead to a model which then has the following key features:

- *Intended HR practices* are those designed by senior management to be applied to most or all of the employees and concern employees' ability, motivation and opportunity to participate. These practices will be influenced by the articulated values of the organisation and found in the HR manual or the appropriate web pages. These also include the ways work is structured and organised since this has an impact on employee attitudes and behaviour.
- *Actual HR practices* are those which are actually applied, usually by line managers (discussed in more detail in Chapter 4). There may often be a substantial difference between the espousal and the enactment of HR practices in an organisation (Hutchinson and Purcell 2003).
- *Experienced HR practices* requires that attention is focused on how employees experience and then judge the HR practices that are applied to them. What they perceive may be different, or the same, as intended and may be judged through a lens of fairness and organisational justice. Experienced HR practices can again be classified using the AMO model. This needs, also, to cover perceptions of overall work climate seen, for example,

in levels of trust (Whitener 2001) and employees' job experience (pace, effort, autonomy, challenge, stress, etc.).

- *Attitudinal outcomes* include attitudes employees hold toward their job and their employer and/or levels of morale or motivation. This especially includes employees' willingness to cooperate and their overall satisfaction with their job.
- *Behavioural outcomes* flow in the main from these attitudinal dimensions. This can be learning new methods of working, engaging in behaviour which is beyond that required, such as organisational citizenship behaviour (OCB) (Coyle-Shapiro *et al.* 2004), or seen in levels of attendance and remaining in the job (or their opposites).
- *Performance outcomes* can be distal or proximal and can be restricted to short-term definitions of performance or can be expanded to include measures of effectiveness.

Relating employee attitudes to behaviour and thence to performance is relatively new in HRM but there are a growing number of studies that have done this (e.g. Ostroff and Bowen 2000; Judge *et al.* 2001). 'This line of research', concludes Gerhart (2005: 179), 'suggests that positive workforce attitudes create value'. In seeking to understand this downstream connection between attitudes and performance, and upstream between HR practices and attitudes, there is much to be gained from the social exchange theory (Coyle-Shapiro *et al.* 2004). In summary, social exchange applied to HRM theory suggests 'HR practices are viewed by employees as a "personalised" commitment to them by the organisation which is then reciprocated back to the organisation by employees through positive attitudes and behaviour' (Hannah and Iverson 2004: 339). Perceived organisational support (POS) may be linked to particular practices of salience to employees but it is the overall effect, or the 'strength' of the HR system (Bowen and Ostroff 2004), and employees' broader conceptions of the employment relationship which are critical.

More precisely the model draws attention to:

- the need to distinguish between intended HR and actual HR practices as experienced by employees;
- the key role played by line managers in the interpretation and implementation of HR practices;
- the link between experienced practices and employee attitudes and behaviours;
- the choice of performance measures that have meaning and significance for the companies and are close to the employee attitudinal data;
- the importance of organisational culture.

This chapter has provided an overview of previous research, outlined some of the key problems with this research and put forward an organising framework to guide our analysis in the following chapters. This concludes the first section of the book. Having established the principal features of this model we now need to develop our analysis further. In the next section we look at the steps in the causal model sequentially in much more detail and demonstrate the insights that they provide by referring to our empirical research. In particular we examine the role of organisational culture, intended HR practices, the role of line managers and the impact on employee attitudes and behaviour. In the third section we then apply the model to three different arenas – the differences between occupations, professional knowledge workers and the financial services sector. The fourth section discusses the implications and conclusions of our research.

2 Culture and values

Introduction

In the search for how human resource management impacts on organisational performance many researchers have looked at the types and coverage of the practices used and linked these to measures of corporate performance like profit or shareholder value. Although, as we have discussed in the previous chapter, there is some evidence of linkages between HR practices and performance we have been left with a problem of understanding why such positive associations exist. In other words, this previous research has been correlative in nature, proving that relationships exist, without being contextually sensitive. If we are to deepen our understanding of the impact of HR practices we need to study four vital components of the HR causal chain. In this chapter we consider the context of the culture and values of the firm, in Chapter 3 we look at these HR practices, in Chapter 4 we examine how these practices are actually implemented by line managers and in Chapter 5 we study the impact of these practices on employee attitudes and behaviour.

In this chapter therefore we explore the notion of organisational culture, showing why it is important yet elusive, how it affects employees, and how they affect it, what particular HR practices are linked to the establishment of a strong culture and what the effects are. We give a number of case histories from among our research companies, draw out some implications for policy and practice and consider how some aspects of values can be measured and managed. We pay particular attention to the organisational context by taking the notion of a strong, unifying mission (referred to here as the Big Idea) forward into its expression through a shared culture.

We begin by discussing why culture is important and then consider the notion of a strongly shared culture, i.e. one where employees can easily explain 'what the organisation is about' and their ability to identify personally with this central mission statement of the organisation. We then link the notion of a strong culture organisation to performance through the concept of extra role behaviour. Here we examine the variability of commitment across a series of organisations. We present the various sets of HRM practices which can be used to manage the organisational culture. Here we express the duality of culture by showing that HRM practices manage culture but that culture is also expressed through the implementation of

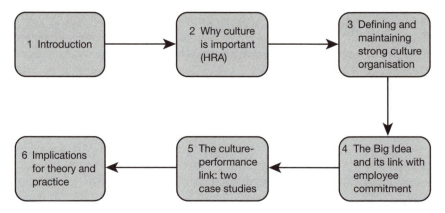

Figure 2.1 Structure of the chapter

these practices. This provides us with the opportunity to discuss the links between culture and performance drawing on our case study material.

We conclude the chapter by discussing the practical implications.

Why culture and values are important to performance: the link with HR Advantage

We need, first, to recall the fundamentals in the link between people management and performance so we can locate the contribution that vision, values and culture make. In particular we need to link the concept of 'Human Resource Advantage' (HRA) (Boxall 1996), which we introduced in Chapter 1, to organisational culture. We can recall that HRA is made up of two linked elements: human capital advantage (HCA) and organisation process advantage (OPA). This comes from the common-sense observation that successful firms are likely to have both better people and better processes. It is based on the distinction between resources and capabilities made by the resource-based view of strategy. The obvious analogy is with sports teams. HCA is at the heart of standard HRM since it points to excellent recruitment and selection, good training and development, appropriate performance management, effective job and team design that encourages learning and avoids boredom, and workable forms of involvement where skills and knowledge have an avenue for expression and growth. OPA is about the ways work and meaningful activity are organised so that people combine together and work with technology to integrate their activities and in dealing with customers, suppliers and responding to competitor threats.

It is often hard to describe how precisely these processes happen, why they are done and where they come from. This is where tacit knowledge is important, for example. Researchers often refer to 'path dependency' meaning the strong legacy of history or to the 'way things are done'. While structures can be designed, behaviours of collaboration or competition, involvement or control, integration or fragmentation, cooperation or conflict are more difficult to order and change. Some companies have highly successful processes which give them an advantage over their competitors whether competing for economic reward, or resources (as in the public and voluntary sectors). Often this process advantage remains hidden from view, is difficult to unravel and so is hard to copy. It also gives added value in a way that no other resource can do. OPA is therefore central to achieving and maintaining sustained competitive advantage. Organisational values and culture are frequently seen as a key ingredient in OPA, especially in knowledge intensive firms as we discuss in Chapter 7.

We need to be clear, too, how this is related to better performance. Before we can explore this in detail it is necessary to reiterate the central proposition in the link between people and performance. Building on the work of American researchers like MacDuffie (1995) and Appelbaum and her colleagues (2000) we show that the function of effective people management is to persuade, induce, cajole, or encourage employees to do as good a job as possible (whether more, or better, or more innovatively) both individually and in working with others. This extra behaviour beyond the minimum can rarely be forced. It has to be given by employees and is therefore discretionary in the sense of 'going the extra mile' or taking responsibility for actions or outcomes that are not strictly part of the job seen in the job description. Organisational effectiveness comes when a significant or large proportion of employees at all levels engage in discretionary behaviour which is valued by the firm and fellow employees. We know from research in the psychological contract and in organisational citizenship behaviour (see Coyle-Shapiro *et al.* 2004) that people with high levels of affective commitment to their organisation and to their fellow workers, and who find their work satisfying, are more likely to engage in discretionary behaviour. Thus actions which help generate commitment are central to the people–performance equation.

The classic definition of organisational commitment is the relative strength of an individual's identification with, and involvement in, a particular organisation. It has three attributes:

- a strong belief in, and an acceptance of, the organisation's goals and values;
- a willingness to exert considerable effort on behalf of the organisation;
- a strong desire to maintain membership in the organisation (Porter *et al.* 1974: 604).

The definitions of HCA and OPA bear strong connections to the definitions of resources and capabilities in the resource-based view described in Chapter 1, and they have similar implications for the use of HR to generate sustained competitive advantage. HCA can be enhanced by improvements in recruitment, selection, training, etc., thereby improving the quantity and quality of the human resources available to the firm. To the extent that HCA is a set of systems and processes for delivering better human capital it can be thought of as a capability. OPA can also be thought of as a capability: an ability to leverage a range of resources, some of which are human and others which are not, to realise sustained competitive advantage.

Defining and maintaining the strong culture organisation

Organisational values and culture first came to prominence in the early 1980s with the publication of *In Search of Excellence* by Peters and Waterman (1982) and *Corporate Cultures* by Deal and Kennedy (1982). The view then was that values were determined by senior management and culture could be designed as something an organisation had or ought to have. Deal and Kennedy showed that successful firms were distinguished from less successful ones through their clearly articulated shared norms and values regarding organisational functioning. The emphasis on *shared* norms and values is the key since this draws attention to the distinction, crucial in HR, between intended and experienced practices. Just as we show in Chapter 4 that front line managers are central to enacting or making practices work, so in studies on culture and values the frequent gap has been noted between what *ought* to happen and does happen. It has often been observed, as O'Reilly and Chatman put it, that 'repetition by top managers of what is important, or the printing of company values on parchment, does not mean that members of the organisation accept these as important' (1996: 166).

This problem of enactment has led researchers and theorists to see culture and values as something that reflects organisational life rather than imposed top down by senior management. Thus, it is often argued that culture is something about what the organisation 'is' rather than what it just 'has' or has been given by senior management. In this sense culture is hard, if not impossible to manage and manipulate at the whim of top management. If senior management want to influence organisational culture they need to be aware of the variety and complexity of existing cultures or culture in the organisation. It is more helpful to identify values and beliefs that are generally and widely shared in the organisation. Senior management can, if they recognise the value of doing so, make these beliefs and values more visible in their communications and especially in their behaviour and in clearly indicating what they expect of others. Thus O'Reilly and Chatman (1996: 160) define culture as 'a system of shared values (that define what is important) and norms that define appropriate attitudes and behaviour for organisational members (how to feel and behave)'. The most famous definition is by Schein:

> Organisational culture is the pattern of basic assumptions that a given group has invented, discovered or developed in learning to cope with its problems of external adaptation and internal integration and that have worked well enough to be considered valid and therefore to be taught to new members as the correct way to perceive, think and feel in relation to these problems.
>
> (Schein 1985)

At the heart of organisational culture are hidden values which are 'unconscious, taken for granted beliefs, perceptions, thoughts and feeling which are the ultimate source of values and action' (Schein 1985). In this sense some part of organisational culture is unmanageable in that it is not capable of being directed but it means that attempts to articulate and reinforce appropriate values and norms need to reflect these hidden values and build on them in part by making some of these values more accessible. For this reason some studies have argued, and shown in field research, that 'shared perceptions of daily practice [are] the core of an organisation's culture' and that 'the values of founders and key leaders undoubtedly shape organisational cultures but the way these cultures affect ordinary members is through shared practice' (Hofstede *et al.* 1990: 311). This daily practice, the influx of new members as well as new leaders, and changing external challenges and uncertainties mean that culture and organisational values are usually dynamic.

Very strong(ly) shared cultures, however, are sometimes seen as too inflexible so a balance is needed between weak cultures which do not reflect or establish common norms and values and strong cultures which can become introvert. If cultures are created by group members and shaped by key leaders it means they are unique to each organisation. What is viable for one could be disastrous for another. Organisations can emphasise different things. Some may give priority to external performance, others to internal integration. Some are based on the primacy of leadership, others are more egalitarian and collegial and yet others may be meritocratic or even elitist (Kabonoff *et al.* 1995). This is very much in tune with the idea that there is no one particular or universalistic way of managing people in every firm. The need is to find the best fit linking people's needs with those of the competitive or resource position of the firm. Whatever the mission or seeming purpose of the company, for values and culture to contribute to a success they must be broadly shared and consistent (Gordon and DiTomaso 1992: 794), enacted in daily practice and contribute to people's desire to contribute and stay with the organisation.

One of the most obvious ways to ensure that a strong culture is maintained is through the 'person–organisational fit'. This is seen first in job choice. Particular kinds of individuals are attracted to particular kinds of organisation and those who do not fit soon leave (Sheridan 1992). This is particularly relevant where the 'fit' is to values based on norms and commitment seen in interpersonal relationships for example, as opposed to instrumental contract compliance. There is clear evidence, certainly amongst studies on accountants, that retention rates were much higher where this fit was achieved (O'Reilly *et al.* 1991). Two implications flow from this. First, people have to know what sort of organisation would best suit them thus placing emphasis on employer branding, becoming an employer of choice and simultaneously having or using realistic job previews and forming realistic expectations of the nature of organisational life. Second, organisations are increasingly moving to recruitment and selection techniques based on attitudinal and behavioural profiling and using different ways of screening applicants, often remotely through highly structured telephone interviews. Interestingly, two of our large companies, both with distinctive cultures and values (Nationwide and Selfridges), had recently adopted this type of selection procedure with excellent results. Some of our smaller knowledge intensive firms did the same only rather more informally. All were concerned to ensure a person–organisation fit based around values and 'belonging' and recognised this was a two-way process.

What is being looked for is congruence between individual values and those of the organisation. This may well be at the crux of the person–culture fit. This fit may be to a generalised value such as 'public service' or to a brand like Jaguar and the primacy of quality, or to the dominant profession employed successfully in the firm like software engineering, or to organisational values like 'mutuality' in Nationwide. Another way of putting this is the search for identity, and these may be multiple – the profession and the organisation. Early experience of work where new members are socialised into prevailing values and culture is crucial in confirming or confounding these shared values (Sheridan 1992). Thus, careful induction of new employees, the use of buddy systems and supportive team members is important in value reproduction. It is here that stories and rituals are learnt and seen to be appropriate in helping to overlay formal controls with social control. Values and culture are a form of social control especially when linked to commitment. When people say they share the values of the organisation they are likely to be expressing a sense of self-fulfilment at work, showing an acceptance of appropriate and expected role behaviour and expressing an identification with the firm and often with their occupation or fellow workers or are identifying with an ideology or wider sense of purpose like 'patient care' or 'public service'. Rousseau (1990) called this 'deep structure identification', beyond the superficial, and showed that this was strongly linked to affective commitment, citizenship and discretionary behaviour.

This, of course, presupposes that organisational values exist in a coherent sense, are known and are enacted or seen in appropriate behaviour. Some of these behaviours will be specific to the organisation in the way it deals with issues such as customer care, handling complaints and reacting to problems and opportunities. Others are more general, reflecting wider societal beliefs about fairness, recognition, support and self-expression. There are often different subcultures within organisations. These can be complementary or conflictual. In particular there may be differences between the executive culture of the top team and that expressed by others whether the engineers or technocrats who design operating systems, and people who fulfil the daily work of the organisation, the operators. Schein (1996) notes that 'the research findings about the importance of team-work, commitment and involvement fall on deaf executive ears because in executive cultures these are not important values to consider'. Thus, there has to be some congruence between executives and employees in expressing values considered to reflect the purpose and social construction of the organisation and these need to resonate with wider social values which members of the organisation think or see as important.

The Big Idea and its link with employee commitment to the organisation

Having set the scene by looking at the previous work in the field we now draw from our own research to provide some illustrations of the important role played by organisational culture and values. Initially we discuss what organisational culture meant in our organisations by proposing the concept of the 'Big Idea' and we illustrate this by reference to two of our cases. We then move on to examine the links between HR practices and culture by focusing on the behaviour of individual employees. In particular we consider the HR practices which are associated with strong cultures.

One of the tests of 'strong' organisation culture is the extent to which there is consistency by which is meant widespread agreement about the organisation of work, the emphasis on human resources, decision-making processes and coordination activities. If consistency is matched with appropriateness the outcome can be powerful. 'A strong culture from the standpoint of consistency, and an appropriate culture from the standpoint of content, will [each] produce positive results, but a combination of the two is most powerful' (Gordon and DiTomaso 1992: 794). A notable feature of our more successful research organisations was the existence of what we came to call the 'Big Idea'. The Big Idea is a clear sense of mission underpinned by values and a culture expressing what the firm is and its relationship with its customers and employees. There are five key attributes to the Big Idea as revealed in the research.

Embedded

First, the Big Idea is not necessarily captured in a formal mission statement agreed at the board level but rather as values which are spread throughout the organisation. In our interviews at all levels we kept on hearing references to these values and to the underlying organisation culture, not always expressed in the same terms, but clearly deriving from a common root. That is, they were embedded into organisational practice. These values and the way they are expressed by different people in different ways in the same firm are a long way beyond trite statements like 'our employees are our most important resources'.

Connected

Second, these values about what sort of organisation the firm sought to be inter-connected the relationships with customers and the organisational culture and behaviour, and thus set the fundamentals on how employees should be managed, their responsibilities to each other and to customers. This linkage between HR and customers, the internal and the external, meant that values were consistent and mutually reinforcing between, for example, HR and marketing. This was particularly evident in customer-facing organisations like Selfridges, Tesco and Nationwide where the logic of the employee–customer–profit chain applied. The most famous example of this is the US chain store, Sears, where strong evidence exists that the organisation became 'a compelling place to invest' when it was seen as a 'compelling place to shop' and was recognised as 'a compelling place to work' (Rucci *et al.* 1998). These issues are discussed in much greater detail in Chapter 8.

Enduring

Third, these values, at their best, were enduring and provided a stable base on which different initiatives and policies could be built and changed as circumstances altered. Strong enduring values, historically derived (sometimes known as 'path dependency'), provided the basis both for the management of performance and the achievement of change. It is a form of historical learning at the organisational level. This was particularly important in sustaining performance and flexibility, but was sometimes hard to achieve. In one of our organisations growing pressure for cost containment was seen by employees to weaken commitment to core values about people. In other cases values remained clear and strong and this was reflected in enduring commitment by employees to their organisation even when difficult decisions had to be made.

Collective

Fourth, the Big Idea has the attributes of strong cultures where the organisational culture acts like glue in binding people and processes together. It is thus a collective endeavour and differs from HR practices in its effect in linking people management to performance. Most HR practices are, of necessity, focused on the individual employee: selection, appraisal, pay, training and development, communication, work–life balance, etc., and the individualization of the employment contract has encouraged this. The outcome of these HR practices, if properly designed and applied, will increase the human capital pool, and provide continuous replacement. This provides the human resource advantage. Values, and in a different sense, organisational routines – how work is done – provide the extra ingredients that can mark out superior sustained performance, what we have referred to as organisational process advantage. Some organisations develop high levels of efficiencies through the creation and continuous refinement of excellent routines so that everyone knows what to do and how to do it, repeatedly. Good examples in our organisations were Jaguar, Tesco, and Nationwide. In Nationwide's case part of the need for routines was the need to satisfy the regulatory requirements in the financial services industry. This collective endeavour, the ability to join people together in one common goal, is reinforced by underlying values about the dominant purpose of the organisation, the way it treats customers and employees. Thus successful organisations combine, in unique ways, values, routines and practices which affect both individuals and the collective endeavour. It is this 'social complexity' which is so hard to copy. Individual HR practices can easily be replicated but it is the mix of these practices with well-developed routines underpinned by values collectively applied and embedded which is so hard to imitate.

Measured and managed

In a number of cases a balanced scorecard (Kaplan and Norton 1996) or the Tomorrow's Organisation approach (Goyder 1998) was used not just as a means of measuring performance in four or five attributes of the business (typically shareholders, customers, employees, operational excellence and, in some, the community) but as a means of integrating different functional areas and decisions into linked processes. This integration was both vertical, linking the top with the bottom, and horizontal, interconnecting HR with marketing, for example, and with operations across the functional areas. In one case when the balanced scorecard just generated performance numbers discussed at a monthly management board meeting it was much less effective than in those cases where processes were integrated informing and influencing decision making and where these decisions were themselves deeply influenced by values associated with the Big Idea.

The existence of the Big Idea in some of our research organisations is, of necessity, a subjective measure that the researchers had to reach in trying to isolate those organisations which had a clear idea that met the criteria of embedded, connected, enduring, collective, measured and managed. The five organisations shown in Figure 2.2 all had clearly articulated a Big Idea which had been in existence for some time, and a balanced scorecard, or had adopted the methodology of the Tomorrow's Organisation approach.

Figure 2.2 shows the mean scores (based on a five point scale where 5 is strongly agree, 1 is strongly disagree) for each of the questions testing organisational commitment from the first year of our survey. These questions were derived from WERS 1998.[1] This allows us to compare our organisations with the national average. All five of the organisations in Figure 2.2 exceeded this. The average for all employees in the remaining case study organisations is shown in the last right-hand two columns. All five organisations with a clearly articulated Big Idea and

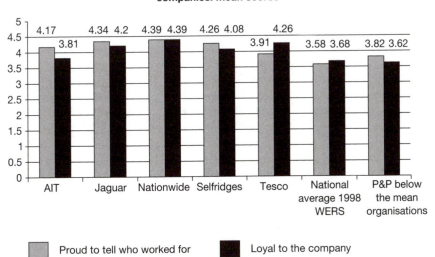

Figure 2.2 Measures of organisational commitment

with the use of some form of balanced scorecard were above average in most or all of the questions.

To get a more accurate comparison we found (in the WERS data bank) the nearest equivalent occupational group in the appropriate sector. For example, we compared the Selfridges Sales Associates with retail trade sales staff and Nationwide Financial Sales Consultants with sales employees in the financial intermediaries sector. Again all outperformed their comparators. However, this was not true amongst the remaining organisations, two of which were below the national average for their comparator.

In other words there is strong evidence in these five organisations that the existence of a Big Idea or mission/culture/values articulation which is embedded and interconnected, and which is linked with a means to measure and integrate, was reflected in the commitment employees showed to their organisation. Organisational commitment was high in each of these organisations.

We can now build on our discussion of the Big Idea and examine the links between HR practices and organisational commitment. Drawing on our research we propose that the link between culture and performance is through the behaviour of individual employees as shown in Figure 2.3. We find that employees who said they had high levels of commitment to their organisation were more likely to be satisfied, often highly satisfied, with HR practices especially training, career opportunities, job challenge and job influence, performance appraisal, rewards and recognition, efforts to help employees achieve a work–life balance, communication and involvement. This, in turn, as we discuss in Chapters 4 and 5, is linked to satisfaction with line manager relationships and high levels of discretionary behaviour.

In our research we found that the extent to which employees agreed, or strongly agreed, with the statement 'I share the values of my company' was associated with specific sets of criteria or conditions. In particular there was a strong likelihood that employees would express high levels of identification with the firm's values when:

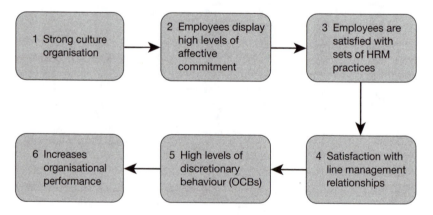

Figure 2.3 The culture–HR practice–performance link

- They were satisfied with the amount of information they received about how well the company was performing, how they contributed to the company achieving its business objects, and believed that everyone in the firm was well aware of the long-term plans and goals of the organisation. Taken together these questions assess the effectiveness of communication.
- They were satisfied with methods used to appraise their performance.
- They were satisfied with their pay, and how their pay compared with others, and with the benefits they received other than pay.
- They felt they were provided with good opportunities to express grievances and raise issues of personal concern. We called this 'openness'.
- They felt their job was secure.
- They felt satisfied with the influence they had in company decisions that affected their job or work. This is a measure of involvement.
- They agreed that managers were good at keeping everybody informed about proposed changes, provided everyone with a chance to comment on proposals, responded to suggestions from employees, dealt with problems at the workplace and treated employees fairly. In short their relationship with their managers was good.
- They also had high levels of satisfaction with the amount of influence they had over their job, the sense of achievement they got from their job and the amount of respect they received. This is a measure of job satisfaction.

Less strong, but still significant associations were found with training, career opportunities, work–life balance and how much effort they made in their job. Taken together these practices constitute an effective HR system which contributes to positive performance. As noted earlier, this mix of HR practices is both a conduit through which values are expressed and enacted and, by their action, express deep-seated shared values.

Using more sophisticated statistical techniques of multi-variant analysis which allow the independent effect of each variable or factor (i.e. each practice) to be assessed, we are able to show that in strong shared value companies a particular set of practices were especially effective in allowing us to explain 40 per cent of the causes of organisational commitment. In the companies with weak or less shared values not only was the level of organisational commitment lower but we could only identify 28 per cent of the causes of organisational commitment. This is shown in Table 2.1.

Added to these was a strong link to commitment where there was satisfaction with the way line managers applied these practices and the quality of the relationship between them and their work group. These practices are important in their own right but taken together we can say two further things. First, they are at the heart of the type and range of activities which mould expectations about what opportunities are offered or promised by the employer for personal development and job growth and security, and help establish what is expected of employees in return. Such practices both reflect and help determine key aspects of the reciprocal exchange between employees and managers. Second, these practices and

Table 2.1 Practices associated with organisation commitment in five strong shared values companies and seven weak shared values companies (rank order)

Strong shared values companies	Weak shared values companies
Organisation Commitment (R^2.403)	Organisation commitment (R^2.278)
Drivers: Communication	Drivers: Openness
Relationship with manager	Rewards and recognition
Career opportunities	Communication
Work–life balance support	Effort
Involvement	
N 325	N 284

Source: People and performance research.

line manager behaviour both reflect and reinforce (or weaken where they are ineffective) organisational values and in a broader sense the culture of the firm. The HR practices are one of the most obvious conduits through which culture and values are expressed or given meaning.

In the organisations where we have high levels of organisational commitment, satisfaction with HR practices and line management relationships, we are also more likely to have evidence of discretionary, or organisational citizenship behaviour (OCBs) (Purcell *et al.* 2004a). Organisational commitment is therefore an important antecedent to discretionary behaviour. As discussed at the start of this chapter, this extra role behaviour beyond the minimum can rarely be forced. It has to be given by employees and is therefore discretionary in the sense of 'going the extra mile' or taking responsibility for actions or outcomes that are not strictly part of the job seen in the job description. This is discussed in greater detail in Chapters 4 and 5.

In summary, levels of organisational commitment are higher in strong shared value companies and can be explained to a greater extent by the practices which fit the values, like communications, the way managers manage, the belief that people have in opportunities for career progression and involvement, and the way the organisation tries to help people achieve a satisfactory balance between work and home. In companies with relatively weak shared values, organisational commitment is lower and it is more difficult to identify the drivers of these. The type of practices we can identify are vaguer like 'openness' – the ease of raising problems with your boss – and rewards and recognition in being how satisfied people are with the way their contribution is recognised. Communication is important but not nearly so strong in its effect as in strong shared value companies. People who put in a lot of effort also show higher levels of commitment in these weak shared value companies. Not surprisingly fewer people in these companies with low levels of shared values are aware of how they contribute to the company achieving its objectives and fewer share the values of the company as shown in Figure 2.2. This, of course, requires people to know and understand the business objectives of their company and its values. No wonder communication in all its meanings comes out as such a powerful link to commitment in firms with high levels of shared values and is central to the articulation of values and culture.

The culture–performance link: two case studies

Although we have found links between HR practices and employee attitudes in several cases it is likely that these detailed interactions will vary between companies. In this section we provide two examples of the Big Idea drawn from contrasting organisations. The first, Selfridges, illustrates a set of culture and values which are very broadly defined to include the perspectives of a variety of stakeholders. Moreover this shows how the multiple stakeholder model was actually worked through in detail and the effect this had on employee attitudes. The Jaguar example shows how a single value, in this instance quality, is interpreted through changes in work organisation and procedures and routines. The changes associated with the increased importance of quality, especially the introduction of group leaders, played a key part in promoting the Big Idea with a consequent positive impact on employee attitudes.

Selfridges plc

Since the mid-1990s Selfridges has embarked on an ambitious renewal and growth programme. During this time the critical strategic choice was about what sort of retailer should Selfridges be and how would internal staff management be linked in to this. The need was to recruit and develop staff who had deep product knowledge and were able to create relationships with customers. The widespread view was that customers were becoming much more discerning than they used to be and increasingly wanted an enjoyable experience beyond the simple transaction of buying. Staff, especially staff associates who serve customers, were seen to be central to creating and achieving this ambience and experience. The creation of a 'store for the next century' as Vittorio Radice, the Chief Executive at the time, demanded, required a major change in almost every aspect of the business including:

- integrated IT Systems linking suppliers to Selfridges and improved communication within the organisation;
- a new team of retail operations managers meeting weekly;
- a new approach to buying with buyers taken off the department floor and no longer reporting to a senior manager in the department;
- moving to seven days a week trading with longer opening hours;
- a new approach to leadership and management style which was to be 'aspirational, friendly and accessible';
- managers would need to take responsibility for people management (in the past even first level disciplinary matters were sent to the Personnel Department);
- new and more accurate performance measures especially in relation to profit per square foot and data on 'foot-fall' and KPIs. This financial information

and data was to be made available down to the lowest level so that economic literacy would improve;

- a different, more partnership-based, relationship with concessionaires and their staff.

Most of all Selfridges had to move from the simple provision of customer service to being customer friendly and beyond that to becoming customer driven. 'Selfridges see themselves at the upper end of the price market with customers prepared to pay a little bit more so the service must be good – people will be critical to that', said the Commercial Controller. Selfridges trades as the 'house of brands' with a strong brand image of its own based around that general presumption. Early in the transformation, the HR Director told us they consciously set out to change the internal brand image of Selfridges amongst the staff making it identical to and conducive with the revitalised external brand image. Culture surveys were undertaken, focus groups were organised amongst staff, a new 360° or 180° appraisal system was introduced. The old Hay job evaluation system was replaced with a broad banding pay arrangement with a performance-based progression replacing age or length of service. A new staff council was created including union representatives from USDAW. Staff representatives were encouraged to head up project teams on such topics as clothing allowances, facilities and the staff restaurant. NVQs for sales associates were introduced with financial rewards for advancement. More care was taken with selection and promotion.

Within the Trafford Park store, where we did our fieldwork, they introduced six-monthly assessment performance reviews (APR). In the period September to October each member of staff was reviewed according to a development plan with the aim to try to maximise people's talents and fit their career to these strengths. In February a second review took place which was more linked to pay and performance bonuses. There was a widespread use of the 'mystery shopper' reporting on staff–customer centred skills. The acronym for this was SHINE (Smile, Help, Inform, New product push, End the sale). Many of the staff associates we interviewed had been mystery shopped and there was a general acceptance that this was the way in which Selfridges encourages performance. Each day, and at the beginning of the late shift, there was a 10 minute briefing break and each month more formal communication events occurred called Team Talk Time. This might, for example, be about the Save As You Earn scheme linked to share purchase. Training was provided at the end of the week in the morning and also at the weekend.

Behind all these innovations in HR and its link with other aspects of the business – a very good example of best fit and best process – there was an explicit effort to model the underlying stakeholder values required in their dealings with customers, employees, the community, suppliers and stakeholders. This is shown in Figure 2.4. The goal is to turn 'values into value' by acting out the values.

The values are expressed in a more articulated form under three goals: *Selfridges should be aspirational, friendly and bold.* Under each of these headings the question is raised about the values required.

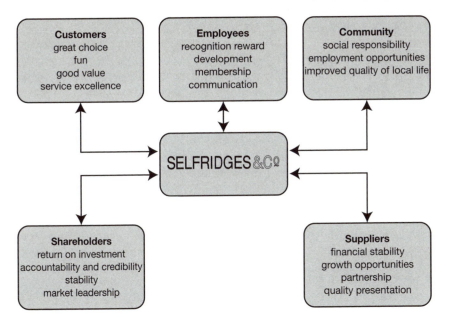

Figure 2.4 The Selfridges stakeholder value model

Employee values:	How does this make me want to work here?
Customer values:	How am I encouraged to shop?
Community values:	How does Selfridges reflect the spirit of the city?
Shareholder values:	Why should we invest in the store?
Supplier values:	What makes Selfridges an interesting proposition?

Figure 2.5 gives an example of how these questions are to be answered in terms of aspirations under the general banner of 'friendly: everyone is welcome.'

These are bold value statements and the development of HR architecture was innovative in trying to turn these into reality. There were, and are, real challenges in making this work. The long opening hours meant that staffing had to be found for weekends and evenings with key staff working under rota. This broke with the traditional working patterns in Manchester at the time. It was not helped by the fact that the public transport system was poor especially at the end of the evening shift so that travel to and from work caused problems. This made it hard to find and to keep staff. Staff turnover was high, particularly in the first few years after opening the Manchester store, although less than the normal for the retail trade (and the organisation successfully reduced turnover from 78 per cent in 2000 to 40 per cent in 2001). In addition there was a heavy reliance on part-time staff. In these circumstances it was more expensive to develop a sophisticated HR system. An added complication was that as the 'House of Brands' a large proportion of the sales associates were concession staff. As shown in Figure 2.5 the value statement

Employee values	Customer values	Community values	Shareholder value	Supplier values
• How does this make me want to work here?	• How am I encouraged to shop?	• How does Selfridges reflect the spirit of the city?	• Why should we invest in the store?	• What makes Selfridges an interesting proposition?
Selfridges is a very friendly place to work. I like my boss and my team.	People at Selfridges are always smiling and helpful – they seem to enjoy working there.	Selfridges promotes an inclusive spirit.	Their annual reports are inviting and easy to read.	We help each other in the continuous improvement of our relationship.
I know my opinion and contribution is welcomed.	I like to buy and browse in Selfridges – I never feel under pressure but rarely come home empty handed.	It is a microcosm of all the different cultures and communities which make up the city.	Their financial information is transparent and their directors are open to any questions.	Their wide and diverse range of quality products adds value to my product.
I feel welcomed and this makes me welcome others.	Selfridges represents the good things about city living.	Through its managers and staff Selfridges gets involves in community projects.	I feel welcome when I attend shareholders' meetings.	My concession staff are treated well and made to feel welcome.

Figure 2.5 Selfridges: an example of the values matrix: friendly – everyone is welcome

and the supplier value says 'my concession staff are treated well and made to feel welcome'. In practice this meant that concession staff join sales teams and take part in communication activities. There were no major differences between the views of concession staff and Selfridges' employees in our survey and 92 per cent of our respondents felt that the relationship between Selfridges' staff and concession staff was good.

Selfridges' staff (including the concession staff) had one of the highest levels of organisational commitment of any of our 12 organisations and in terms of a comparison with the attitudes of retail trade staff nationally, taken from the WERS 98 survey, were markedly better. For example, figures from our first year survey show:

97% are proud to tell people who they work for (WERS 98, 56%)
93% are loyal to Selfridges (WERS 98, 70%)
83% would recommend a friend or relative to work in Selfridges
72% say they share the values of the organisation (WERS 98, 50%)

If we examine the correlations between HR practices and employee attitudes in Selfridges (Table 2.2) it is clear that what was really important in the first year in linking in to commitment, motivation and job satisfaction were aspects of the job – job challenge and teamwork. The feeling that the job was secure and that there were career opportunities linked with appraisal, and most of all satisfaction with the degree and style of communication, levels of involvement and the way managers managed. The key design features of the HR system are clearly reflected in this bundle of people management practices. One of the written values is 'Selfridges is a store where there are many career opportunities'. Satisfaction with these opportunities for those who wanted them was clear in the survey and this fed through into motivation and commitment. Another written aspiration in

Table 2.2 The relationship between HR practices and employee attitudes in Selfridges. First year correlation results (N= 40)

	Job satisfaction	Motivation	Commitment
Job security	*		
Training			
Career opportunity	*	**	
Appraisal	*		
Pay satisfaction			
Job challenge		**	*
Teamwork			*
Involvement	**		
Communication	*	**	*
Openness (ability to raise concerns)	**		
Work–life balance			
Management behaviour	*	*	*

* significant at .05 level (2-tailed)
** significant at .01 level (2-tailed)

the value statement is 'I like my boss and my team, and I know my opinion and contribution is welcomed'. These too, were reflected in our survey under team-work, involvement and management behaviour, and in the opportunity to raise a concern, which is a test of openness.

The correlations show that those staff who were satisfied with their manager and the way they were managed had high levels of commitment, motivation and job satisfaction. Since it was the managers who undertook the daily and monthly communication sessions and it was these managers who did the appraisals the strong correlations here in these segments also reflect management style and management behaviour. However, according to our respondents, there were not enough managers undertaking this type of people management to the level expected by the staff. As we discuss in Chapter 4 this is an important part of people management, and Selfridges took this on board as a result of our first year feedback.

The importance of the line manager in delivering people management comes out even more clearly when we look more closely at the drivers of commitment, motivation and job satisfaction. For example those who felt they received a lot of coaching and guidance from their line manager were much more likely to show commitment to Selfridges, and this was true too if they thought management were good at dealing with absenteeism and lateness. This active role of managers was also linked to people's sense of having a career opportunity and their satisfaction with the appraisal system. Since the managers we are referring to are mainly team leaders (the immediate line manager) not surprisingly there was a link also with the staff's satisfaction with teamworking.

Jaguar

The Big Idea in Jaguar is quality. The organisation's position in the J. D. Power league table and other consumer tests was just one part of it, albeit crucial for performance in the marketplace. Quality was not just an outcome seen in product reliability, design and build, it was also about processes and routines. It drives down costs by reducing reworking, eliminating the need for an army of quality inspectors and reduces accidents and injuries. This latter issue was a major focus at the Browns Lane plant in Coventry, where we did our research, as the work-force was long established (a third of those we interviewed were over 50) and with outsourcing of some areas it was harder to move people off the track to different, slower jobs. Thus the pursuit of quality had many meanings and many outcomes. Everyone in the plant we talked to recognised the need for quality. The unions raise quality issues with senior management in their regular meetings, and workers had pride in the product.

Ford took over Jaguar in 1989. The recession of the early 1990s led to major difficulties with big redundancies many of which were compulsory. The union officers still remember that time with horror. 'Sitting down with senior managers to decide who was going to be made compulsorily redundant was very painful – we decided we did not want it to happen again.' A flexibility deal was agreed then with the unions and they have subsequently worked in partnership with the organisation helping to bring in quality measures while still keeping their distance and independence when they feel it necessary. One aspect of quality has been the use of metrics to measure everything and to identify appropriate actions often listed as eleven steps, or eight goals or seven plus one wastes (interestingly the eighth waste is 'under-utilization of our people, their skills and knowledge'). These metrics are linked with the typical hardware of lean production systems as we described in an earlier CIPD report (Hutchinson *et al.* 1998): statistical process control (SPC), value stream analysis (VSA) with value stream mapping (VSM), FTPM (Ford Total Preventive Maintenance) and so on. Most of these measures are Ford driven and provide benchmark standards across the Group but especially within Ford Europe and the Premier Automotive Group which now includes Volvo and Land Rover. The success of these quality initiatives and the launch of new models led to a substantial expansion in the Jaguar manufacturing capacity with the opening of the old Ford Halewood plant on Merseyside and with a further capacity at Castle Bromwich.

The most important of these quality measures in the 1990s as Jaguar recovered and retooled with the help of Ford investment and Ford management expertise was Q1, the Ford Quality Standard. This standard was mandatory. At first Jaguar was bottom of the league but by the time we did our interviews they were top. They also won the J. D. Power Gold Award for the best quality plant in Europe (shared with Porsche). Since then there has been the progressive adoption of the Ford Production System (FPS) covering all aspects of work in great detail, and the introduction of 6 Sigma, a quality management tool involving project focus and analysis using trained employees full-time on this work for two years (the black belts) and part-time team members (brown belts). Quite a number of brown belts were manual workers, and it was not unusual for manual workers to meet suppliers as part of problem solving.

The people management dimensions of the pursuit of quality were not to be found in a battery of new HR practices. In some ways there was a continuity in the basics of HR. People queued up for jobs in Jaguar, although it was only until very recently with the new model launch that there was any need to recruit. Training in quality standards was necessary but there was no appraisal system, no performance pay and no attitude surveys for manual workers on the line or such like. Communication about quality problems and the meeting of targets was important but beyond that, in terms of wider plant issues, it has proved difficult to get it right.

What was important, however, was the reorganisation of employees on the track and in the trim shop into teams with one of their number chosen by management as a team leader, known as a group leader, and paid a supplement. There remained some resistance to this, with some of the older employees seeing group leaders as 'gaffers' narks', but the team leaders themselves who we interviewed were positive and enthusiastic. Eventually there will be a ratio of one group leader to eight employees with groups becoming more self-managed, for example doing their own job timing and work-study. This was a form of empowerment to some but was not necessarily welcomed by others. Teams do their own quality measures, enter data onto charts in the team area, spot variances, undertake statistical analysis and take corrective action, all as part of SPC. Group leaders entered issues on the Countermeasure Boards on behalf of the team. There were set time limits for a management response. Some middle managers found it hard to deal with this sort of employee involvement. 'The real skill is learning how to say no and explaining it, if no is the correct answer' said the Production Manager. Initially when group leaders were introduced the track stopped at 11 a.m. each Friday for 15 minutes to discuss issues on quality, cost, health and safety and employment matters and so on. The practice was then changed so that the track stopped once a day for five minutes with a set topic for each day. Teams do routine maintenance as part of FTPM. Some saw this as work intensification, others as empowerment, where group leaders had a key role in work allocations dealing with quality and communication and 'owning' the work processes.

This focus on 'ownership' influenced how new production lines and new models were introduced. In the mid-1990s an innovative line was installed by a specialist design team but it turned out to be defective. The people who were to work on that line were not consulted. This was, according to the Production Director, 'a really hard lesson' and led to the idea that people had to be involved in both big things and little things in order to achieve the level of quality which Jaguar had to reach. 'Measurement' and 'ownership' came through frequently in our interview notes with senior managers and with group leaders as the key processes in achieving quality.

We interviewed 41 manual workers in the first year, mainly from track and assembly but some from the trim shop. Another 37 were interviewed in the second year. Compared with the national data for manufacturing operatives taken from WERS 98 there was a higher level of job satisfaction (64 per cent compared with 52 per cent) and very high levels of commitment with 95 per cent being proud to tell people who they work for compared with 47 per cent nationally and 85 per cent felt loyal to the organisation (WERS 98, 55 per cent). This underlying historically derived commitment to Jaguar, and its distinctive green logo, as opposed to the blue of Ford's oval, as a form of value provided a strong base for people management. This was the case even when a large number of respondents felt they had to work very hard, and double the number in the WERS survey worried about their job outside work. Three quarters of our respondents said that their sense of team working was very or fairly strong and an equal number felt that membership of teams helped them improve their performance. It is important to recall that teams were only introduced relatively recently.

When we asked about employees' attitudes to their managers it was important to differentiate between the levels of management. The key management level was the immediate manager and many people included the group leader as one of these people even though group leaders are manual workers and formally do not have management responsibility for such things as discipline. Higher-level management began at the level of the superintendent. Thinking of their immediate manager:

61% felt managers were good at dealing with problems (WERS 98, 33%)
68% felt managers were good at treating employees fairly (WERS 98, 35%)

Commitment was particularly (and significantly) associated with people's good experience of teamworking, involvement and communication. The other main links, also seen in the way they helped trigger job satisfaction and motivation, were people's satisfaction with their training and development, the career opportunities they had and their job challenge. This was especially true for group leaders themselves who were much more positive than other manual workers belonging to their team. However, where workers felt their immediate manager provided help and guidance in how they did their job they were more likely to show high levels of commitment to Jaguar and to find their jobs satisfying. The new organisational form of teams and group leaders was confirmed in our results. While work intensification had occurred, interestingly it was those who found their jobs challenging who were more likely to express strong commitment to the firm and to have higher levels of job satisfaction. In this case the values associated with working for a high quality leading car manufacturer were translated into commitment and job satisfaction especially when the relationship with immediate line management was good, and where people felt they had a challenging job, beyond the monotony of the line, and had training and development to help them with their job and career aspirations. For them working for Jaguar was more than just doing a job day after day. All this was especially true for group leaders, manual workers on the first rung of management.

In this section we have demonstrated that 'going the extra mile' is likely to be present when employees share the values of their organisation. They believe what the organisation stands for and they can identify with the values of the organisation. We illustrated here that the 'sense of shared value' can be achieved through:

1   establishing person–organisation fit;
2   excellent line management relationships;
3   sets of HRM practices that reinforce the culture.

Organisational effectiveness comes when a significant or large proportion of employees at all levels engage in discretionary behaviour which is valued by the firm and fellow employees. We know from research in the psychological contract and in organisational citizenship behaviour (see Coyle-Shapiro *et al.* 2004) that people with high levels of affective commitment to their organisation and to their fellow workers, and who find their work satisfying, are more likely to engage in discretionary behaviour. Thus actions which help generate commitment are central to the people–performance equation. We discuss this further in Chapter 5.

Implications for HR practice

In a study of employee attitudes in a New York based bank, Bartel and her colleagues concluded that:

Employee attitudes differ significantly across branches in ways that cannot be explained by branches randomly drawing workers from a distribution of workers with different innate attitudes. Newly hired workers adopt the favourable or unfavourable attitudes that the branches exhibited before they arrived. Moreover, branches with less favourable attitudes have higher turnover rates, lower levels of sales and lower rates of sales growth than where workers have more positive attitudes.

(Bartel *et al.* 2004: 24)

The implication is that employee attitudes do matter and these reflect, in part, organisational culture and values. Thus measuring employee attitudes has become a much more important feature of the HR toolkit, and needs to be integrated with measures of customers' views, and those of suppliers and other stakeholders. It is interesting to note that a survey of firms listed in the 100 best places to work (as Nationwide is) found that employees in those companies had more positive attitudes than employees in a matched sample of companies and better financial performance (Fulmer *et al.* 2003). We can confidently assert that these companies are very likely to have a strong culture (measured in a high level or consistency of agreement among participants) and with an appropriate content for their purposes (i.e. vision and values must be appropriate for the fundamental aim of the firm). Thus, we have illustrated here that strong culture organisations have a system of shared values and beliefs about what is important in and for the company, what behaviours are appropriate (and what are inappropriate) and values that guide their relationships, for example, towards customers and fellow workers. In these firms there will be an extensive use of HR practices since these are the key conduits which allow vision and values to be reflected and reinforced in daily practice, for example in recruitment and selection to achieve the person–organisation fit, in performance management to define what is meant by effective performance and individual responsibility for it, in training and development to provide opportunities for relevant skill and competence growth, and in communication and involvement to provide priorities for action, information and participation. Culture and values provide the basic parameters for specific policy development without which they can remain generalised wish-lists of 'good practice'.

We noted in our research that the 'Big Idea', to be effective, has a number of attributes.

1   It needs to be *embedded* across the organisation and widely understood or referred to, not as part of a learnt script but as a reflection of everyday life in the organisation. This is why in our study of strong shared value companies communication came out as so important in employees' perceptions of HR policy. Most employees were able to say that they shared the values of the company.

2   It is nearly always *integrated* or interconnected with customer-facing values or those relating to the desired relationship with clients, patients or other external stakeholders. While cultural perceptions of a company or organi-

sation can vary between those held inside by employees and those on the outside by customers in strong shared value organisations there is a base of societal values like honesty, fairness, respect, etc. which apply to both. Since employees are themselves consumers, failure to apply standards from one domain to another can cause commitment to the firm to fall.

3   Values need to be *enduring*. The strong shared value companies in our sample had built, consciously or unconsciously, their Big Idea on a legacy which allowed people to respond to the idealised values of the past while reflecting present and future states. By being built on the historic values of the organisation they are more likely to be seen as relevant and appropriate. Thus, 'mutuality' goes back to the origins of the building society movement; 'quality' is the very essence of the Jaguar marque; 'Friendly, bold, accessible and aspirational' as Selfridges values had their origin in the values expressed by the founder of the firm 100 years ago.

4   The implication of studies of organisational culture, vision and values is that sensible firms build on what they have, what is sometimes called 'social architecture'. Senior managers know they cannot dictate what culture their firm should have but they can influence it, for example, in the way HR practices are designed and the importance attached to their effective implementation. Since values, to be meaningful, must influence behaviour firms with strong shared values that will then tend to have *habitual, collective or routine patterns* of behaviour expressed in everyday life. These relate to interactions between people and norms of conduct and to accepted definitions of wider responsibilities and priorities seen in organisational citizenship behaviour and expressed in organisational commitment.

5   While many aspects of organisational culture are hidden, tacit and intangible, organisations have increasingly sought ways to *measure and manage* aspects of their Big Idea. The growing sophistication of attitude surveys and the regular collection of marketing, operational, financial and HR metrics and an ability to integrate their interpretation has allowed much deeper understanding of the value of 'values' in influencing productive behaviour.

This chapter set out to identify the enabling context of the people–performance link. We have done so by conceptualizing the HRM environment as the culture of the organisation which would have a direct impact on *which* practices are adopted and also on *how* they are implemented. The very notion of paying attention to the context of practice implementation is therefore important. This quality makes our research specific and sets it apart from other valuable quantitative work which is more focused on the 'presence' of HR practices. As discussed in the introduction and Chapter 1, we are interested in the Organisational Process Advantage (OPA) of the firm and not merely in the Human Capital Advantage. However, before we turn to this we must first consider the research into the impact of these HR practices which is the subject of Chapter 3.

3   Intended HR practices

Introduction

In the previous chapter we drew attention to the importance of culture and values in setting the context within which HR practices operate. This chapter shifts the focus directly on to the HR practices themselves. These practices, as we have said, have often been the centre of attention for much of the research in the field. Moreover, practitioners have also typically emphasised HR practices, often with extensive attempts to get a particular practice 'right'. Typically a problem will be identified, such as a high level of turnover of new graduates, and attempts will then be made to investigate the problem and make changes for example to the method of selection. At other times practitioners will seek to make changes to a combination of practices, for example, as part of a change management programme.

The result of the extensive academic interest is a vast amount of research which is difficult for the uninitiated to navigate. Therefore this chapter aims to:

1   stand back from the detail to provide an overview of the types of research in the field;
2   examine the research into the impact of combinations of practices at the level of the organisation;
3   evaluate this research;
4   discuss results from the people and performance research into the external and internal alignment of HR practices and employee attitudes;
5   identify key areas of research which will be addressed in later chapters.

Classifying the types of research into the links between HR and performance

In Chapter 1 we distinguished broadly between the research in the field aimed mostly at practitioners and that targeted at a more academic audience. Our focus now is on the academic research, although even allowing for this restriction we find that the sheer volume of research creates a problem in mapping out the area. There have been various attempts to provide this overview. Guest (1997) distinguished between:

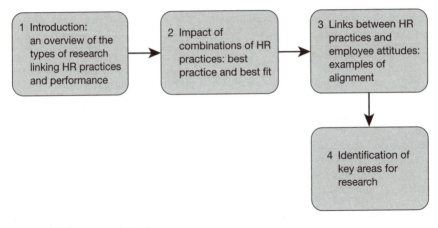

Figure 3.1 Structure of the chapter

- descriptive theories of HRM such as Beer *et al.* (1985) and Kochan *et al.* (1985) which set out to identify key areas of HRM practices and the related outcomes;
- strategic theories of HRM such as Hendry (1995) which looked at the relationship between external contingencies and HRM;
- normative theories of HRM put forward by Walton (1985) and Guest (1987) were more prescriptive in their approach and advocated the use of particular types of HR practices.

This approach is useful but fails to capture the diversity of approaches which have been taken since it focuses too much on studying combinations of practices at the organisational level.

Wright and Boswell (2002) provide a more comprehensive overview because they distinguish between studies based on their level of analysis and the number of practices studied. They recognise two important levels of analysis: macro studies where the organisation is the unit of analysis and micro studies which focus on the individual or the small group (Wright and Boswell 2002: 249). In addition research can either examine the impact of a single practice (e.g. a type of selection method used) or a combination of HR practices, sometimes referred to as an HR system (Wright and Boswell 2002: 249). This produces a classic two by two as shown in Figure 3.2.

Our focus in this chapter is on the top left quadrant where multiple practices have an impact at the organisational level. However, before we examine this we need to set this in context by looking at the other types of research.

The individual level of analysis is the typical habitat of the psychologist. For example in the lower left quadrant there is the well established research into the impact of HR practices on the psychological contract led principally by the work of Rousseau (1995) in the US and Guest (1998) in the UK although other researchers have been active in this area (Coyle-Shapiro *et al.* 2004). The lower

		Number of HR practices	
		Multiple	Single
Level of analysis	Organisation	Strategic HR IR High performance work systems	Isolated functions (i.e. research aimed at demonstrating a relationship between a particular functional area and firm performance)
	Individual	Psychological contract Employment relationships	Traditional/functional HRM Industrial/organisational psychology

Figure 3.2 A typology of HRM research (Source: Wright and Boswell (2002). Reproduced by permission of Sage Journals.)

right quadrant is the home of extensive amounts of research into the impact of particular practices on individual employees such as recruitment and selection, training and development, compensation, performance management and involvement and participation (See Wright and Boswell (2002: 255–61) for a discussion of these).

Research into the impact of individual practices on organisational performance has been more limited. Perhaps the best-known examples are the studies looking at the impact of personnel planning (Koch and McGrath 1996), recruitment and selection practices (Terpstra and Rozelle 1993), compensation practices (Gerhart and Milkovich 1990), performance related pay (Dowling and Richardson 1997; Lazear 1996; McNabb and Whitfield 1997), training and development (Kalleberg and Moody 1994) and internal career possibilities (Verburg 1998). Wright and Boswell (2002: 255) are critical of this last approach because of the failure to control for the combined effect of HR practices. Indeed, we share this view and hence devote much of our discussion to this area of research.

Impact of combinations of HR practices on organisational performance

The emphasis by researchers on the impact of multiple practices at the macro level of analysis has both an academic and a practical rationale. From the research point of view it is difficult to disentangle the impact of changes to one practice from the rest of the practices (MacDuffie 1995). As Lepak *et al.* (2006: 218) argue, 'the failure to consider all of the HR practices that are in use neglects the potential explanatory value of the unmeasured HR practices'. This also has a practical justification because organisations rarely use HR practices in isolation but more typically employ them in combination. For instance a change to a performance management system will usually require changes to be made to the payment system.

The impact of this is that we need to adopt an HR systems approach to study the links between HR practices and performance (Lepak *et al.* 2006). Indeed, this emphasis on clusters, bundles or combination of practices has dominated much of the research in the area. These combinations have come to be known by a bewildering series of names and acronyms such as HPWS (High-Performance Work Systems) (Huselid 1995; Appelbaum *et al.* 2000; Berg 1999), HCM (High-Commitment Management) (Walton 1985; Guest 1997; Arthur 1992; Lepak and Snell 2002) and High Involvement HR (Lawler 1992; Wood and De Menezes 1998). Although the need to study HR Systems is clear many questions remain unanswered. Lepak *et al.* (2006: 218–19) note there is uncertainty over the content of these systems, the interactions between these component practices and their relationships with organisational performance.

Broadly speaking the research in this area can be divided into two groups. First, those who argue that a set of HR practices can be identified which can be applied in a wide variety of circumstances and will have a positive effect on business performance, an approach usually referred to as 'best practice'. The second view, referred to as 'best fit', is that the effectiveness of HR practices depends on the external and internal context of the organisation. We review each of these using illustrations from the principal studies.

Best practice

As we have mentioned research which adopts a best practice approach has a long heritage and can be easily traced back to the early 1980s (Walton 1985) and well before then (McGregor 1960). This view has a strong intuitive appeal and suggests there is a set of practices which can and should be adopted by firms which will lead to improvements in performance. Indeed, it might be argued that most textbooks in the field put forward a set of practices which can be applied in all circumstances, with only a relatively few statements about how these might be modified to fit particular contexts. Tables and lists of best practices abound. Advocates of this approach argue that the task is first to identify the best practices, then gain sufficient support from senior managers to adopt these (since they often involve significant expenditure) and then to implement them (Boxall and Purcell 2003: 61). Researchers have also highlighted the need to avoid what they referred to as 'deadly' combinations, for example the introduction of individual perform-ance pay and teamworking (Delery 1998).

What these approaches have in common is that they identify a distinctive set of successful HR practices that can be applied successfully to all organisations irre-spective of their setting. Pfeffer (1994, 1998) is perhaps the best known of these developing a list of 16 best practices which were subsequently narrowed down to seven (1998). The seven practices are: employment security, selective hiring, self-managed teams/teamworking, high compensation contingent on organisational performance, extensive training, reduction of status differentials and sharing information.

As we noted earlier, Huselid (1995: 644) highlighted the need for an integrated system of work practices to fit the needs of the organisation. This research involved counting the number of practices a firm employs with data usually collected by means of a postal questionnaire completed by a single respondent representing the company as a whole. Impressive results are available linking the number of practices and various forms of performance – typically profit and market value. Delery and Doty (1996) and Wood and Albanese (1995) also provide some support for this view.

Rather more mixed results have emerged from recent research by Guest *et al.* (2003) drawing on a survey of 366 UK firms. They found that greater use of HR practices was associated with lower labour turnover and higher profit per employee, but not with higher productivity. However, these associations ceased to be significant once profitability in earlier years is taken into account (Guest *et al.* 2003: 306). Although the association between HR practices and organisational performance is confirmed, there is no evidence to show that the presence of HR practices causes a change in performance (Guest *et al.* 2003: 307).

This school of thought has been the subject of extensive criticism (see Boxall and Purcell 2003: 63–4). Broadly speaking there are questions about the theoretical base of this research and the practical application. From the academic perspective three kinds of criticism can be identified. First, these lists do not actually agree on what these practices actually are, some mention four or five while others have as many as sixteen (Dyer and Reeves 1995; Becker and Gerhart 1996). Boselie *et al.* (2005: 72) identified 26 general categories of practices used by researchers. Most researchers construct a list of practices but there is no agreement on what or which practices to include. While core practices associated with recruitment and selection, training and development, and performance management (appraisal and variable pay) are nearly always included, others like job design and involvement are much more sporadic. If the authors cannot agree on which practices are important, it creates doubt in the mind of the practitioner over the applicability of the findings. There is little debate on where lists of practices come from or what criteria to use in their construction. The lists appear to emerge from sets of practices normally associated with activities undertaken by well-staffed, sophisticated HR departments in large firms often linked to so-called 'transformational' approaches to the management of labour. These predetermine what type of HR practices are hypothesised to lead to outcomes of higher performance as made clear by Pfeffer's list of seven practices 'for building profits by putting people first' (1998).

Second, the unanswered question in this is whose goals are being sought (Paauwe 2004: 66–73)? Marchington and Grugulis (2000) note that the voice of the employee is largely silent in this analysis. While there is a focus on selection, training, appraisal and pay, representative systems are often absent from the research. Indeed, Purcell (1999: 27) notes that much of the best practice discussion is taking place at a time of growing use of contingent labour and income inequalities where the concern for employee voice is especially important. This then leads on to the final criticism which is the failure to take account of the context within which organisations operate. This draws attention to the differing HR needs of the architectural practice, the sophisticated manufacturing firm and the corner shop. More generally Boxall and Purcell (2003: 64–8) note the failure to take into account the contexts at the national, sectoral and organisational levels. For example while the union role has been drastically reduced in many parts of developed economies there are some parts of these economies (e.g. the public sector in the UK and parts of the manufacturing sector in Australia, Canada and New Zealand) where unionised interests remain active (Boxall and Purcell 2003: 63).

A series of practical questions have also been raised. First, there are those concerned with the existence of the kind of planning which this view assumes (Marchington and Grugulis 2000). Indeed, Purcell (1999: 27) comments that 'what is most notable about the best practice model is that there is no discussion of company strategy at all'. This then links to the second point which is the lack of any systematic evidence that these practices are being widely used and have the desired effect. Purcell notes that not only does the WERS 1998 research reveal limited adoption of best practices and that it is not only firms with high commitment practices which show evidence of high performance (Wood and De Menezes 1998). Indeed, he argues that 'the control or cost minimization type of human resource management can be equally successful in performance terms' (Purcell 1999: 28). The final concern relates to the groups of staff to whom these best practices are applied. For example are these practices used for all employees or only some of them, if so which groups are included or excluded? If a flexible firm model is adopted then are the best practices reserved for those privileged enough to work in the core group while the peripheral employees and outsourced groups are treated differently (Purcell 1999; Marchington and Grugulis 2000)? These questions have led to the research into HR architecture which is discussed in Chapter 6.

Lepak *et al.* (2006) provide a useful corrective to the best practice–best fit discussion when they point out the need to identify more precisely what it is that these practices are seeking to achieve. Indeed, they note that the highly technical discussions over research design and measurement in many of the studies may be premature. They believe that it is important to establish key 'policy domains' and then examine the kinds of practices which are most clearly linked to them. These policy domains, as we have discussed earlier, are concerned with the ability of employees, their motivation and their opportunities to contribute to the business (Appelbaum *et al.* 2000; Boxall and Purcell 2003; Purcell *et al.* 2003). For example although HR practices can have multiple purposes some can have a particular focus: staffing and training are likely to be linked to ability, performance management and reward to motivation and work structure and participation to opportunity (Lepak *et al.* 2006: 236).

To sum up, although the best practice view has gained a great deal of publicity because of the simplicity of the message it has also attracted widespread criticism. Indeed, Purcell (1999: 36) has characterised research in this area as leading into a 'utopian cul-de-sac and ignores the powerful and highly significant changes in work, employment and society visible inside organisations and the wider community'. This emphasis on the importance of context leads us to discuss the second perspective, referred to as best fit, which regards the most effective HR practices as those which take account of the organisational, sectoral and national contexts.

Best fit

This perspective is derived from the contingency view that argues that the effectiveness of HR practices depends on how closely they fit with the external and
internal environment of the organisation. Business performance, it is argued,
improves when HR practices mutually reinforce the choice of competitive
strategy. This is the concept of vertical integration between the competitive
strategy, the objectives of the firm, the HR practices and individual objectives
(Fombrun *et al.* 1984; Wright *et al.* 1994) and it helps to explain the lack of
diffusion because the appropriate practices will depend on the context. There
are different views on the influence of particular contexts on HR practices: some
stress the 'outer context' of the competitive strategy or the 'inner context' of
existing structures and strategy (Hendry 1995) while others emphasise the stage
in the life cycle of the organisation.

Perhaps the best-known examples of this perspective draw on the classic analysis
(Porter 1980) on the sources of competitive advantage (Miles and Snow 1978,
1984; Schuler and Jackson 1987) which argues that HR practices work best when
they are adapted to the competitive strategy. Miles and Snow (1984) identify three
types of strategic behaviour and link these to various HR practices: 'defenders'
will have narrow, relatively stable products and will emphasise internal, process
oriented training and internal pay equity; 'prospectors' have changing product
lines and rely more on innovation leading to the use of external recruitment,
results oriented compensation and external pay equity; 'analysers' have changing
and stable product lines leading them to use internal and external recruitment and
pay equity measures and process oriented performance appraisal.

Schuler and Jackson (1987) and Jackson and Schuler (1995) developed probably the
best known of these approaches where they identified the different competitive strategies of organisations and the role behaviours which were needed with each of them. In
particular they drew attention to the different kinds of behaviours needed for innovation, quality enhancement and cost reduction and the types of HR practices which are
needed to achieve these. For example a strategy based on cost leadership will result in
minimal levels of investment in human capital with low standards for recruitment and
poor levels of pay and training. In contrast, a strategy based on innovation calls for HR
practices that encourage risk taking and cooperative behaviour. Youndt *et al.* (1996)
and Delery and Doty (1996) provide some support for this perspective.

This is perhaps best shown in studies carried out in a single sector where
most firms are operating within the same industrial context. Arthur (1994)
showed how steel mini-mills firms pursuing cost leadership business strategies adopted cost minimization command and control type approaches. While
those pursuing product and quality differentiation pursued HCM or HPWS
approaches with emphasis on training, employee problem solving, teamworking, higher pay, higher skills and attempts to create a work community.
Batt and Moynihan (2002) examined call centres in the US telecommunications
industry and found that HR practices emphasizing investment in employees
were more successful in the parts of the industry that required employees to
exercise their discretion.

Thompson (2000) conducted two surveys of firms in the UK aerospace industry. His first survey in 1997 found that establishments with higher levels of value added per employee tended to have higher penetration of innovative working practices among their non-management employees. These workplaces tended to be more heavily engaged in specialist production for niche markets and employed a richer mix of technical and professional employees. The second survey in 1999 revealed 'compelling evidence that firms introducing a greater number of high performance work practices have much improved business performance' (Thompson 2000: 10). Indeed, firms moving from less than five to more than six innovative practices made a 34 per cent gain in value added per employee.

Other research has highlighted the influence of the network of relationships within which firms, especially knowledge intensive and professional service firms, are working (Swart and Kinnie 2003; Beaumont *et al.* 1996; Sinclair *et al.* 1996). Firms increasingly form relationships with clients, suppliers and collaborators and often these other parties will influence the HR practices pursued by the focal firm both directly and indirectly. They may influence these practices directly, for example through shaping recruitment and selection criteria or through requiring certain types of training to be conducted, or more indirectly by setting performance targets that can be reached only by adopting, for example, team-based forms of work organisation (Kinnie and Parsons 2004).

Labour markets are also likely to be important because in certain industries and geographical areas firms find they have to compete much more intensively than others. Tight labour markets, as seen where call centres are concentrated, will put pressure on particular HR practices such as recruitment and selection and reward (Kinnie *et al.* 2000).

Others argue that HR practices need to fit with and complement other important strategies and structures within the organisation. The size of the organisation will be important – larger firms will have complex internal structures often with multiple layers and more generally just the resources needed to fund certain approaches, for example a formalised salary structure or recruitment scheme. There is also a need to take account of the influence of the manufacturing strategy of the firm (Purcell 1999; Boxall and Purcell 2003: 56–8; Baron and Kreps 1999).

Some authors (Kochan and Barocci 1985; Baird and Meshoulam 1988) argue that there needs to be a fit between the HR practices and the stage in the business life cycle. For example the HR practices of a start-up are likely to be highly informal whereas during the growth phase there will be increasing formalization and emphasis given to recruitment, training and development. Mature organisations where growth is slowing will need HR practices which control costs while those in the decline phase will need to cut costs and move staff. Most organisations will have a series of products that are at different stages in their life cycles producing the situation familiar to many managers whereby certain parts of their business are growing whereas others are shrinking producing quite different pressures on HR practices. This then poses questions about the nature of internal fit or consistency of practices across different employee groups.

The best fit approach has been subject to extensive review and a number of issues have been raised. Perhaps the most basic point of all is the assumption that firms have a competitive strategy with which HR practices can fit (Legge 1995; Ramsey *et al.* 2000). Even if the firm does have a strategy, this view assumes that the one they have is the most appropriate for them. The second and related point is that it is possible to typify the firms in the way that has been suggested. Purcell (1999) suggests this is unlikely for a variety of reasons. In practice organisations may pursue a mix of competitive strategies for example seeking both cost leadership and differentiation leading to confusion over the most appropriate HR practices. Firms may also lack sufficient knowledge of their external environment or they may have misinterpreted the information that they have gathered. Moreover, most firms are faced with a fast-changing external environment which in turn has implications for business strategy and HR practices. Wright and Snell (1998) neatly summarise the need for 'fit and flexibility' and note the tensions between the two. Fit is related to competitive strategy now, and thence to financial performance; flexibility is building adaptability for future purposes. Increasing turbulence in the business environment and seemingly growing frequency of exogenous shocks place a premium on the latter.

It is for these reasons that Purcell (1999: 37) regards the search for 'best fit' as a chimera 'limited by the impossibility of modelling all the contingent variables, the difficulty of showing their interconnection, and the way in which changes in one variable have an impact on others, let alone the need to model idiosyncratic and path dependent contingencies'.

Links between HR practices and employee attitudes: examples of alignment

The criticisms of the best fit view of the kind we have discussed need not invalidate this perspective indeed, they can strengthen it. As Boxall and Purcell (2003: 58) have argued 'Much of the problem with the contingency theorising in strategic HRM stems from the tendency for researchers to look for correlations between two variables such as competitive strategy and HR strategy. Such models are attractively simple, but are "too thin". They miss out much of the interactive, multi-variate complexity of strategic management in the real world.' Consequently they propose an approach which sees business strategy as a configuration of competitive, operational, finance and HR strategies. They go on to argue that a superior business strategy is one which 'links all of these pieces in a more effective configuration' (Boxall and Purcell 2003: 58). This throws attention on the issues of interactions and alignment of HR practices, especially external and internal alignment. External alignment refers to the extent to which HR practices support the corporate strategy and in particular the sources of competitive advantage. Internal alignment refers to the degree of internal consistency or synergy between the HR practices themselves (Purcell 1999).

The importance of the impact of external and internal alignment of HR practices and employee attitudes is best illustrated by reference to two of our case studies. The first, Tesco, illustrates the beneficial effects of both external and internal alignment. The external alignment is achieved through their own version of a balanced scorecard which provides a link between the sources of competitive advantage and HR practices. Internal alignment of formal practices is sought by the use of a common set of HR practices across all of their stores. The second example is of AIT, a software firm, where the attempts to achieve close external alignment were driven by the views of the founder of the firm. Internal alignment is achieved by a strategically placed HR activity.

Tesco

Tesco, the UK's largest food retailer, underwent considerable change in the mid-1990s in order to improve its competitive position by placing much greater emphasis on a customer-facing culture. As one senior head office manager remarked, '1995 saw the evolution of a customer-focused business … with quality and price being very much the same across the sector, people and our service were seen as the differentiator'. With the help of Gemini consultants Tesco developed its own version of the balanced scorecard (Kaplan and Norton 1996) to help define their business more strongly and bring about this culture change. The scorecard was translated into a 'steering wheel' with four quadrants – people, finance, customers and operations and each store's performance is measured against specific targets in each area. In the people quadrant, for example, targets include recruitment, development, retention, labour turnover, absence and staff morale (taken from their staff attitude survey) which help to achieve external alignment. Although the four quadrants are not weighted, one retail director we interviewed considered the 'people' quadrant to be the most important, as he explained 'if we can recruit, maintain and deliver fantastic people then operationally we can deliver'. The measures are updated each quarter and link to the corporate measures which underpin the organisation's strategic objectives. In each store there was a large 'steering wheel' on display, which was highly visible to staff who could monitor their own store's performance using a traffic light system (red, green and orange to show if performance is below, above, or on target). The introduction of this approach brought about a much greater focus on people and customer issues in the stores which historically had been driven by financial and operational results, and a consequent change in culture which was seen as a major catalyst for Tesco's recent success.

Delayering took place as part of the restructuring exercise and within the stores there are currently four levels: store manager, senior managers, section managers and general assistants. Each store was run by a store manager whose job it was to provide coaching, guidance and support and to deliver the Tesco 'standard'. As one store manager explained 'my role is to mobilise the team with a goal, to be energetic and to be able to motivate people'. There was a senior management team in each store which included operational managers responsible for departments and in an average-sized store (employing around 400 staff) this comprised five to six managers which typically would include the store manager, personnel manager, customer services manager, fresh foods/ambient manager and an out-of-hours manager. Each member of this team, including the personnel manager, took a turn in managing the store for around 20 per cent of their working time so that they gained an understanding of the business issues. The personnel function within the stores (over two-thirds of stores have their own personnel manager) had undergone considerable change over the last five to six years, moving from a predominantly administrative and welfare role to a store level senior management position. The role of the personnel manager included taking responsibility for the payroll and controllable expenses and ensuring that the store maintained productivity levels. This means focusing on the people measures within the steering wheel such as absence management, employee appraisal and development, resourcing and succession planning. One of the benefits of the steering wheel has therefore been to make the role of the personnel manager much clearer within the stores and enabled the function to measure themselves against specific goals.

A more recent change to pursue internal alignment within Tesco has been the drive for consistency across stores and all practices, procedures and processes were centrally determined and their implementation closely monitored. Each store was governed by the organisation routines handbook which provides detailed information on how every task was to be performed – this was down to the minutest detail even including details on office layout, such as where pictures should go on the wall, and where the waste paper bin should go! On the HR side all practices and procedures are highly centralised and controlled. The wages budget, for example, was fixed for each store and there was very little local flexibility on pay – something which was obviously a cause of great frustration in some of the stores we visited where recruitment, retention and staff quality were ongoing major problems. Although the stores cannot function without these routines it was the way in which the rules and routines were implemented that was considered a key ingredient to success. It was management, in particular the general manager, who were responsible for how the practices and processes were implemented and their behaviour was therefore critical to a store's performance. We discuss this in more detail in Chapter 5.

Our research focused on the section manager population which was a first line manager position within the store. Spans of control were normally 12 general assistants to each section manager and in an average size store there were about 20 section managers covering different areas such as produce, bakery, non-food, and checkout. In addition to being responsible for the day-to-day running of their areas section managers took responsibility for a range of people management tasks such as recruitment, training, performance appraisal, disciplinary and grievance issues, and pay enquiries. The nature of the job was therefore fairly demanding, particularly on the people management side and this may partly explain why many stores face recruitment and retention difficulties with this position.

Interestingly, like staff in the other retail organisation in our study (Selfridges), Tesco section managers displayed one of the highest levels of organisational commitment of any of our case study organisations, and were highest in terms of sharing the values of the organisation. Comparisons with the WERS 98 survey data for retail trade staff also show that Tesco's staff had significantly higher levels of commitment.

74% felt proud to tell people who they worked for (WERS, 56%)
88% felt loyal to Tesco (WERS, 70%)
86% would recommend a friend or relative to work in Tesco
88% shared the values of Tesco (WERS, 50%)

This was particularly interesting given that Tesco section managers scored highest of all our case study organisations in terms of working hard (91 per cent felt they worked very hard), and were one of the highest in terms of feeling that their job was challenging (88 per cent). This undoubtedly reflects the inherent nature of what is a very demanding job – staff have to work long hours (two thirds, for example said they worked, on average more than 10 hours overtime a week), perform a wide range of tasks and struggle to fill vacancies and absences on the shop floor. As one store manager remarked:

Section managers have to work bloody hard ... they are more task orientated than the senior team ... ideally section managers should spend 70/80 per cent of their time managing but they do not always do this because of the demands of the job, especially if they have gaps. It's one of the more pressurised roles.

When we look at the correlations in Tesco (Table 3.1) we see that there is a positive association between job challenge and job satisfaction and commitment. This is borne out by the following quote from a section manager:

Table 3.1 The relationship between HR practices and employee attitudes in Tesco. Year 1 correlation results (N=43)

	Job satisfaction	*Motivation*	*Commitment*
Job security			*
Training	*		*
Career opportunity	*		
Appraisal	*		
Pay satisfaction		**	**
Job challenge	*		*
Teamwork			
Involvement			*
Communication			*
Ability to raise a grievance			
Work–life balance			
Management behaviour		**	

* significant at 0.05 level (2-tailed)
** significant at 0.01 level (2-tailed)

I believe in the organisation. The grass isn't greener on the far side … the organisation looks after their staff well although they expect a great deal from people and stretch people.

In terms of HR practices, the above correlations suggest that training and development and career opportunities are linked to job satisfaction and commitment. This is not surprising considering these are first line managers, most of whom have been promoted from the shop floor, and many of whom were keen to progress further in the organisation. Satisfaction with pay is strongly associated with motivation and commitment and one possible explanation for this is explored in the following chapter.

AIT[1]

The 'Big Idea' in AIT stems from the beliefs of their founder and current chairman. This was seen not only in the steps they took to establish and preserve their organisational culture but also in the way the organisation sought to achieve external and internal alignment through the way it was structured as well as their HR practices. The organisational culture was very important to the chairman and it was captured by their aim of being, 'the best organisation in the world to work for and the best organisation in the world to work with', a view which in many ways gets at the very heart of external alignment. Indeed, the chairman held strong views about the role of business in society because he did not see a separation between business or work and society. This then produces a particular need to make the workplace a good place to work. Moreover he believed that it was something of a challenge to make organisations good places to work. When asked to sum his philosophy he suggested it was to 'have fun and make money'.

The fast growth of the organisation especially in the late 1990s presented serious challenges to the ethos and culture of the organisation as the number of employees increased. Indeed, the chairman suggested that 'There is a danger that the culture of the organisation will wash away with a tide of new people'. However, he also commented that 'what survives depends on what you choose to let go of last'.

The importance of organisational culture is shown in a variety of ways. In practice they sought to apply these principles equally to their customers and to their employees. This was seen as a mutually reinforcing marketing advantage. The Director of Intellectual Capital expressed her version of external alignment in the following way: 'It allows us to attract good people who want to work for AIT and provide excellent service for the customer, it is all about forming the right relationships and these are easily transferred between employees and customers.'

This culture was supported in various ways including a 'Visionaire' whose job it was to improve social relations between employees through organising team away days, an annual organisation social for all employees, together with a strong social and sporting set of shared activities. Sustained attempts were made to align the HR practices internally to support the culture and the competitive strategy. Recruitment and selection assumed central importance in the maintenance of the organisational culture especially because much of the entry was new graduates. Indeed, the key criterion for their selection was not their level of technical skills but whether they fitted with the organisational culture. The local labour market made it difficult to recruit experienced staff but there had been a move to employ more of these because of the changing demands of clients. Traditionally most staff had been recruited straight from university with a variety of backgrounds and then provided with intensive training in the firm. Labour turnover at around 10 per cent was low for the industry.

The emphasis on graduates was continued with the training and development programmes, and a third of the budget was devoted to graduate training which lasted around three months. Training and development for other employees were also important and they averaged around six days' training per year. However, as with recruitment and selection, this training was not client specific, instead it was designed to increase the 'stock' of intellectual capital so that AIT was better able to meet and anticipate the needs of a variety of clients and to attract and develop employees they needed.

Again in the words of the chairman,

> We want people to be effective when they come to work, we want teams to work together effectively, we want them to be able to communicate well with one another and with the customer, they are more likely to do this if they are happy at work and they socialise with the rest of their team. It is important that these relationships are robust, that they are grown internally so that they can withstand challenges which are placed upon them.

This emphasis on organisational culture was also shown by the reliance on direct employees who made up nearly 90 per cent of the staff rather than using large numbers of subcontractors or offshore working. Teamworking was emphasised with employees usually being members of three teams organised around the current project, their profession and the social organisation of the firm. In addition there was active management support for extramural clubs and societies.

The HR structure itself was well developed and broken down into human capital (the skills and knowledge of employees), structural capital (the fixed systems which are in place for collecting, storing and transmitting information for example the database and the intranet) and training and development. Critically, the HR department controlled the allocation of staff onto different projects rather than the operational director and this allowed them to pay particular attention to the career development needs of employees. Line managers had a clear responsibility to carry out their HR responsibilities, most importantly the appraisal of their employees and they were closely monitored to ensure that they were doing this as part of the development of the employees who worked for them.

The HR strategy was influenced indirectly not so much by the needs of individual clients as by the conditions within the industry as a whole which, at the time of the research, were characterised by skill shortages and the fast pace of technical change. More importantly, AIT had a clear HR strategy which was aimed at maximising and developing intellectual capital and playing a key role in managing its relations with its clients. The principal aim here was to develop and retain the skills, such as non-technical business analysis skills which were critical to satisfy client needs. The focus of the activity was on looking forward to try to anticipate client needs rather than simply on managing the present problems or looking back.

The pay and performance management systems also reflected this approach which was not client specific. The salary structure was not directly affected by clients since it reflected increases in the skill, knowledge and experience of employees. Up to 20 per cent of the activities which contributed to the acquisition of these attributes can be carried out outside for example, on community projects. The performance management system rewarded performance against project related objectives, but typically the resulting bonus counted for only around 5 per cent of the total employee reward.

The internal structure of the organisation was built around a series of communities. The operational communities were the project teams, which were developed to work for a particular client. These typically lasted for around six months, although some could be much longer, and involve around 12 people including business analysts, software developers, builders and testers. The vocational communities were effective across these projects teams and they were made-up specialists such as builders or testers. These groups met together regularly to discuss issues of common interest across the project teams. The staff communities which were referred to as T Groups were the principal means of internal communication. They were non-hierarchical and cross-functional. The social communities were very strong and included social and sporting teams as well as the staff away days.

There were extensive knowledge management activities across the organisation both through the use of formal systems such as an intranet and a document database but also through semi-formal systems which included regular lunchtime briefings and addresses to the whole organisation by the MD. These activities were coordinated by the knowledge manager who was assisted by knowledge mediators whose task it was to stimulate the sharing of knowledge both within and between project teams.

This ability to combine all aspects of human resources and organisational processes together and build a strong value-based organisation was reflected in our interviews with employees. These were a group of young professional software designers in the main. We interviewed 36 in the first year and 33 in the second year. Job satisfaction was especially high – and much higher than the national average for associated professional employees.

> 85% were satisfied with the influence they had over their job (WERS, 54%)
> 61% were satisfied with the sense of achievement they got from their work (WERS, 58%)

When we look at the correlations between HR practices and various measures of employee attitudes in AIT we find results as shown in Table 3.2.

Thus for these young professionals knowing what was going on, having a say

Table 3.2 The relationship between HR practices and employee attitudes in AIT. Year 1 correlation results (N=36)

	Job satisfaction	Motivation	Commitment
Job security			
Training			
Career opportunity	**		**
Appraisal			
Pay satisfaction			
Job challenge	*		
Teamwork	**		
Involvement			
Communication			
Ability to raise a grievance			
Work–life balance			
Management behaviour			

* significant at 0.05 level (2-tailed)
** significant at 0.01 level (2-tailed)

in organisational decisions that affected their job or work, working in a supportive team environment, and doing challenging work that helped develop their career skills were all important to them in terms of providing job satisfaction. This is a typical young professional view. In addition AIT was able to generate high levels of organisation commitment. Particularly important here were people management skills of managers and the way the organisation tried to create a work–life balance for its staff. To quote two of our respondents:

> It's a good place to work, people generally feel valued – you're not just another number and there's scope for advancement. They encourage you to make more of your skills and abilities.

> It's a nice working environment. The most important things are that everyone is helpful and friendly ... and competent – there's no blame culture, which you can't take for granted.

The issues associated with managing professionals in knowledge intensive firms are discussed in much greater detail in Chapter 7.

Remaining problems in the links between HR practices and organisational performance

Our review of the strategy and HRM literature has revealed a number of tensions between the best practice and best fit perspectives. The question remains therefore of how these might be resolved. Boxall and Purcell (2003: 69) propose one helpful way forward to reconcile these tensions by drawing attention to the circumstances in which the best fit and best practice views are helpful. They argue that the best fit view is most appropriate at the 'surface level' of HR policy and practices in a firm. At this level, contingent factors at the societal, sectoral and organisational levels are inevitably going to be important. However, they believe that the best practice view is more relevant at the 'underpinning layer of generic HR processes and general principles of labour management'. This suggests that there are some principles of best practice, for example the use of structured selection interviews which research suggests will in most cases be more effective. They conclude their discussion therefore with the observation that 'both general principles and specific contexts play an important role in the theory and practice of strategic HRM' (Boxall and Purcell 2003: 70).

This view represents a step forward because it effectively resolves the best practice–best fit debate by saying that both are important. Despite this helpful proposal two further problems in the research remain unresolved. For us these problems are linked to two, often unstated, assumptions: (a) that HR practices are always implemented as intended and (b) employees experience these practices as they were intended. One of the principal arguments of this book and one which underlies the HR causal model is that we cannot make these assumptions. We believe that a discussion of these assumptions is fundamental to understand the links between HR and performance.

Research into the gaps between what should happen and what actually happens is hardly new. Argyris and Schon (1974) referred to the differences between espoused theory and theory-in-use, while Brewster *et al.* (1983) spoke of espoused and operational practices and Legge (1995) drew attention to the differences between rhetoric and reality. However, much of the HR and performance literature seems to neglect these points tending to assume that HR practices will be implemented as intended. For example Lepak *et al.* (2006) draw very helpful distinctions between HR policies which represent the broad objectives in a particular area, for example highly selective selection, and the HR practices which are needed to achieve these (such as the use of competency-based criteria in selection interviews). However, they fail to distinguish between what we refer to as intended HR practices, how these practices are actually implemented and how these are experienced by employees.

As we discussed in Chapter 1 these differences have been identified by Boxall in his discussion of the Human Resource Advantage. This comprises a human capital advantage (HCA), which is made up of superior people and HR practices and organisational process advantage (OPA) which is concerned with the implementation of these practices. Thus rather than being distracted by an ultimately pointless debate over whether a best fit or best practice view is somehow 'better', we have to realise that, critically, it is the 'process' that employees experience not the intended practice. The search, therefore, is for the 'best process' which must be in the hands of the line managers rather than the designers of the practices. For us, therefore, OPA lies at the heart of the black box linking HR practices and performance and it is to these issues of process that we now turn.

4 Bringing practices to life

The vital role of front line managers

Introduction

In our causal chain model outlined in Chapter 1 we drew attention to the need to distinguish between the *intended* practices that are designed by senior management and the practices *experienced* by employees, indicating that any differences between the two will be influenced by the action of front line managers (FLMs) who put the intended practices into operation. We also highlighted the importance of employee discretionary behaviour in any analysis of the people management–performance link, suggesting that line management behaviour could influence the likelihood of employees engaging in discretionary behaviours. Despite this, however, a detailed examination of the role of FLMs has tended to be overlooked in the literature and it appears rare for organisations to identify line managers, especially FLMs, as an occupational group worthy of special care or attention. This was perhaps understandable in the 1970s and 1980s when there was talk of 'forgotten supervisors' (Thurley and Wirdenius 1973) and 'lost managers' (Child and Partridge 1982) but this was before the substantial growth in people management roles of FLMs.

Our own research, however, seeks to address this gap and the central purpose of this chapter is to explore this issue of FLM behaviour in people management by drawing on survey and case study material from three research projects. Here we use the term 'people management' to cover all aspects of how people are managed. This includes not only the HR duties which FLMs undertake, such as selecting, appraising, developing and communicating but a wider set of leadership behaviours which aim to influence employee attitudes and behaviours.

Data collected from 12 organisations in the People and Performance project (Purcell *et al.* 2003; Hutchinson and Purcell 2003) are utilised plus evidence from two more recent case study-based projects which focus directly on the role of FLMs in people management. One of these considers their role in two aspects of people management (reward and training, learning and development) and is based on research in six organisations (Purcell and Hutchinson 2007a, 2007b; Hutchinson and Purcell 2007). The second (research in progress) considers FLMs' people management roles in the NHS, and looks at five acute hospitals and two ambulance trusts.

We first consider who the front line managers are, identifying a number of common characteristics in the managers we studied across the three projects and note the increasing workload, pressure and tension in the role. We then assess how the roles in people management have evolved in recent decades, put forward some explanations for the recent trend in devolvement to the line and report on the frequently observed gap between what is formally required in HR policy and what is actually delivered by FLMs – in other words between the rhetoric and the reality (Legge 1995). Using the literature, we then explore why FLMs' role and behaviours are important and use theory on social exchange to consider the link with employee attitudes. Results from our employee survey are then assessed to provide a link between employee outcomes, as seen in commitment, job satis-faction, motivation and job discretion, and FLM behaviour. Case study material from one organisation, Selfridges, is then presented to illustrate the critical role that FLMs play in the HRM–performance causal chain. Despite this importance, however, our own research, and that of others, shows that in practice devolution to the line is problematic. In the final sections we consider the effectiveness of FLMs in delivering people management before concluding with some observations about support.

Who are the front line managers?

We define this group of managers as those who have direct supervisory responsi-bility, normally for non-managerial employees, and are placed at the lower levels of the management hierarchy, often the first line level. They are responsible for the day-to-day running of their work area rather than strategic matters and are normally engaged in general management work, but could also be specialists in a functional area, such as sales or finance. Traditionally referred to as 'supervi-sors', these managers have a variety of titles in the organisations we researched, including team leader, group leader, section manager, project manager, and in the NHS, ward manager. Spans of control varied according to the context but typically

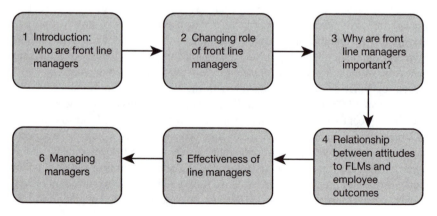

Figure 4.1 Structure of the chapter

ranged between 5 and 20 employees, but could be as small as one, and as great as 80. Where spans of control were large, these FLMs usually had deputies, or some administrative assistance. For example in the NHS, where ward managers could be responsible for multiple teams, junior sisters typically help share the responsibility for conducting performance appraisals, and sometimes other people management duties such as absence management and organising training.

Despite these variations however, the FLMs we interviewed in the three research projects shared a number of characteristics. First, the scope of their job typically covered a combination of traditional management duties such as providing technical expertise, monitoring performance, planning, work allocation, providing leadership and more recent activities in the form of people management and cost control or budgeting. Significantly, these newer activities had been taken on without relinquishing the old roles. Second, these multiple duties inevitably created tension in the role. Pressure to manage the business aspects of the job and meet service or production targets would invariably conflict with the softer people management requirements of the job. Not surprisingly it was the more pressing 'harder' priorities which dominated (Cunningham and Hyman 1999; Gratton *et al.* 1999; Whittaker and Marchington 2003; Hutchinson and Purcell 2007). This was particularly acute in the NHS, where managers faced constant pressure to deliver service targets, reduce costs whilst at the same time meet the NHS Plan of becoming a model employer.

Third, there was often ambiguity surrounding the people management role and our interviews revealed a gap in understanding of what this role encompassed between FLMs and their own managers and/or the HR department. Other studies have made similar findings. In their research of Hilton International UK hotels Maxwell and Watson (2006) found that HR managers believed there to be greater line management involvement in HR activities than did line managers, and that differences existed in HR priorities across line manager and/or HR manager groups. Significantly this had implications for business performance – where there were differences in views between line managers and HR specialists, there was poor hotel business performance. Conversely convergent views were evident in effectively performing hotels. In other research by the CIPD (CIPD 2007b) into the changing HR function, the great majority of HR respondents report that their line managers took less responsibility for people management than had been intended.

Fourth, in many organisations these FLMs were individuals who had been promoted from the ranks of the shop floor. This could create further tension as managers found themselves 'caught between the opposing forces of management and the shop floor, torn by competing demands and loyalties' (Child and Partridge 1982: 8). As one of the team leaders we interviewed remarked 'you are a piggy in the middle' – expected to be the voice of management on the one hand and yet, on the other, the champion of the team's interests (Boxall and Purcell 2003). Furthermore, in most cases these people were members of a team, often doing the same work as other team members in addition to their own management duties. It was not uncommon to hear of managers having to cover for sick team members or for unfilled vacancies in the team, as these two managers explain.

> You never get anything completed. There's so much to do, covering areas ... doing the work of my team.

> It feels like a treadmill at times. I have lots of staffing issues, trainees and absentees ... Its about keeping your head above water.

The picture we have of the FLM role, therefore, is one of increasing responsibilities, work overload, role ambiguity and dilemmas concerning competing priorities. Line managers often have other more immediate business priorities than managing the people working for them, and consequently people management may be taken less seriously. It is this aspect of the job we now turn to.

The changing role of line managers in people management

Numerous studies testify to the increasing devolution of people management activities to the line over the last few decades. In the mid-1990s Hutchinson and Wood (1995) found greater line management involvement in personnel issues compared to five years previously and WERS 98 found that supervisors were more likely to play a part in HR type decisions than previous surveys showed. More recently, an IRS survey (2006) found that in six in ten organisations' FLMs had taken on more responsibility in the past three years, and in a recent CIPD survey of HR/training specialists almost three quarters of respondents reported that line managers had increased involvement for learning and development activities in the last two years (CIPD 2007c).

This is not a new phenomenon. Line managers have always had some responsibility for people management and indeed this seems quite logical – they are after all closest to employees, having direct responsibility for managing them on a regular basis and being accountable for their performance. Back in Victorian Britain supervisors enjoyed extensive delegated powers including sole charge for the hiring and firing of employees, and the docking of pay (Child and Partridge 1982). Over the next century, however, these powers diminished as we witnessed the emergence and development of the personnel function as a profession, and consequent removal of these responsibilities from line managers. Since the 1990s, however, we have seen this trend reverse dramatically as we have witnessed a return of HRM to the line, or 'relocating the line'.

How do we explain this recent increase in involvement? Undoubtedly some of these changes are linked to the changing role of the HR function, particularly the emergence of the concept of 'Human Resource Management' in the 1980s. A consistent theme in models of HRM is that line managers are key players in the delivery of HRM, arguing that the management of people should be increasingly 'integrated' and shared with line management rather than being the sole responsibility of some specialist function (Guest 1987). As Karen Legge explains

'In the HRM models, HRM is vested in line management as business managers responsible for coordinating and directing all resources in the business unit in pursuit of bottom line results' (Legge 2005: 113). More recently we have seen the emergence of the HR shared services model in which HR becomes a strategic business partner and centre of expertise (Ulrich 1997), and transfers day-to-day responsibility for HR matters to the line. Alongside this has been the growth in e-HR which has facilitated devolution to the line.

There are also other factors at play to explain this recent trend. Decentralisation of decision making, organisational restructuring with the consequent decline of the middle manager (Hales 2005), the growth of teamwork giving a heightened role to team leaders in motivating and leading people, pressure on costs and speedier decision making have all influenced devolvement to the line. Within the employment relationship the trend toward individualism, in particular the spread of performance pay and appraisals systems, alongside the decline in collective bargaining and reassertion of management prerogatives have also contributed to this shift.

The conclusion from many studies is that HR specialists and line managers now work in conjunction with each other on a range of people management issues (Hutchinson and Wood 1995) but that, for FLMs, this aspect of the job is broadening and deepening (Purcell and Hutchinson 2007a, 2007b). Many of the traditional day-to-day activities we associate with HR are now in the hands of FLMs, such as appraisal, absence control, recruitment and selection, communication and involvement, training and development and discipline and grievance handling. Our own research suggests this is extending to other areas like career development and reward and that FLMs have a much greater role to play in informal practices than formerly recognised (Hutchinson and Purcell 2007). In some organisations we studied, for example, where FLMs appeared to have little discretion over the formal reward system we found strong evidence of 'unofficial' practices creeping in as a means of motivating people such as allowing time off, access to training, and providing more challenging work. Training and development was another area where there was plentiful evidence of informal approaches. This has implications not just for workload, but raises questions about consistency and control. The administrative burden has also increased for FLMs, and in our own research this was particularly evident where a shared services model of HR had been adopted (Hutchinson and Purcell 2007). As we discuss later, this is often resented by FLMs. There is also a suggestion that line managers may be having more involvement in policy design. The CIPD 2007 learning and development survey finds that 51 per cent of respondents claim line managers have some involvement in determining learning and development strategy, and 4 per cent say the main responsibility rested with line management (CIPD 2007c).

Research also points to a difference between formal intended HR practices and those which are experienced by employees – or between the rhetoric and the reality (Legge 1995), with the gap often explained by FLMs' variability in behaviour (Marchington 2001; Hutchinson and Purcell 2003; McGovern *et al.* 1997). Part of the explanation for this is provided by McGovern *et al.* who, in a study of performance appraisal found that, 'management implementation was uneven within organisations and that the actual quality of practice was also subject to significant variations' (McGovern *et al.* 1997: 26). They asked line managers in the seven companies studied to 'rank in order what motivates you to be involved in personnel activities' (McGovern *et al.* 1997: 21). The first ranked answer in each case was 'personal motivation', as opposed to targets, company values, career advancement and other possible reasons. The authors went on to note from their qualitative research on 'the rules of the game' in each organisation that 'people management, either in the form of carrying out HR policies or in general, did not emerge in the list of unwritten rule/measurement priorities within any of the organisations' (McGovern *et al.* 1997: 23). In other words FLMs' people management roles often rely for their fulfilment on the manager's own sense of motivation and commitment, particularly in the absence of any perform-ance criteria to consider HR issues seriously (Whittaker and Marchington 2003; Gratton *et al.* 1999). Significantly, it is therefore likely to be more discretionary than other aspects of FLM duties especially those related to the primary task of the work unit.

Other explanations offered for this gap are lack of training, lack of interest, work overload and conflicting priorities (Fenton O'Creevy 2001; Harris 2001; Whittaker and Marchington 2003). We consider these issues in more detail later.

Why are front line managers important?

Another body of research asserts that line managers can influence employee atti-tudes and behaviours. Social exchange theory, as we discuss in more detail in Chapter 5, emphasises the importance of leadership behaviour and tells us that a reciprocal relationship exists between employees' perceptions of the degree of support the organisation provides to meet their expectations and their own behav-iour. This is seen in the psychological contract. One key element in this contract is the interpersonal relationships between leaders and their subordinates – known as 'leader–member exchange' (LMX). Uhl-Bien *et al.* (2000: 138), focusing on lead-ership behaviour within social exchange theory, assert that 'one critical element of HR systems that has not been well addressed ... is the role of interpersonal relationships'. Managers and subordinates research, they suggest, 'shows that more effectively developed relationships are beneficial for individual and work unit functioning and have many positive outcomes related to firm performance' (2000: 143). Ostroff and Bowen (2000: 209) see this as establishing 'alignment or congruence between individual and manager goals', and thus managers as agents can play important roles in the transmission of values and climate. Thus leader–member exchange and the influence of line managers, especially front line managers, form a key part of people management (Tekleab and Taylor 2003) and 'the immediate supervisor plays a critical role as a key agent of the organisation through which members form their perceptions of the organisation' (Liden *et al.* 2004). Truss (2001: 1136) uses the concept of agency and shows that 'managers act as powerful mediator between individuals and HR practices'

In a study of 1000 employees Guest and Conway (2004: 19–32) showed that supervisory leadership was the strongest factor associated with organisation commitment. Supervisory leadership was also the strongest, or among the most important factors, explaining positive psychological contracts, work satisfaction, loyalty to customers, colleagues and supervisor, and felt 'excitement' at work. Other work by Guest (Guest and King 2002) found that chief executives felt that front line supervisors, team leaders and middle managers were key to effective people management. A study by Kidd and Smewing (2001: 37) found that 'respondents who saw their supervisor as engaging in feedback and goal setting behaviours were more committed to their organisation, as were those whose supervisor trusted them and gave them authority to do the job'.

Others have also observed that employees' perceptions of FLMs' leadership behaviour influences affective organisation commitment and job experiences.

> Supervisors are able to jointly influence the exchange relationships that they have with the employee and that the employee has with the organisation. Because the supervisor is an important source of information, she is able to influence whether employees attribute favourable or unfavourable treatment to the actions of the supervisor, the organisation or both.
>
> (Eisenberger *et al.* 2002)

It is the proximity and immediacy of the relationship which is important as confirmed in studies on commitment where commitment to the FLM is often greater than to the organisation (Becker *et al.* 1996). As Redman and Snape note (2005: 304) 'there may ... be a general tendency for the more cognitively proximal focus (i.e. supervisor or team) to exert greater influence over employee behaviour'. It is, in HR terms, not just the quality of this LMX relationship but the extent to which FLMs are perceived to be the provider of HR practices.

Despite these findings, however, the role of FLMs in people management and in eliciting employee engagement has been largely ignored in the huge volume of research on the HRM–performance chain (see Boselie *et al.* 2005). As we explain earlier in Chapter 3, while a list of HR practices in use and their coverage can be generated, these cannot be related to either the actual practices applied by the line manager or to the employee responses to them and to leadership behaviour. The steps in the chain cannot be ignored.

Our HR causal chain model seeks to address this. In this we distinguish between intended and experienced practices drawing attention to these. While some HR practices may have an impact on employees directly, most rely on line manager action or support, as we have demonstrated. Employee perceptions of HR practices are therefore likely to be influenced by how their managers implement and enact these HR practices, or 'bring practices to life' to quote a senior manager in one of our research companies, and show leadership. These perceptions and experiences of HR practices will influence employee attitudes and behaviours as seen, for example, in commitment, job satisfaction, and job discretion which in turn will have an impact on performance. The following analysis which uses data from the People and Performance research (Purcell *et al.* 2003) seeks to test this proposition. We first assess data from the employee survey before considering one of our case studies.

Analysis: the relationship between attitudes towards FLMs and employee outcomes

In order to explore the relationship between employee attitudes towards FLMs in their role in people management and employee attitudinal outcomes we combined five questions which rated the behaviour of managers over certain aspects of people management into one factor.[1] These questions asked employees how good managers were at:

- keeping everyone up to date about proposed changes
- providing everyone with a chance to comment on proposed changes
- responding to suggestions from employees
- dealing with problems at the workplace
- treating employees fairly.

We refer to this as 'relationship with FLM'. Table 4.1 shows clearly that there is a strong association between those employees who felt their managers were good in people management and their feelings toward their employer (commitment), the satisfaction they get from their job, their motivation and the extent to which they are given freedom to do their job or have discretion and choice over how it is done.[2] As one employee said:

> My motivation and satisfaction varies from job to job depending on the client and the manager and crucially how much influence I have over my job.

We then conducted more sophisticated analyses to assess the association between employee attitudes and behaviours, and perceptions of front line management behaviour and perceptions of HR practices. Using multiple regression analysis we find that the factor 'relationship with FLM' is the most important factor in explaining the variation in job satisfaction and job discretion and one of the

Table 4.1 Correlations between 'relationship with managers' and employee outcomes (N=609)

Employee outcomes	'Relationship with managers'
Commitment	0.417**
Job satisfaction	0.524**
Motivation	0.360**
Job discretion	0.278**

** Significant at the 0.01 level (2 tailed)

most important in developing organisational commitment. In other words the better employees rate FLMs in terms of the way they manage people, the more committed and satisfied those employees will be, and the higher their levels of job discretion (and vice versa).

To gain a greater understanding of this relationship we have looked at differences between 12 organisations (Table 4.2).

It is evident that all companies showed a significant correlation or association between 'relationship with FLM' and at least one employee attitudinal outcome (commitment, motivation, job satisfaction), and in all but one organisation there was a link with two employee attitude outcomes. The widespread results give us confidence in asserting that in all types of organisations the way FLMs undertake their people management roles plays a significant part in influencing employees' attitudes toward their organisation and their job.

One of the major limitations to surveys of this sort, however, is always that by being cross-sectional it is impossible to identify trends or establish causality. We were able to do quasi-longitudinal research by repeating fieldwork in a second year. Three of the above companies responded to the first year employee survey results by taking action to improve the quality of FLM people management behaviour as reported in Hutchinson and Purcell (2003). We report next on one of these (Selfridges) where a wide ranging set of actions was implemented and where we were able to follow up with further senior management interviews in the third year.

Selfridges & Co

We discussed in Chapter 2 the changes in culture and values made by Selfridges facilitated by an HR strategy which was integrated into the company's vision and goals. We can now study the implementation of these changes in more detail

Table 4.2 Association between 'relationship with FLM' and employee attitudinal outcomes.

Company	Commitment	Job satisfaction	Motivation	Job discretion
AIT (38)	0.333**	0.354**		
Clerical Medical (38)		0.672**	0.446**	0.432**
Contact (55)	0.429**	0.336*		
Jaguar (61)	0.445**	0.613**	0.315**	0.316**
Nationwide (61)	0.435**	0.554**	0.382**	
OMT (45)	0.672**	0.436**	0.502**	
PWC (52)	0.305**	0.318*		
Royal Mint (58)		0.430**	0.281*	0.337**
RUH (54)	0.323*	0.493**	0.353**	
Selfridges (61)	0.448**	0.718**	0.569**	0.317*
Siemens (27)			0.428*	
Tesco (58)	0.391**	0.554**	0.376**	

* correlations are significant at the 0.05 level (2 tailed)
** correlations are significant at the 0.01 level (2 tailed)

by focusing on one store. This store provides an excellent illustration of the changes in the role of line managers and their impact on employee attitudes and performance.

Our research focused on the Trafford Park store on the outskirts of Manchester which was the first store to be opened outside London (in 1998) and became a test bed for the development of future stores. At the time around 650 staff worked in the store comprising a mixture of directly employed staff and concessionary staff – these are staff employed by concession owners but present an identical presence to the customer as Selfridges' staff. An extensive range of HR practices was in evidence including extensive training and development (Investors in People accreditation), a staff forum for consultation, generous staff discounts and extensive communication.

Our first attitude survey in 2000 of 40 staff in two units of analysis (women's wear and household departments) showed some very positive employee attitudes. There were high levels of organisational commitment amongst sales associates (including concessionary staff) which compared favourably with commitment levels in the other 11 organisations in the study (Purcell *et al.* 2003) and were substantially higher than for retail staff nationally using identical WERS 98 questions. Further analysis showed a positive relationship between satisfaction with various HR practices and measured employee attitudes. For example, employee perceptions of teamworking, career opportunities, performance appraisal, involvement and communication showed positive correlations with job satisfaction and/ or organisational commitment.[3]

Team leaders

Nevertheless, the survey did reveal some less positive attitudes and experiences. Only 58 per cent were satisfied with the performance appraisal system, with views of dissatisfaction centring mainly on the behaviours of FLMs, and there was clear evidence of a policy–practice gap in terms of the frequency of appraisals. Company policy specified biannual appraisals (one for pay purposes and one for training and development) yet employee experiences of formal appraisals revealed an inconsistent approach with variable frequency and some employees never having been appraised. There was further evidence of poor leadership behaviour. For example, 46 per cent said they wanted more recognition and appreciation shown by management, two thirds said they were hardly ever asked by managers for their views. As one respondent remarked 'management should have a more relaxed, approachable attitude ... do more floor work, and ask staff what problems they have. They should be more involved on the shop floor'. These results were of concern to the company, particularly since they had recently invested in a leadership programme for these managers (referred to as the 'boot camp') to instil the company culture and values into management style. To the HR manager it was clear that 'team leaders' behaviours were not in line with Selfridges' expectations' and that they were not living the espoused values of the company (Purcell *et al.* 2003: 19–25).

Following these results the store focused on making improvements to the team leader role, redefining it into one single role (there had previously been two grades). All team leaders were required to reapply for new positions through a new selection process which focused on behaviours as well as skill sets, and inevitably this meant some lost their position. Improvements were also made to the FLMs' performance appraisal process linking it more to development and career opportunities and including a core requirement to undertake staff appraisals and give emphasis to leadership behaviours. The second attitude survey, conducted a year later, showed improved employee attitudes in terms of job satisfaction, commitment and job influence as shown in Table 4.3. Since there had been no changes to the job content of sales associates in the intervening period the marked improvements to job influence and satisfaction can only be explained by changes in the way FLMs managed their staff. This was clear in the qualitative comments of respondents. For example:

> [I am very satisfied with the sense of achievement I get in my work] … because I now have a good manager who appreciates the work done – I get constant praise – we have a good rapport, respect each other … a good manager makes all the difference

> We now have a good team leader who gives us a chance to give our views and do our own thing.

The survey also revealed improvements in attitudes towards employee perceptions of leadership behaviour and certain HR practices (most notably performance appraisal) as shown in Table 4.4. As one respondent put it, 'We now have a manager that gets appraisals done … and we get praise now and little gifts, such as perfume'.

Performance also improved in the store with sales increasing by 23 per cent compared to the previous year, payroll costs down 5 per cent and 'contribution' – the key measure of sales against payroll costs – up 31.7 per cent. Labour turnover fell to well below the average for retail, in part because it became one of the indicators used to assess FLM performance. Significantly, senior store managers

Table 4.3 Employee attitudes (sales associates) in Selfridges

Employee outcomes *% agree or strongly agree*	*Percentage of employees*	
	Year 1 *(N=40)*	*Year 2* *(N=41)*
A lot of influence over the job	35	56
Satisfied with level of job influence	68	73
Satisfied with sense of achievement	68	83
Commitment: 'I feel loyal to Selfridges'	81	93
'I would recommend a friend or relative to work in Selfridges'	83	90

Table 4.4 Employee attitudes (sales associates) towards management leadership behaviour and certain HR practices in Selfridges

Employee attitudes % agree or strongly agree	Percentage of employees	
	Year 1 (N=40)	Year 2 (N=41)
Managers are good at:		
• Keeping everyone up to date about proposed changes	58	61
• Responding to suggestions from employees	43	59
• Treating employees fairly	58	68
Satisfied with respect from immediate line manager	88	92
Line manager provides coaching and guidance to help improve your performance *(% to a great extent or some extent)*	58	78
Satisfied with performance appraisal	59	84
Satisfied with career opportunities	70	88

themselves attributed these improvements to the changes made to the team leader role and continued to focus on this group of managers.

A year later the FLM job was again reviewed and team leader role guides were issued giving greater clarity and more emphasis to people management activities. These included recruitment, coaching, counselling, monitoring absence and lateness, handling discipline and grievances, leading, delivering daily team briefings, communicating, conducting development reviews, and giving recognition. In terms of recruitment and selection, for example, a task formerly undertaken by the HR department, team leaders were required to interview applicants, advise on the job evaluation and make the final decision to select. Team leaders had other responsibilities such as dealing with customer complaints, ensuring excellent standards on the shop floor, drawing up the weekly rota and helping out on the floor. In order to prepare them for this new role all team leaders went through eight days of training, covering mainly aspects of people management.

The recruitment of team leaders was also re-examined as the HR manager explained:

> We looked at behaviours as well as skill sets such as body language, communication skills, how people say things, how they identify with people and connect with the team.

This was in line with the company policy of recruiting for attitude rather than skill to ensure that all staff fit and deliver the culture and values of the organisation. Potential recruits were initially tele-vetted (as are all staff) – a telephone screening process that aims to do behavioural screening around the company values, before going on to a half-day assessment including individual and group exercises, role playing, conducting interviews, etc. With this emphasis on the need for 'fit' it is not surprising that the company aimed to recruit 60 per cent of staff to team leader level from within. At the same time the HR function was moved off-site to a shared service centre. The store's effort to improve the performance of team leaders also included addressing how the team leaders themselves were managed. Four areas in particular were focused on: involvement, coaching and guidance, career opportunities and management support. At the team leaders' initiative a forum was set up, meeting twice a month to discuss common issues and problems to which 'experts' may be invited for advice and guidance. Assistant sales managers (ASMs – those who manage the team leaders) took on the role of coaching and developing team leaders through both formal and informal means. On the formal side, development reviews were conducted twice a year focusing on monitoring team progress against key performance indicators such as absence and customer service (mystery shopper results). In addition, weekly formal meetings were held with team leaders to assess their training needs. On a more informal basis the ASMs conduct weekly floor walks with the team leaders to assess sales and performance issues.

This, therefore, is further evidence of the company attempting to influence attitudes and behaviour, this time those of the team leaders themselves, through improving HR practices which applied to them and also focusing on the leadership behaviour of their managers – the ASMs. This whole process was considered a success by senior managers. As one senior manager rather bluntly explained 'forcing the team leaders to be more disciplined, more planned and forcing them to be less reactive ... partly because the HR team are no longer available on site to wipe their back sides!'

We have explored the relationship between FLMs and performance, showing that the way in which FLMs implement and enact practices by 'bringing them to life' and show leadership plays a significant part in influencing employees' attitudes towards the organisation and their jobs. The way FLMs carry out their people management responsibilities is directly related to levels of commitment, motivation and satisfaction which, as we show in the next chapter is linked to discretionary behaviour. The employees' judgement of their FLM leadership behaviour was directly related, where positive, to higher levels of affective commitment and to better aspects of job experience.

Having identified the critical role that FLMs play in the HRM–performance causal chain we now address some more practical considerations.

The effectiveness of line managers

Numerous studies, including our own research (Marchington 2001; McGovern *et al.* 1997; Fenton O'Creevy 2001; Hutchinson and Purcell 2007), have raised concerns about the effectiveness of line managers in supporting and delivering people management activities. The CIPD 2006 reward management survey found that front line managers' skills and abilities are perceived to be the main inhibitor to the successful implementation of a reward strategy (CIPD 2006). In another survey of training/HR specialists (CIPD 2007c) 44 per cent of respondents felt that line managers were not very effective or ineffective in relation to learning and development despite 96 per cent expressing the view that line managers are important in supporting learning and development in their organisation. The fact that line managers may be problematic has obvious implications for the people–performance link. We now consider briefly three main areas of concern (CIPD 2007c): lack of skills and knowledge, lack of commitment to people management and competing priorities.

Lack of skills and knowledge

One the most consistent themes from all three research projects was the widely expressed concern over FLM capability, with many arguing that line managers lack the necessary skills and competencies to perform the people management aspects of their role. Problematic areas where skill gaps were identified include discipline and grievance handling, performance appraisal, involvement and communication and training, learning and development. Indeed many managers themselves admitted to the need to improve skills if they were to do the job well, and cited a lack of training and support in this area as a key contributory factor (Cunningham and Hyman 1995; Gennard and Kelly 1997; Hutchinson and Purcell 2007). Financial constraints, workload and lack of commitment (which we consider next), and even the low educational and technical base of line managers in Britain (McGovern *et al.* 1997), have been identified as impediments to training.

Nearly all of the organisations we studied placed great emphasis on management training courses as a means of equipping managers with the necessary skills to deliver their people management roles, although these tools were not always used and were insufficient on their own to skill managers. There will, of course, always be managers who feel that they do not actually need training in people management, believing that competencies are best gained by a mixture of 'learning by doing' or are nothing more than common sense (Cunningham and Hyman 1995), or that they, as managers, know what is best for their team – what motivates them, what pressures they face and so on (Hutchinson and Purcell 2007).

Lack of commitment to people management

There are also concerns that some line managers do not take their role seriously or value this particular aspect of their job. The CIPD learning and development (2007c) survey found that almost a quarter (23 per cent) of respondents felt that line managers do not take their responsibility in learning and development seriously, as this senior manager from a consultancy organisation (Hutchinson and Purcell 2007) suggests.

> Most people around here are not interested in managing people. They are engineers with low interpersonal skills, poor at communication, less behavioural. They cannot deal with underperformance, can't manage change so we are locked into stasis.

This may, in part be down to the dominance of the 'harder' more immediate business priorities which we discussed earlier, and the fact that the people management role is more discretionary than other aspects of line managers' work. Failure on the part of the organisations to rate people management highly by, for example, placing it in any formal or informal performance expectations is no doubt a contributory factor here (Whittaker and Marchington 2003; Gratton *et al.* 1999).

Other explanations are offered for this lack of commitment. Maxwell and Watson suggest that 'the line managers' lack of understanding of the business and HR strategy may curtail their involvement in HR activities' (2006: 1162). It was clear from some of our interviews (Hutchinson and Purcell 2007) that some line managers were unclear about HR strategy and policy, for example on the performance management process, particularly where there were linkages with pay. Research on individual performance related pay (Harris 2001) reveals that middle managers often do not share the stated objectives or principles of the system they are required to operationalise. This highlights the need for HR specialists and the line to work more closely together, and for HR to consider the line when designing practices. We consider this further in Chapter 9.

Another impediment to commitment may be lack of ownership. In our study on reward (Purcell and Hutchinson 2007a) we found that lack of involvement in final performance-related pay decisions was regretted by line managers and a cause of frustration.

Competing priorities and work overload

Related to these issues are ones of excessive workloads, lack of time and competing priorities. As we have already indicated, people management is often seen as an extra to the main parts of the job and only addressed if urgent, and very often these are 'additional' responsibilities which have been taken on without any reduction in the more traditional activities. A common theme running through our interviews with line managers were complaints of heavy workloads and resentment about added administrative work and bureaucracy. This is borne out by this remark from a line manager in an organisation which had recently restructured the HR function to a single serve delivery model (Hutchinson and Purcell 2007), with consequent implications for line managers in terms of taking on greater people management responsibilities:

> Although I agree with the responsibility of the line manager in the recruitment of staff I feel that the administrative burden placed on line managers by the new system is intolerable and a very inefficient use of expensive resource.

In this particular organisation many of the managers we spoke to provided the example of having to place flowers in a vase on the table in the interview room – a task formerly undertaken by HR!

Managing the managers

It is possible to identify a number of supportive conditions necessary for effective line management involvement. If the secret to linking people management to performance is to 'unlock' or trigger discretionary behaviour in employees in the way they do their work, the same must be true for the FLMs – in fact it may be more important since it will have an impact on those they manage. In other words the way line managers are themselves managed will be likely to influence their discretionary behaviours positively or negatively (Hutchinson and Purcell 2003). Further analysis of our employee data (Purcell *et al.* 2003) reveals that it is the FLMs' relationship with their manager, and more generally senior management, which is key and makes a difference. In our subsequent research on line managers we also observed the importance of senior management support (Hutchinson and Purcell 2007) and of the need for senior managers to act as role models or champions.

The HR function has an influential role to play, partly in the design of particular people management strategies which are most appropriate for managing FLMs such as in the provision of training and development. Care also needs to be taken in the selection of line managers, paying particular attention to behavioural competencies, and consideration needs to be given to rewarding good people management skills. HR can also provide mechanisms to measure, monitor and support line manager effectiveness including the provision of a well designed performance management system. In the design of people management practices HR need to take account of the fact that they are delivered and 'brought to life' by the line. Interestingly few of the organisations we studied did this.

Central to the question of HR support is the role of HR and this is considered in greater depth in our CIPD-sponsored piece of research (Hutchinson and Purcell 2007). In some of these organisations studied, the transfer of activities to the line was linked to the development of a shared services model of HR as HR seeks to add value to the business (Ulrich 1995). The danger, however, is that this can be resented by line managers who feel they have been dumped upon, and perceive it as a cost-cutting exercise with the removal of the friendly HR Manager down the corridor.

In Chapter 2 we show the importance of creating a strong and positive organisational culture. In this we argued that in addition to adopting high commitment HR and employing effective line managers, successful organisations have operated a positive culture. These issues and other practical implications are considered further in Chapter 9.

Conclusion

Earlier research on the HRM–performance link, which focused exclusively on a count of HR practices in place and the proportion of employees covered by such practices, had the danger of giving the misleading impression that it was the number and mix of practices that were important. Once the model of the causal chain is proposed, hypothesising the steps between intended practices and performance outcomes, it is clear that the crucial link is between the employee experiences of people management, the formation or modification of attitudes toward the employing organisation and the job, and the inducement these provide to engage in certain types of discretionary behaviour. It is not, however, simply the quality of the HR practices per se which causes this chain reaction, but crucially the way in which FLMs apply these practices. Employees' experience of these is inexorably linked with their relationship with their FLM who is seen as the agent of the organisation and the deliverer of the people management practices. Organisations therefore need to recognise the potential impact that FLMs can have on employee engagement and as such are an occupational group worthy of special treatment and support.

5 Employees' perceptions, attitudes and discretionary behaviour

Introduction

Our analysis of the HR causal chain so far has examined the importance of culture and values, HR practices and the role of line managers. We now turn to a discussion of the next part of the chain which focuses on the factors which influence employee attitudes and behaviour. We are particularly interested in what is referred to as discretionary behaviour (Appelbaum *et al.* 2000), that is, behaviour which is over and above the minimum which is demanded and what Fox (1974) some time ago referred to as behaviour which is 'beyond contract'. This is behaviour which employees choose to engage in rather than that which they are required to and which has a clear link with performance (Podsakoff *et al.* 2000).

Once we have established what discretionary behaviour is and why it is important we then look at the drivers of this behaviour. In order to do this we need to return to the ability–motivation–opportunity model that we discussed in Chapter 1. We can recall that this argues that employees must have the skill needed to exercise discretion (ability), the desire to do so (motivation) and they must be given the opportunity to do so by their organisation and their line manager (Boxall and Purcell 2008: 5; Appelbaum *et al.* 2000; Lepak *et al.* 2006). Our particular focus in this chapter is on motivation: what determines whether an employee will exercise whatever discretion they have in ways which will benefit the organisation? This involves distinguishing between what the employee *can* do and what they *will* do (Boxall and Purcell 2008: 173). This chapter argues that employee perceptions and experiences of HR practices are vital for understanding the answers to these questions. We will explore these influences at three levels: the individual, the individual and their line manager, and their interaction with the wider organisation. We argue that this multilevel approach gives good insights into the influences on employee attitudes and behaviour. Once we have established these we then examine the Tesco case in some detail to provide an illustration of the links between employee attitudes and behaviour and organisational performance. In doing so, we hope to provide an accessible way to access the key themes of this chapter as well as set the stage for the more detailed application of the HRM causal chain model in Chapters 6 to 8.

Thus this chapter aims to:

1   establish the importance of discretionary behaviour and its links with performance;
2   examine the drivers of discretionary behaviour at three levels;
3   illustrate the links between employee attitudes and behaviour and organisational performance.

Discretionary behaviour

Interest in discretionary behaviour is not new. According to LePine *et al.* (2002) research into discretionary behaviour can be traced back to Barnard (1938) and Katz (1964). Over 30 years ago Fox (1974) identified what he called the 'managerial problem' of motivating employees to perform the minimum requirements of the job and ideally to perform above the minimum. Since then the notion of discretionary behaviour has become central to many contemporary studies on the people and performance link, such as the work of Appelbaum and her colleagues in manufacturing in the USA (2000), Wright *et al.* in their study of a single customer service firm (2003) and our own research (Purcell *et al.* 2003).

In any situation, work (or otherwise) employees have a degree of choice and discretion over how they perform their tasks and responsibilities. As Appelbaum *et al.* noted 'in any formal system of work controls, some effort remains that workers contribute at their discretion' (2000: 25). Fox (1974: 16) distinguished between two characteristics of work roles: 'task range' and 'discretionary content'. Task range refers to the variety of tasks in a job and can be highly specific or diffuse. Discretionary content looks at the extent to which the behaviour needed in a job is highly specified or diffuse. Fox argued that 'every job contains both prescribed and discretionary elements' and that the discretionary elements 'require not trained obedience to specific external control, but the exercise of wisdom, judgement

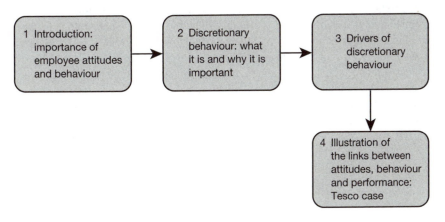

Figure 5.1 Structure of the chapter

and expertise. The control comes from within: it is in a literal sense, self-control. The occupant of the role must himself [*sic*] choose, judge, feel, sense, consider, conclude what would be the best thing to do in the circumstances, the way of going about what he is doing' (Fox 1974: 19). Taylorism and scientific management focus on limiting discretion by breaking down jobs into simple component elements and tightly prescribing the way in which tasks were performed through close supervision and rules and regulations. In contrast, exhibiting discretionary behaviour or effort means making choices about the way the job is done, such as the speed, care, innovation and style of job delivery. As we suggest in our earlier report (Purcell *et al.* 2003: 5):

> This behaviour is at the heart of the employment relationship, because it is hard for the employer to define and then monitor and control the amount of effort, innovation and productive behaviour required. The most obvious example here is front-line service work dealing with customers either face to face or over the telephone. It concerns the sort of everyday behaviour that the employer wants but has to rely on the employee to deliver. It may involve emotional labour (smiling down the phone), using knowledge to solve a problem or suggest an alternative to the customer, or it may be internal to the work of the organisation, such as co-operating with team members, helping probationers learn shortcuts or sharing new ideas on work processes.

The choice of how and how well to do things is not necessarily made deliberately for it can be unconscious – just part of the way people behave in their organisation. Discretionary behaviour can certainly be withdrawn, in response, for example, to a belief that 'the firm no longer cares about me, my future or my opinions'. Ultimately, whatever the incentives or sanctions the firm tries to use, it lies with the employee to 'give' discretionary behaviour and to withdraw it. Although this is described in terms of the action of an individual (we all have bad days), it is the collective withdrawal of discretionary behaviour that is so damaging.

Discretionary behaviour is closely associated with 'organisational citizenship behaviour' (OCB) which is strongly linked to people's perceptions of their employer, how satisfying they find their job and how strongly they feel motivated to undertake it (Coyle-Shapiro *et al.* 2004). Organ (1988) defines OCB as a type of job performance that is discretionary, not directly recognised by the formal reward system, and promotes organisational effectiveness. The concentration on beyond-role actions is evident in the focus on 'helpful, but not absolutely required, job behaviors' in Smith *et al.* (1983: 656). Organ *et al.* (2006: 16) indicate that this 'operationalization' took shape in a set of semi-structured interviews conducted by Ann Smith in which she asked supervisors of manufacturing plants, 'What are the things you'd like your employees to do more of, but really can't make them do, and for which you can't guarantee any definite rewards, other than your appreciation?'.

The measurement and dimensionality of OCB have been the subject of a great deal of research. Organ (1988) separated OCBs into five categories: altruism, courtesy, civic virtue, conscientiousness and sportsmanship. Podsakoff *et al.* (1990) extended this work by developing a measure of OCB that consisted of subscales for each of the five dimensions proposed. Williams and Anderson (1991) further advanced the theory by proposing a two-dimensional structure for OCB, with one dimension focused on discretionary behaviours directed at individuals (OCBI) and another on discretionary behaviours directed towards the organisations (OCBO). Williams and Anderson's conceptualization of OCBI included Organ's notions of altruism and courtesy, while the conceptualization of OCBO captured sportsmanship, conscientiousness and civic virtue. Hoffman *et al.* (2007) use meta-analysis tools to examine the accumulated evidence from OCB studies, and they suggest that it is possible to reduce this dimensionality to a single factor model of OCB that is 'distinct from, albeit strongly related to, task performance' (Hoffman *et al.* 2007: 563).

In addition to academic discussions of the dimensionality of OCB, the literature is also filled with a wide range of measures. These behaviours are typically chosen to fit a specific research setting, though they tend to fit within the broad categories identified by Organ and others. A good example of this is the work of Bettencourt *et al.* (2001), who tailor an OCB measure to a service environment. The questions used are distinct from those used elsewhere, but they map neatly on to key categorisations identified by the previous literature (Bettencourt *et al.* 2001: 41).

Organ *et al.* (2006: 200–202) cite several reasons to suspect that high OCBs are linked with improved organisational effectiveness. These include: increases in the productivity of managers and co-workers; the saving of resources that would otherwise be used in production or in maintenance activities (e.g. team building); improved coordination across team members and work groups; improved recruitment and retention of the best people; better adaptability to environmental changes; and more stable organisational performance. They also provide a summary of evidence for the connections between OCBs and workgroup productivity. Outcomes which have been shown to depend (at least to some extent) on OCBs include: workgroup productivity, sales team performance, customer satisfaction, sales revenue, profitability and operating efficiency.

Drivers of discretionary behaviour

Having discussed both the desirability and dimensionality of organisational citizenship behaviours, one is naturally drawn to understand the key attitudinal determinants of these behaviours. This is a growing literature, and we report here only on the main attitudinal determinants of OCB, upon which there is substantial agreement. Much of the discussion in the literature is (of course) based on agency theory and incentives drawn from organisational economics. Rather than follow this well trodden path (see Grimshaw and Rubery (2007) for a summary) we have chosen to examine the influence of social and psychological processes since these are more directly related to the HR causal chain. Our analysis looks at the psychological contract, leader-member exchange and perceived organisational support.

Psychological contract: breach and fulfilment

Recent debates in the HRM literature have used the concept of the psychological contract to examine job satisfaction, motivation and discretionary behaviour. The psychological contract was first introduced by Argyris (1960) and defined by Schein (1978: 48) as a 'set of unwritten reciprocal expectations between an individual employee and the organisation'. He argued that successful employment relationships involved matching organisational and individual needs (1978).

Rousseau (1995: 9) takes a different view and defines the psychological contract as, 'individual beliefs, shaped by the organisation, regarding terms of an exchange agreement between individuals and their organisation'. For her the psychological contract 'exists in the eye of the beholder' (Rousseau 1995: 6). This contract is therefore subjective, unwritten and often not discussed or negotiated and goes beyond any formal contract of employment. The terms of this contract may vary by individual and over time, as they 'emanate from perceived implicit or explicit promises by the employer' (Robinson 1996: 575). Rousseau (1995: 91–2) distinguishes between transactional and relational contracts. Transactional contracts are based primarily on economic incentives, have limited personal involvement and well-specified commitments, tend to be for a time-specified period and use existing skills on jobs with limited flexibility. Relational contracts include a personal and emotional attachment as well as an economic exchange, have open-ended commitment for jobs which are subject to change and often affect the personal lives of employees. The psychological contract is effectively therefore a set of personal expectations which are influenced by a series of HR practices, most notably recruitment, selection and induction. Rousseau (1995: 162) argues that 'HR practices send strong messages to individuals regarding what the organisation expects of them and what they can expect in return'.

Guest (1998) disputes Rousseau's model because her emphasis on the subjective means that it cannot be seen as 'contractual'. He defines the psychological contract as the 'perceptions of both parties to the employment relationship, organisation and individual of the reciprocal promises and obligations implied in that relationship' (Guest 2007: 133). Indeed as Boxall and Purcell (2008: 191) argue 'to have a psychological contract must mean that the employer and employee *share* some common understandings that go beyond what is written in the employment agreement'. Guest and Conway's survey work for the CIPD (2002) refers to the concept of the *state* of the psychological contract which they define as 'the extent to which the promises and obligations that form the psychological contract have been met, whether they are fair and the trust that they will continue to meet in the future' (2002: 1). Their model suggests that the state of the psychological contract and consequent attitude and behavioural outcomes, such as motivation, satisfaction and intention to quit are influenced by a set of individual and organisational factors plus a range of HR policies and practices. Where the psychological contract is positive, increased employee commitment and satisfaction will have a positive impact on performance. However, failure by the organisation to deliver on the contract terms such as broken promises or failure to deliver on commitment can be thought of as 'breach', which has a negative effect on job satisfaction, commitment and individual effectiveness.

Boxall and Purcell (2008: 192–193) draw on the work of Grant (1999) which highlights the dynamic nature of the employment relationship by referring to the concept of psychological contracting. This is based on expectancy theory (Vroom 1964) which argues that employees will be motivated where they believe their efforts will lead to successful performance, this performance will be recognised and rewarded and the rewards are desirable. This, therefore, is the key link back to the HR causal chain because it focuses on employees' perception of HR practices (Guest 2007: 133). As Boxall and Purcell (2008: 192) argue 'our *ongoing* motivation at work is affected by the expectations we form *and* our experience of whether these are met over time'. On a practical level therefore if employees perceive there is a gap between what they expected to receive (based on the intended practices) and what they actually experienced then they are likely to feel that their psychological contract has been violated and be less likely to deliver the desired discretionary behaviour or indeed leave the organisation altogether. As we have seen in Chapter 4, line managers play a critical role in this because the actual delivery of HR practices is often in their hands.

Grant (1999: 331) identifies four types of psychological contracts which may affect employee performance and motivation: congruent contracts where intended practices are experienced, mismatched contracts where there is a gap between intended and experienced practices, partial contracts where some expectations are met and others are not and trial contracts where the contract is given a chance to prove itself. Indeed, he argues that employee feelings may contribute towards a general view of management's competence and trustworthiness which he sees as a kind of collective contract.

As we have seen in Chapter 4, writers on the psychological contract are increasingly using social exchange theory (Gouldner 1960; Blau 1964) to draw attention to the reciprocal nature of the employment relationship. This requires a discussion of interactions between employees and their leaders and the extent of perceived organisational support. However, before we do this we need to discuss the more general attitudes of organisational commitment and job satisfaction.

General attitudes

At several points in the earlier chapters we have established links to general measures of employee 'affect' like organisational commitment and job satisfaction. This is because the general employee attitudes towards their jobs and employers have been shown to have meaningful links with employee discretion.

Organisational commitment

We defined organisational commitment in Chapter 2 as the relative strength of an individual's identification with, and involvement in, a particular organisation. Organisational commitment has three attributes:

- a strong belief in, and an acceptance of, the organisation's goals and values;
- a willingness to exert considerable effort on behalf of the organisation;
- a strong desire to maintain membership in the organisation (Porter *et al.* 1974: 604).

Theory suggests that committed employees feel some affinity with the activities, aspirations and even identity of the organisation they work for, and that this affection translates into a willingness to exert discretionary effort in the interests of the organisation. Support for the existence of connections between OCB and commitment is extremely common in the literature, and Frenkel and Sanders (2007), Sinclair *et al.* (2005) and Riketta and Landerer (2005) are a few of the many recent academic articles supporting this view.

Job satisfaction

There has been a long-running view that workers who are satisfied with their jobs will perform their jobs better. This view is well entrenched amongst academics, practitioners and laypeople, despite relatively limited evidence of direct links between job satisfaction and productivity (Organ *et al.* 2006: 69). However, there is ample evidence that satisfaction generates performance benefits through its effects on OCB.

Relationships with the organisation

Social exchange theory (Blau 1964; Adams 1965) posits that voluntary actions of individuals are motivated by both intrinsic and extrinsic returns that these actions are expected to produce: typically through the reciprocal actions of others. The functioning of these social exchange relationships is enhanced by job satisfaction, as this makes it more likely that employees feel that their organisation, or at least the part of the organisation with which they are most closely associated, is a 'just world' (Lerner 1980) and that any efforts they make will subsequently be rewarded.

Leader–member exchange

Leader–member exchange (LMX) is a theory closely linked with social exchange theory. It is based on the idea that the same leader may have different social exchange relationships with different subordinates. Uhl-Bien and Graen (1998) argue that the character of these relationships, or *dyads*, are important because they can be linked to employee trust in leaders, commitment to a leader's vision and other desirable employee attitudes. LMX conceptualises the relationship between leader and subordinate as an *exchange* with each party both giving and receiving through the relationship. Leaders may give things like power, influence and access to resources, while members typically reciprocate with things like loyalty, high effort and increased workloads. High levels of LMX lead employees to engage in OCBs by creating a sense of obligation and a consequent desire to reciprocate received behaviours. Scholarly evidence of this link includes Hui *et al.* (1999) and Uhl-Bien and Maslyn (2003). High levels of LMX are associated with improved employee performance across a range of occupations at the individual, group and organisational levels of analysis (Gerstner and Day 1997). In addition to OCBs, performance may include other subjective measures like supervisor ratings of competence as well as objective performance measures (e.g. sales levels) or performance against set targets.

Perceived organisational support

Social exchange theory also suggests that employees have exchange relationships with people other than their manager. This view is consistent with the suggestion by Eisenberger *et al.* (1986) that employees form a global belief about the extent to which the organisation values their contributions and cares about their well-being. This belief is called perceived organisational support (POS). Social exchange theory suggests that POS enhances discretionary effort by building emotional commitment towards the organisation, as well as a sense of obligation associated with attaining organisational objectives (Eisenberger *et al.* 2004). A recent meta-analysis of the research into POS has revealed that high POS enhances employees' organisational commitment, reduces employee withdrawal and improves both job performance and organisational citizenship behaviour (Rhoades and Eisenberger 2002).

Organisational justice

Fairness in the workplace has been linked with OCB by several researchers. Researchers often conceptualise fairness with measures of organisational justice. Colquitt (2001) separates justice into four factors: procedural, distributive, interpersonal and informational justice. Each of these is the subject of a substantial literature beyond the scope of our review here, but the theoretical link between OCB and measures of organisational justice is an outgrowth of both social exchange theory and the existence of the reciprocity norm (Peterson 2004). Earlier studies suggest that employees will have higher levels of commitment when they are treated fairly (Witt 1991; Korsgaard *et al.* 1995) and employees are likely to identify with fair procedures because they benefit from them and because they identify with an organisation which treats its employees fairly. Beneficial actions directed at employees create a reason for employees to reciprocate with their attitudes and their behaviours. For example, studies of the relationship between organisational commitment and justice perceptions suggest that they are positively and significantly related (Meyer *et al.* 2002; Cohen-Charash and Spector 2001). Kamdar *et al.* (2006) find that employee-level differences in justice perceptions are linked to the observed levels of OCBs these employees exert as well as the extent to which employees are likely to perceive their roles more 'widely' (i.e. they are more likely to indicate that OCBs actually are an expected part of their jobs).

We have argued that exchange relationships exist between employees and their managers and organisations, the character of which can influence discretionary effort, but it is also important to recognise that similar arguments can be constructed for the relationships between co-workers, and we consider these separately from the hierarchical relationships addressed earlier. The concepts of team–member exchange (TMX), group cohesiveness and perceived team support (PTS) are three examples of the way these collegial relationships can influence discretion.

Team–member exchange

Like leader–member exchange, team–member exchange conceptualises employee relationships through the lens of social exchange theory, but here the dyadic relationships are between co-workers rather then between a manager and his/ her subordinate. Evidence for the importance of TMX is convincingly presented in Kamdar and Van Dyne (2007), where they examine matched data on 230 employees, their co-workers and their supervisors to understand the combined effects of LMX and TMX on task performance and OCB. Their results suggest that good quality social exchange relationships are associated with enhanced OCB and task performance, and also yield the intuitive result that TMX is particularly linked with citizenship behaviours that are directed at co-workers while LMX is associated with behaviours directed towards the organisation.

Group cohesiveness

Group cohesion refers to the affinity of group members for one another and their desire to remain a part of the group (Organ *et al.* 2006: 117). Highly cohesive groups typically have high degrees of friendliness, mutual liking, cooperation, and positive feelings about the group's tasks (Janis 1982; Shaw 1981). This provides several reasons to expect links between group cohesion and discretion. The strong sense of shared identity associated with high levels of cohesion leads to the exercise of discretion, and provided these group agendas are linked with organisational objectives the organisation should see performance benefits associated with cohesion. This links back to the ideas we presented in Chapter 2 surrounding the 'Big Idea'.

Perceived team support

Perceived team support (PTS) is similar to group cohesion but is more focused on the work relationships between team members rather than their emotional attachments. Indeed, PTS is typically measured using the same set of questions as perceived organisational support but with the referent changed from 'organisation' to 'team'. Again, social exchange theory suggests that PTS should be linked to discretion because it builds feelings of affection and obligation to the team through a desire for reciprocity.

There are, of course, other factors besides employee attitudes that influence the exercise of discretion. Much research has investigated the effect of personality traits on discretion, though their ability to predict behaviour is limited, particularly in organisations with strong cultures (Organ *et al.* 2006). In these environments the characteristics of employee relationships with the organisation, its leaders and their co-workers tend to influence discretion. That said, the exercise of discretion requires not only a willingness but also an ability and an opportunity, as we have mentioned previously. As such, there are a range of organisational constraints that may inhibit the relationship between employee attitudes and discretion described in this chapter. Poor training, isolation, job routinisation, excessively high work-loads, etc., all may limit the ability and/or opportunity of workers to exercise discretion in ways that could benefit their employers.

Employee attitudes, behaviour and performance in Tesco

In Chapter 3 we referred to the example of Tesco to illustrate the ways in which the company sought to align its HR practices internally and externally. In this chapter we build on this example to discuss the interactions between employee attitudes and behaviour and organisational performance. The case illustrates two important findings in particular. First, we saw variations in employee attitudes (in this case, section managers) between the four stores we studied in ways that we might not have expected given the identical intended HR practices. Second, this pattern of attitudes was matched by significant differences in performance between the stores measured using a variety of criteria.

Employee attitudes

We carried out our research in four Tesco stores. Each was in a market town and demographics, labour market and income patterns in these towns were generally similar. As we have seen, Tesco is a centralised, highly successful retail giant with clear routines and policies emanating from Head Office designed to guide management behaviour at store level. We would expect there to be a low level of variation in the exercise of managerial discretion in this environment at store level but in practice there were significant differences. These variations seem to be about the way in which senior managers at store level were exercising their discretion when putting Head Office routines into operation. This is a particularly important area of discretionary behaviour since, as one store manager in Tesco explained: 'The routines should be viewed as providing a focus and structure ... they are necessary in terms of delivering best practice but it is the way in which the rules and routines are implemented that makes them effective.'

We interviewed 43 section managers in these stores representing around two thirds of the population. Table 5.1 shows distinct differences between the section managers' perceptions of the various aspects of their line manager's role: enact-ment, controlling and leadership in the four stores. Levels of job satisfaction, motivation and commitment are shown at the base of the table. It is clear that store C in particular is out of line with the others. How can we explain this?

Table 5.1 Employee satisfaction with aspects of HR practice: Tesco four stores compared. Percentage of respondents who said 'very satisfied' or 'satisfied'

	Store A	Store B	Store C	Store D
1 HR practices	%	%	%	%
Training	46	82	36	90
Career opportunities	64	91	55	70
Pay	46	64	9	60
Appraisal	50	82	64	90
2 Controlling				
Influence over how job is done (% a lot)	64	64	27	50
Job influence	82	82	36	100
Sharing knowledge (% good)	64	82	18	70
3 Leadership (% good)				
Chance to comment on changes	53	72	18	30
Respond to suggestions	27	82	18	60
Deal with problems	73	82	55	70
Treating employees fairly	64	100	64	70
Provide coaching/guidance (% to a great extent)	46	55	27	40
Respect received from your boss	100	91	64	90
4 Outcomes				
Job satisfaction	64	73	64	80
Motivation (% 'very' and 'fairly' motivated)	55	46	36	40
Commitment (% proud to tell people who I work for)	91	73	46	90

N=43

Enacting HR practices

Perhaps most intriguing of all is that this pattern of satisfaction and commitment is also reflected in terms of attitudes towards certain HR practices in Tesco as shown in the table. Both stores A and C have low scores for satisfaction with levels of training, opportunities for career advancement and satisfaction with the appraisal system. Variations in the levels of satisfaction with pay are especially interesting given that the pay rates for these employees are standardised across all 4 stores yet as few as 9 per cent of employees in store C are either satisfied or highly satisfied with their pay compared with 64 per cent in store B. Employees who suffer poor levels of satisfaction and motivation in general may well be transferring their feelings over to specific HR practices. This has profound implications for the focus on HR practices in providing the necessary environment for discretionary effort since perceptions on and satisfaction with these policies is clearly influenced by the context in which they are applied.

Controlling

The table also shows variations along the controlling dimensions of discretion. For example, there are marked differences between the stores on the extent to which employees claim they have influence over their job. 27 per cent of employees in store C say they have a lot of influence over their job compared to 64 per cent who say this in stores A and B and half who say this in store D. Only around one third of employees in store C are satisfied with their level of influence they have over their job and 18 per cent are dissatisfied. This compares with the other stores, especially store D where all the employees are satisfied with the level of influence over their jobs. These two measures are likely to be highly influenced by the way local managers implement the rules and job descriptions set by Head Office. This applies too to sharing knowledge with store C being particularly poor. However, there are fewer variations in the extent to which employees find their jobs challenging, perhaps because this reflects the inherent nature of what is basically a very demanding job which is less susceptible to local interpretation in terms of what has to be done but the local interpretation is how the job can be done.

Leadership

The table shows that there is a high level of variation in employees' perception of the exercise of managerial discretion in the way line managers carry out their jobs in people management terms, what we call leadership. Employees in store C consistently have a poor perception of the way their senior managers exercise their discretion; the responses in this store are either the lowest or equal the lowest across all of the measures. This suggests that senior managers in store C had, at the time of our interviews, a very controlling style of managing which is considered poor in terms of, for example, allowing staff to comment on changes and responding to suggestions from employees. This compares to around three quarters of employees in store B who think their managers are good at these things. The relatively poor results for store C were repeated, but in a less noticeable way, when their results were compared with others in terms of how good managers were at dealing with problems in the workplace, treating employees fairly and showing respect. The other distinct pattern was the consistently good performance of store B across all the measures.

The impact of local store managers is clear to see here. Even though there is a heavy standardisation of routines, local senior managers are able to exercise their discretion in how they put these into practice and this is clearly reflected in employee perceptions. The following quotes from our interviews reflect this:

> It's a good organisation to work for but the management within individual stores varies and … in terms of their style of management – there are different styles in different stores.
>
> (Section Manager)

> Store managers have to interpret what Head Office wants … and there is a lot of room for discretion. Effectively the store manager is the interface between the Head Office and those who work in the store. The key is how you apply the Head Office policies – that's very different.
>
> (Store Manager)

Getting the right managers into the right store is the biggest issue I have to deal with.

(Regional Director)

Comparing store performance

We have seen that employee attitudes varied across the four stores we studied in ways we might not have anticipated given the common set of HR practices. The question now is whether there are similar variations in performance between the stores.[1]

A variety of measures have been used, although most of these are operational because they most closely reflect the actual performance of each store. These performance measures are among a group of the key indicators used by Tesco on their Steering Wheel to assess operational efficiency and they link these to their business strategy and financial success. Some of these, such as waste and shrinkage can be regarded as proximal to employee performance, whereas others, for instance profit contribution, are more distal. These measures are:

- Availability: stock availability on the shelves
- Known loss: wastage
- Shrinkage: unknown loss resulting from theft and stock errors
- One in front: a measure of how often the store achieves its set target of one or less customers in the queue at the checkout
- Payroll costs as a percentage of sales
- Profit contribution
- Turnover (£ million).

The results are presented in Table 5.2. Though we based our work on the raw numbers from the stores, we present them here as performance in percentage terms relative to the regional average. A negative score indicates performance which was below the regional average while a positive score is above average. This means that we can compare these four stores to a wider set of stores as well

Table 5.2 Tesco performance data: percentage variation from regional average (20 stores)

	Store A	Store B	Store C	Store D
Availability	−0.1	0.6	−0.8	0.3
Waste/known loss	−5.5	4.7	−11.8	7.1
Shrinkage/unknown loss	5.4	63.5	−59.5	44.6
Operating expenses as percentage of sales	2.4	2.4	−28.2	−11.7
Waiting to be served	2.4	−6.9	−0.6	−3.3
Payroll costs as percentage of sales	−4.3	14.8	4.3	0.1
Profit contribution	−13.0	21.4	−33.7	−0.1
Turnover £m	42.6	71.1	48.2	54.8

as to each other. Inspection of the results suggests that the performance of these stores is fairly typical for the region. We can see clear evidence that the superior employee responses for Store B and Store D presented above are matched by superior performance in many of the key measures.

For example, Store C was the poorest performer in a number of key areas: its expenses were 28 per cent higher than the average and its profit contribution was 34 per cent lower. In contrast Store B had expenses which were 2.4 per cent lower than average and profits which were 21 per cent higher. Store A had profits which were 13 per cent below the regional mean and Store D had profits which are almost at the mean. Shrinkage is much lower in Store B and Store D compared with Stores A and C. The differences in waste are less dramatic. This is unsurprising as we would expect the performance measures that are proximal to employees would show greater links with employee attitudes than those which are more distal, such as profit contribution.

The findings from Tesco are clear: even though it is a highly standardised organisation seeking consistency in all its practices, we have evidence of variations in the implementation of HR practices and of employee views of the ways managers exercise their discretion. Stores A and C were generally lowest in terms of managerial behaviour, employee discretion, employee attitudes and overall performance compared to Stores B and D. There was a strong pattern between employee attitudes on a wide variety of job design and HR practices, employee views on the quality of HR management applied to them, especially the opportunity to participate, and store performance. It was possible to trace a pattern of results which were repeated through the different kinds of data which linked the exercise of discretion, employee attitudes and store performance. Indeed, we argue that the ways in which store managers exercised their discretion affected the willingness of employees to go 'beyond contract' and consequently to improve or sustain business performance. Given the location of the stores in four similar market towns and the application of common practices, the most credible explanation for the variation in store performance was the difference in the way people are managed.

As we have discussed the employees interviewed were section managers who had some freedom over how they carried out their jobs, particularly in the people management area. We suggest that the way section managers exercise this discretion is particularly affected by the many ways store managers undertake their leadership responsibilities. The section managers meet the store manager frequently and these meetings can be intense if there is a short-term operational problem to be solved virtually immediately. Not only is interaction frequent and intense but store managers have a high degree of freedom over how they handle issues such as allowing employees to comment on proposed changes, responding to suggestions for change and providing coaching and guidance as well as how they implement HR practices such as conducting appraisals. Thus store managers have high choice over how they manage their people, within standardised routines, and this in turn affects the way section managers exercise their discretion, which is also mostly over people management issues.

The store manager is particularly influential in setting the tone for the way of managing employees across the store. They provide a role model through their own way of managing their staff and set the expectations for achieving certain goals and behaviours which are acceptable when dealing with individual employees. It is possible that the power of the store manager is unusual and characteristic of ways of managing within the retail sector.

This chapter has attempted to illustrate the importance of employee perceptions of HR practices. We have done this with a review of the literature focused on how employees can be motivated to exercise discretion in positive ways and what happens when their expectations are not met. We have also illustrated this litera-ture with research done in four stores in the Tesco supermarket chain. While these results are not in any way intended to be definitive, they do provide interesting and accessible evidence of the variety of employee responses to an identical set of HR practices, and they provide case study evidence of the links between these differences in perception and important operational indicators of employee discretion. Chapters 6 and 7 will investigate the formation of the attitudes of different employee groups while Chapter 8 will examine the performance impli-cations of employee perceptions of HR practices in a contrasting organisation (Nationwide).

6 HR architecture and employment sub-systems

Practices and perceptions

Introduction

In this book we have so far drawn on our research to develop and discuss a model to analyse the links between people management and performance. This was briefly explained in the first chapter and then the key components of the model were discussed in more detail looking at culture (Chapter 2), intended HR practices (Chapter 3), the role of line managers (Chapter 4) and the impact on employees' attitudes and behaviour (Chapter 5).

This chapter is the first of three which applies this basic model to different contexts. We use this model to explore the influences on the attitudes of employees in different occupational groupings by drawing on survey and case study evidence. In particular we ask: do employees in different occupations have different needs and respond in different ways to HR practices as reflected in their commitment to their employing organisation? This discussion of the importance of employee occupational groupings serves as an important foundation for the following two chapters. The next chapter looks at the influences on the attitudes and behaviour of a key group within organisations – professional knowledge workers. The final chapter in this trilogy examines the links between HR practices and the attitudes and performance of employees working in the financial services sector examining evidence from a major retail bank, Nationwide Building Society, in detail (See Figure 6.1).

Rationale for the chapter

Much of the research in strategic HRM has assumed that all employees are managed in the same way and that HR practices have the same effect on all employees. This

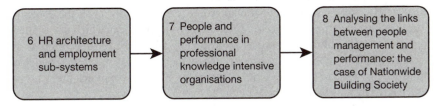

Figure 6.1 Links between chapters 6, 7 and 8

approach is seen most clearly in the best practice perspective (Pfeffer 1994, 1998; Becker and Gerhart 1996) which, as we saw in Chapter 3, argues that a set of practices can be identified which have a positive effect on all organisations and by extension all employees. However, we need to question this assumption and consider the importance of occupational groupings for three reasons.

First, the best practice approach, if it applies at all, is most likely to be applicable in organisations where there are large groups of similar employees, as in law and accountancy firms. However, in other organisations the workforce is more heterogeneous making it less likely that a best practice approach will be effective. Recent evidence (Kersley *et al.* 2006: 23) shows that on average there are four occupational groups in each workplace. Indeed, the largest occupational group (excluding managers) typically accounts for only two-thirds of the employees in a workplace. We need to consider, therefore, the extent to which these employees have differing needs and respond in different ways to HR practices.

Second, various authors are now pointing to the dangers of assuming that all employees within an organisation are managed in the same way. Lepak and Snell (1999: 32) note that 'most strategic HRM researchers have tended to take a holistic view of employment and human capital, focusing on the extent to which a set of practices is used across all employees of a firm as well as the consistency of these practices across firms'. They go on to argue that by ignoring the diversity of employee groups strategic HRM literature may be seen to be somewhat 'monolithic'. Wright and Boswell (2002: 264) go further arguing that the assumption of homogeneity is 'naïve and detrimental to the development of the field'.

Boxall and Purcell (2003: 50) note that 'we should not assume that HR strategies are uniform within firms. It is wrong to conjure up the image of a single set of critical practices for managing people in the firm'. The evidence, they say, suggests that firms rarely adopt a single style of management for all their employee groups. 'In a nutshell, the pattern of strategic choice in a firm's employment relations is variegated'.

Third, the differing needs of these various groups may create tensions within HR practices which need to be explored. Lepak and Snell (2007: 210) note that on the one hand there is clear evidence of the positive impact of, for example, high commitment practices on business performance. On the other hand we have evidence of increasing externalisation of the workforce and the use of internal employment sub-systems within organisations. Our discussion of these sub-systems and their effect on employees will identify the nature of these tensions.

In this context the chapter has four aims. First, it charts the emergence of differing HR practices and occupational groups. Second, it discusses the contemporary evidence of the existence of differentiated HR practices which are applied to these groups. Third, it examines the extent to which the tension referred to actually exists by considering whether the commitment of different groups is influenced by the same or different HR practices. Fourth, it explores the ways in which any tensions between these might be overcome.

In brief we find that there is clear evidence that the commitment of different groups is affected by different HR practices. This implies that these groups should be managed in different ways to improve business performance. This then requires us to explore how this need for differentiated practices might fit with the need for consistent practices.

Structure of the chapter

This chapter draws on survey and case study evidence to study the influence of HR practices on the commitment of different occupational groups. As shown in Figure 6.2 it does this by:

1 examining the historical development of occupational groups and in particular the emergence and decline of internal labour markets;
2 discussing existing theory, in particular the HR architecture model, which draws attention to the heterogeneity that exists within the workforce and the differing HR practices which are used to manage them;
3 explaining the data which are used to examine the way different occupational groups respond to HR practices;
4 analysing this data and discussing the HR practices which have the greatest impact on the commitment of various groups of employees;
5 considering the implications of these findings for how these different groups should be managed.

Emergence and decline of internal labour markets

Boxall and Purcell (2003: 115–121) usefully draw our attention to the rise and disintegration of the internal labour market (ILM). They note that in the UK at least in the mid-nineteenth century the whole idea of the employment contract was unusual. Gospel (1992: 16) says that the typical late-nineteenth-century firm 'was

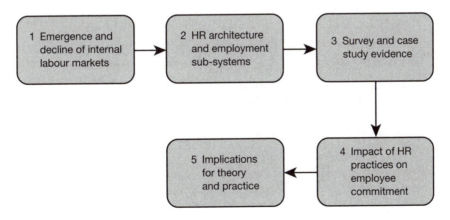

Figure 6.2 Structure of the chapter

a small or medium-sized single plant operation, employing tens of workers and with limited capital assets'. Consequently, there was a strong reliance on external labour markets of often skilled craftsmen with all its associated characteristics of insecurity and unpredictability for workers. The use of casual employment also had its drawbacks for employers. For example, many management responsibilities were delegated to senior skilled workers, internal sub-contractors or gang leaders who had control over recruiting and paying workers and monitoring production (Gospel 1992: 19). Even by the end of the nineteenth century there were relatively few large firms and 'hierarchies remained particularly rudimentary and traditional' (Gospel 1992: 18).

However, heavy investment in emerging industries such as the railways, engineering, shipbuilding and cotton meant that firms grew in size and there was demand for greater predictability and permanency. 'Capital accumulation, economies of scale and the development of national and even international markets led to the creation of the large firm, the requirements of a cadre of managers and the development of "rules" of employment exclusive to, and inside, the firm' (Boxall and Purcell 2003: 116). In short the ILM was born, something which Marsden (1999: 3) saw as one of the great innovations of the modern enterprise. Gospel, (1992: 101) however, notes that the growth of the ILM was slow in the UK and even by the 1940s and 1950s there was still a reliance among many small firms on externalisation and employers' associations. It was only really the growth of workplace bargaining in the post-war period which stimulated firms to develop much more elaborate internal arrangements for managing employees.

The ILM provided employers, trade unions and government with a mechanism for managing the employment relationship. Osterman (1987: 48–9) points to four sets of rules which were crucial to the regulation of ILMs. Job definition rules involved the codification of job descriptions which were changed relatively infrequently. Career development rules laid down the entry points into the organisation and the subsequent steps up the promotion ladder which might be expected. These were most elaborate in 'cradle to the grave' employment systems often associated with salaried employees. Job security rules spelled out the explicit commitments made by employers about the expected time employees could spend with the firm. Finally, the wage rules defined the effort–reward bargain and the mechanism for settling this was via the employer alone, collective bargaining or reliance on bureaucratic systems such as job evaluation.

Boxall and Purcell (2003: 118) note that by the 1960s and 1970s the 'ILM became the defining feature of sophisticated personnel management' as illustrated by Foulkes (1980). However, times were changing and ILMs became associated with various problems. First, ILMs became associated with divisions within the workforce, classically between management and staff or blue collar and white collar employees. There were often clear status differences in terms of conditions of employment such as holidays, sick pay and job security and various perks and benefits. As times changed it became increasingly difficult to justify these. Second, ILMs were profoundly gendered (Wacjman 2000) and failed to keep pace with changes in the wider society. Women were often trapped in low skilled jobs with little opportunity for training and promotion. This sexual division of labour was challenged by changes in labour law and the education system as large numbers of well-qualified female graduates entered the workforce.

Grimshaw *et al.* (2001) point to changes in points of entry to organisations, promotion systems and the growth of temporary employment. More generally we see how firms began to pursue a mixed pattern of employment involving both internalisation and externalisation. Employers therefore faced a choice of how they might design their employment system. Boxall and Purcell (2003: 121) characterise this as a choice between internal and external primary and secondary labour markets. In essence the choice can be likened to a particular application of the decision to 'make' or 'buy' inputs to the production process, where this decision depends on the attendant transaction costs associated with transaction frequency, uncertainty and specificity (Williamson 1979: 245).

Transaction frequency reflects the number of hours of work required in the production process. Greater scale enhances the likelihood of employment because it allows for more intensive use of human capital. For example, very small firms are unlikely to hire a lawyer on a full-time basis and instead are likely to purchase legal services from individuals who serve a range of clients. Uncertainty enhances the desirability of formal employment because in the presence of uncertainty the costs of constant re-contracting with an external agent may be high relative to the costs of signing a long-term contract with an employee in which the employee agrees to carry out the commands of the employer (Coase 1937: 391; Simon 1951).

Boxall and Purcell (2003: 135) conclude that 'the old certainties ... are melting as are the traditional divisions between manual, staff and managerial workers'. These uncertainties have grown still further with the rise of the networked organisation, as we discuss in more detail in Chapters 7 and 9. Here we find that many organisations operate within complex multi-party networks of clients, suppliers, partners, intermediaries and regulators. As a result, we find that the boundaries of the firm are becoming increasingly permeable (Marchington *et al.* 2005; Swart and Kinnie 2003). Indeed, as we will argue, managers of HR have to manage across these organisational boundaries if they are to be successful.

Employment subsystems

There have been a number of attempts to characterise the heterogeneity of employee workgroups. One of the best known is the core–periphery model put forward by Atkinson (1984). This distinguishes between the core group of workers and two different types of peripheral groups. The first peripheral group includes agency workers such as clerical, IT, catering and distribution staff who are present on the employer's site but are not employed by them. The second peripheral group is made up of employees who are on temporary or fixed-term contracts. Inside this is a core group of employees who are expected to demonstrate high levels of functional flexibility. The implication is that employers would differentiate between their employment policies based on the group of employees in question.

More recently various authors have begun to tease out the differences which might exist between occupational groups. Marchington and Grugulis (2000: 1117) in their evaluation of the best practice literature note that 'so much depends on the categories of staff that employers are trying to recruit'. They cite the work of MacDuffie (1995) who notes that HR policies are likely to contribute to improved performance only where 'employees possess knowledge and skills that managers lack, where employees are motivated to supply this skill and knowledge through discretionary effort; and when a firm's business or production strategy can only be achieved when employees contribute such discretionary effort'. They argue that these conditions are quite specific and will not be met when training is brief, work is boring and easily monitored and when there is a plentiful supply of labour (Marchington and Grugulis 2000: 1118). Consequently 'the best practice model may be relatively unattractive or inappropriate in some industries or certain groups of workers'. Earlier work has also argued that HR strategies may vary by occupational group, thus resulting in a segmented internal labour market (Osterman 1987; Pinfield and Berner 1994; Purcell 1987). Indeed, Osterman and Burton (2005: 441) argue that such occupational organisation is likely to increase in coming years as ties between employees and firms are loosened by the spread of structural careers outside of traditional firms.

HR architecture model

The development of the HR architecture model (Lepak and Snell 1999), as shown in Figure 6.3, represents one attempt to deal with the issue of different employee groups. This is based on the configurational view which argues that it is unlikely that a company will use a single approach for all its employees. Indeed, they argue that 'the most appropriate mode of investment in human capital will vary for different types of capital' (Lepak and Snell 1999: 32). This suggests that the 'best fit' approach is too simple because there is a need to focus on desirable within-firm combinations of practices: in essence linking the bundle of integrated HR practices (horizontal fit) with business strategy (vertical fit) (Delery and Doty 1996).

Lepak and Snell (1999) draw on theories of transaction cost economics and the resource-based view to identify four employment modes. At the heart of their model they characterise a firm's human capital in terms of its value and uniqueness to the firm. The value of human capital is 'inherently dependent on its potential to contribute to the competitive advantage or core competence of the firm' (Lepak and Snell 1999: 35). They also differentiated between core and peripheral employees, defining the former as those who are vital to the competitive advantage of the organisation. These employees have the skills which enable the firm to enact effective and efficient strategies which are especially valuable. The uniqueness refers to the extent to which the skills and knowledge are specific to a particular organisation. If this human capital cannot be duplicated then it is likely to be a valuable source of competitive advantage. An example of unique human capital would be tacit knowledge of a firm's operating system which cannot be bought in from the external labour market.

	Quadrant 4	Quadrant 1
High	Employment mode: alliance Employment relationship: partnership HR configuration: collaborative	Employment mode: internal development Employment relationship: organisation focused HR configuration: commitment
Uniqueness of human capital	Quadrant 3 Employment mode: contracting Employment relationship: transactional HR configuration: compliance	Quadrant 2 Employment mode: acquisition Employment relationship: symbiotic HR configuration: market based
Low		
	Low High Value of human capital	

Figure 6.3 HR architecture (Source: Lepak, D. and Snell, S. (1999). Reproduced by permission of the Academy of Management)

By combining these concepts of value and uniqueness into a single model Lepak and Snell are able to identify four employment modes or HR subsystems: develop, acquire, contract and alliance. Each of these has associated employment relationships (organisation, symbiotic, transactional and partnership) and HR configuration (commitment, market based, compliance and collaboration) (Lepak and Snell 1999: 37).

More recently, Lepak and Snell (2007) have refined this model further by adopting a knowledge-based view of employment. The high value and uniqueness of core knowledge workers means they contribute to the firm's success through what they know and how they use their knowledge. This would include staff such as managers, planners, engineers and analysts (Liu *et al.* 2003: 142). Firms tend to invest in commitment-based approaches characterised by employee development, empowerment and high job discretion. Long-term financial incentives are also used to retain employees. The second group of employees have high strategic value but low levels of uniqueness which means that staff can easily move in and out of the organisation. This typically includes staff such as accountants, administrators, account managers and HR professionals (Liu *et al.* 2003: 142). Employment tends to be more job-based and linked to immediate performance. Recruitment and selection decisions emphasise the need to begin work immediately in relatively standardised jobs. Employee incentives focus on efficiency and productivity stressing a short-term results-based orientation.

The third group of tasks is characterised by low value and uniqueness where there are few incentives to internalise employment. These jobs include clerical, maintenance, support and junior staff (Liu *et al.* 2003: 142). These jobs may well be contracted out and managed by a predominantly compliance-based approach. There will be an emphasis on preset rules and procedures and a focus on productivity and efficiency. Kersley *et al.* (2006: 105) noted that nearly 90 per cent of all workplaces subcontracted out at least one service. This was most likely in large establishments and the most common services to be outsourced were building maintenance and cleaning. The final group of tasks demands knowledge which is firm specific but is of low value. This kind of work is typically externalised but often is not easy to find in the marketplace. Consequently long-term partnerships are likely to be formed with suppliers to build up trust and ensure collaboration. The emphasis here is on forming alliances with a substantial investment in relationships (Lepak and Snell 2002).

Lepak and Snell (2007: 215) note that the architecture model has received some empirical support in Lepak and Snell (2002) as well as in Gonzales and Tacorante (2004). Lepak and Snell (2002: 536) found 'whether intended or emergent, there appears to be a clear pattern in the resource allocation and HR configurations used for different kinds of workers. For example the commitment based HR configuration is significantly greater for knowledge-based employees than for employees within the three other modes' (Lepak and Snell 2002: 536). Indeed, they found evidence that the commitment-based approach was limited to knowledge-based workers. Gonzales and Tacorante (2004: 67) found that high value employees were more likely to have rigorous selection, extensive training, performance management systems, greater autonomy, flexibility and participation in decision-making compared to employees who had lower value to the organisation. Lepak and Snell (2007) do go on to note that this differentiation of HR practices raises a variety of practical and ethical issues. They also refer to the tension that exists between this kind of heterogeneous approach and the broader need to gain the widespread commitment of employees to the goals of the organisation. We discuss these issues further in Chapter 9.

Links between the experience of HR practices and the organisational commitment for different employment subsystems

We have so far established that different combinations of HR practices are used for various employment groups. However, we need to go further than this if we are to understand the links between HR and performance for these heterogeneous workgroups. In order to do this we need to return to the causal chain model and recall the importance of the links between employees' experience of HR practices and their commitment to the organisation.

In Chapters 1 and 5 we argued that employee experiences of HR practices are central to the HR–performance causal chain. Individual HR practices have a functional role (such as training or performance management) but they can also have a non-instrumental role in both reflecting and reinforcing the wider organisational climate when considered at a systematic level (Bowen and Ostroff 2004). Positive employee experience links to employee affective commitment and leads to better or more discretionary behaviour and better task performance. Negative employee experiences have the opposite effect.

Hannah and Iverson (2004: 339) suggest that 'HRM practices are viewed by employees as a "personalised" commitment to them by the organisation which is then reciprocated back to the organisation by employees though positive attitudes and behaviour'. Eisenberger *et al.* (2002) provide empirical support for this view as they demonstrate that employee perceptions of organisational support (as seen in HR practices) are connected to high degrees of organisational citizenship behaviour and retention and attendance.

If we put the research on the heterogeneity of workgroups and the importance of employee attitudes together then we need to investigate whether employees (rather than firms or workplaces) have different needs and respond in different ways to HR practices as reflected in their affective organisational commitment.

If we accept that it is misleading to assume that HR practices should be applied in the same way across all employee groups the question then is how might employees be disaggregated? Wright and Boswell (2002: 265) suggest that this problem could be avoided by looking at the key or core jobs 'or at least attempting to assess practices for more coherent job groups than simply managerial vs hourly'. Alternatively they suggest looking at the nine different categories for which the US Equal Employment Opportunity Commission requires reporting demographic information since 'this would provide for much clearer understanding of HR configurations and variations' (Wright and Boswell 2002: 265). Here we classify occupations according to the Standard Occupational Classification system of 2000 (SOC 2000). This assigns occupations individual numbers and groups these numbers into nine main categories:

1 Managerial occupations
2 Professional occupations
3 Associate professional and technical occupations
4 Administrative and secretarial occupations
5 Skilled trades
6 Personal service occupations
7 Sales and customer service occupations
8 Process, plant and machine operatives
9 Elementary occupations.

The data we use comes from employees and managers who were present in workplaces included in the 2004 Workplace Employee Relations Survey.[1] This survey allows us to examine the influences on organisational commitment based on a sample that is representative of the UK economy as a whole. Our unit of analysis is the employee and we merge information on each workplace (e.g. industry, size, HR practices, etc.) into this employee information. We complement this survey data with references to our own case study research conducted as part of the People and Performance research project.

We examine data from employees in the non-managerial occupations and we anticipate differences in the reactions of the members of these occupational groups to various practices, because the groups have very different stocks of human capital and are often performing different roles in their organisations. We have chosen to focus on organisational commitment because of an extensive literature (e.g. Kacmar *et al.* 1999; Balfour and Wechsler 1996; Mowday *et al.* 1979) on its links with employee behaviours such as turnover, attendance, in-role performance and organisational citizenship behaviour (e.g. Meyer *et al.* 2002).[2]

HR practices are not the only things that can influence employee commitment towards their organisations. Meyer *et al.* (2002) undertook a comprehensive meta-analysis of the antecedents, correlates and consequences of organisational commitment and we adopt a conceptual model of the determinants of commitment consistent with this work. This model is presented as Figure 6.4 and it shows the determinants of commitment in three broad categories: HR practice-related determinants, employee characteristics and workplace characteristics.

The first of the practice-related influences is social support for employees. This can come from both supervisors and peers, and both should increase commitment levels. Job stress is another important influence on commitment and the model includes measures of role ambiguity, employee unease and workload. All of these are thought to decrease commitment to the organisation. Job involvement is another important determinant of commitment, as programmes like quality circles, attitude surveys and joint consultation committees have been shown to influence employee outcomes. The provision of career opportunities and training are also thought to increase employee commitment, as they both represent opportunities for growth and development within the organisation, thus diminishing the need to look outside the organisation for such opportunities. Various job design features may also influence commitment. These include: autonomy, routinisation, job challenge and flexible working arrangements. Lastly, we include job satisfaction in the model as it is a well-established correlate of organisational commitment, though there is substantial debate regarding the direction of causation (e.g. Meyer *et al.* 2002: 22; Rayton 2006). We include it here as an indicator of employee perceptions of relevant practices (e.g. satisfaction with pay, training, etc.), thus helping us to disentangle the different practice-based effects of several important HR 'levers'. Further details of the independent variables used in our model are given in the technical appendix to this chapter.

Impact of HR practices on employee commitment

We now discuss the results of our analysis of the survey data (as shown in Table 6.1) and, in the interests of brevity, we restrict our analysis to the most interesting results.[3] We look first at the job-related influences and then move on to discuss the influence of social support from managers.

The analysis reveals that each occupation shows some evidence of association between approximately four of the eight job-related variables, though there is substantial variety in the results. Satisfaction with 'the work itself' is positively

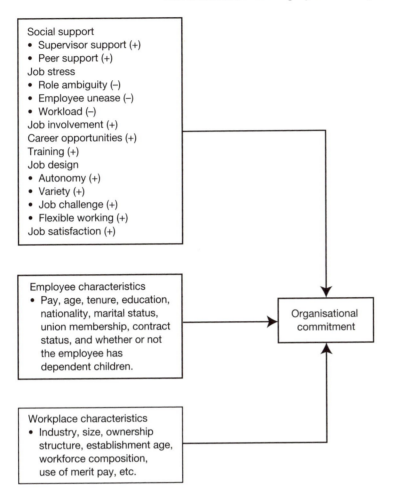

Figure 6.4 Summary of the empirical model illustrating hypothesised effects of a range of variables on organisational commitment

related to the commitment of workers in seven out of eight occupational groups with the exception being administrative workers. This was nicely captured by one of the workers in Jaguar who said:

If I ever get unhappy I look upon it as my own car. I wouldn't stamp it off if I wasn't happy with it.

Satisfaction with the sense of achievement from work matters to the commitment of workers in three groups: administrative, skilled and operatives; while job challenge is significant for two groups: associated professionals and skilled workers. We see that neither satisfaction with training nor satisfaction with the

Table 6.1 Regression results

Regression results from analysis of the organisational commitment of employees in the largest occupational group of their workplace using the WERS 2004 data. Estimates calculated using the SPSS complex sample general linear model. Estimates weighted using the employee weights. Cells report regression coefficients. Significance levels flagged at the 95 per cent (*) and 99 per cent (**) levels. All regressions include unreported intercepts, employee controls and workplace controls.

	Professional occupations	Associate Professional & Technical	Administrative & Secretarial	Skilled Trades	Personal Service	Sales & Customer Service	Process, Plant & Machine Operatives	Elementary
Number of observations	739	687	798	352	488	523	559	439
Sampling design d.f.	116	114	110	56	101	111	115	92
R-squared	0.685	0.603	0.556	0.812	0.666	0.633	0.721	0.717
(Constant)	4.536**	−0.849	3.126**	5.202**	2.151	1.562	0.839	0.402
Employee trust in managers (4-item scale)	0.211**	0.169**	0.086**	0.141**	0.135**	0.080*	0.133**	0.124**
Employee reported quality of relations with management (1-item scale)	0.275*	0.279*	0.477**	0.301	0.358**	0.106	0.426**	0.229
Proportion of LOG that works in teams (scale)	0.018	−0.042	−0.074	0.263**	0.099**	0.008	0.061	−0.002
Role ambiguity (4-item scale)	−0.043	−0.023	0.036	−0.061	0.059*	−0.059	−0.014	−0.053
Employee unease (ewellsc - r)	0.006	−0.023	−0.029	−0.083**	−0.053*	−0.012	−0.023	0.015

	Professional occupations	Associate Professional & Technical	Administrative & Secretarial	Skilled Trades	Personal Service	Sales & Customer Service	Process, Plant & Machine Operatives	Elementary
Usual weekly hours	0.003	0.053*	0.007	0.002	-0.017	-0.044	-0.047	-0.006
Usual weekly hours squared	0.000	-0.001*	0.000	0.000	0.000	0.001*	0.001	0.000
Workplace has quality circles	0.139	0.352*	0.020	0.273	0.080	0.002	0.127	0.494*
Workplace does employee attitude survey	0.011	-0.131	-0.017	0.046	0.044	0.181	0.075	0.509
Any functioning JCC?	-0.294*	-0.044	0.323	0.321	-0.423	-0.238	0.361*	0.469
Workplace selects via attitude/personality tests	0.061	0.003	-0.106	0.298	-0.219	0.292	0.396	-0.630*
Workplace selects via performance tests	0.555**	-0.313	0.212	-0.221	-0.128	0.141	-0.505**	-0.079
Proportion of non-managerial employees who are regularly appraised	0.120	0.042	0.175*	-0.111	0.100	0.117	0.132*	0.120
Vacancies filled from within	-0.094	-0.016	-0.314	-0.106	-0.324*	-0.201	0.263*	-0.055
Workplace is Investor in People	-0.092	-0.012	-0.072	0.267	0.288	0.029	0.177	0.396*
Standard induction programme for LOG	-0.292	1.171**	-0.172	-0.370	0.328	-0.443	0.444	-0.127

Table 6.1 Continued

	Professional occupations	Associate Professional & Technical	Administrative & Secretarial	Skilled Trades	Personal Service	Sales & Customer Service	Process, Plant & Machine Operatives	Elementary
5 or more days' formal off the job training in LOG	0.332	0.417	−0.816*	−0.949**	−0.142	0.477	0.256	−0.265
Employee report of own training in last year	0.065	0.084	0.057	0.038	−0.072	0.118	0.082	0.105
Employee report of skill match	0.081	0.075	0.064	0.152	−0.030	0.023	0.085	−0.002
Employee reported level of autonomy (5-item scale)	−0.011	−0.015	0.002	0.047*	−0.051*	0.006	−0.015	−0.032
Employees in LOG have variety in their work	−0.123	0.165	0.227	0.150	−0.181	0.192	0.036	−0.217
Job challenge	0.033	0.118 **	0.091*	0.193**	0.081*	0.002	0.092*	0.053
Employee says home working is available	−0.170	0.183	0.561*	−0.112	1.693**	−0.155	0.597	0.059
Employee reports opportunity to reduce from FT to PT	0.017	0.078	0.022	−0.520	−0.150	0.623**	−0.101	0.098
Employee reports opportunity to increase hours from PT to FT	−0.038	−0.045	0.473*	0.181	0.020	0.060	0.132	0.114

	Professional occupations	Associate Professional & Technical	Administrative & Secretarial	Skilled Trades	Personal Service	Sales & Customer Service	Process, Plant & Machine Operatives	Elementary
Employee says job-sharing available	-0.236	0.184	-0.134	0.055	-0.276	0.185	-0.713**	-0.340
Employee says flexitime available	0.317	-0.271	-0.023	0.236	-0.019	-0.071	0.085	-0.155
Employee reports ability to change working patterns, including shifts	0.651**	0.280	0.474*	0.004	0.157	0.255	-0.085	0.247
Employee reports ability to work the same number of hours per week across fewer days	-0.694**	-0.357	-0.613**	0.164	0.142	-0.421*	0.369	-0.021
Any employees on annual hours contracts	-0.348	0.422*	0.105	-0.562	-0.064	-0.188	-0.207	0.356
Any employees on zero hours contracts	-0.632**	-0.264	-0.188	2.588**	-0.677*	0.994**	-1.591**	0.625
Any employees entitled to work term-time only	0.084	-0.127	-0.411	-2.535**	0.552	-0.238	-0.468	0.137
Managers lead employees to expect long-term employment	0.200	-0.119	0.141	-0.159	0.044	0.602*	0.690**	-0.077
Workplace has quality targets	-0.284*	-0.019	-0.194	0.407	0.101	-0.030	-0.312*	0.504*
Specificity of human capital in LOG	0.144*	-0.009	0.036	-0.040	-0.007	0.083	-0.034	0.053

Table 6.1 Continued

	Professional occupations	Associate Professional & Technical	Administrative & Secretarial	Skilled Trades	Personal Service	Sales & Customer Service	Process, Plant & Machine Operatives	Elementary
Job security guarantee for respondent's occupation	0.217	−0.138	−0.508*	0.712	0.346	0.602**	0.501	0.130
Satisfaction with sense of achievement from work	0.071	0.077	0.761**	0.754**	0.318*	0.135	0.547**	0.224
Satisfaction with scope for using own initiative	0.378**	0.198	−0.290*	0.008	0.325*	0.172	0.028	0.003
Satisfaction with amount of influence over own job	−0.056	−0.057	0.158	−0.108	0.065	−0.130	−0.078	−0.130
Satisfaction with training received	−0.040	−0.180*	0.032	0.092	0.094	−0.189*	0.047	0.164
Satisfaction with amount of pay received	0.040	0.169*	0.154	0.307**	0.209**	0.110	0.200*	0.287**
Satisfaction with job security	−0.008	0.070	−0.008	−0.253**	0.042	0.068	0.341**	0.093
Satisfaction with the work itself	0.516**	0.728**	0.229	0.287**	0.457**	0.881**	0.298**	0.935**
Satisfaction with involvement in decision-making at workplace	0.190*	0.244*	0.209	0.248*	0.244*	0.276*	0.230*	−0.177

	Professional occupations	Associate Professional & Technical	Administrative & Secretarial	Skilled Trades	Personal Service	Sales & Customer Service	Process, Plant & Machine Operatives	Elementary
Has dependent child(ren)	0.009	0.037	0.167	0.263	-0.271	0.097	-0.145	0.343*
Single	-0.065	-0.309	0.064	0.047	-0.218	0.023	0.034	-0.383
Widowed	-0.257	0.315	-0.195	-1.162*	-0.432	-0.462	-0.588	1.181**
Divorced	-0.077	0.198	0.156	-1.083**	-0.172	-0.081	0.129	0.455
Male	-0.077	-0.017	-0.451	-0.553	0.126	0.016	0.699**	-0.320
Postgraduate degree	-5.192**	0.202	-0.822	-0.075	-0.367	0.248	1.751**	-0.321
Undergraduate degree	-5.158***	-0.147	-1.057*	-0.284	0.774**	-0.248	-0.359	0.112
A levels in the A–C range	-5.184***	-0.052	-0.872	0.291	0.242	-0.722*	-0.341	0.432
A levels below the A–C range	-5.594**	-0.540	-1.185*	0.774	0.276	-0.266	0.221	0.051
GCSE results A–C	-5.508**	0.100	-0.952*	0.367	0.044	-0.149	-0.552*	0.574**
GCSE results below A–C	-5.397**	0.417	-0.741*	-0.011	-0.097	-0.141	-0.304	0.657*
Other academic qualification	-5.562**	-0.149	-0.482	-0.574*	-0.053	0.101	-0.495**	0.890**
Vocational qualification	0.544**	-0.282	-0.089	-0.428*	0.048	0.196	0.069	-0.447*
Self-identified as British	-0.105	-0.122	-0.214	-0.864**	-0.088	0.032	0.098	0.204
Union member	-0.340	0.168	-0.669*	0.369	-0.135	-0.780**	0.267	-0.536*
Union member in the past	-0.095	0.197	-0.456	-0.248	-0.220	-0.306	-0.223	0.178
Fixed-term employee	0.165	-0.493	0.131	-0.389	0.291	1.023*	-0.793	-0.754
Temporary employee	-0.123	-0.185	-0.825	0.238	0.338	0.198	-0.029	-0.622
Aged 16–17	0.435	0.763	-0.153	-4.717**	-1.486**	-0.505	5.539**	-0.377

Table 6.1 Continued

	Professional occupations	Associate Professional & Technical	Administrative & Secretarial	Skilled Trades	Personal Service	Sales & Customer Service	Process, Plant & Machine Operatives	Elementary
Aged 18–19	1.124	0.227	0.260	-2.644**	-0.637	-0.051	-0.294	0.464
Aged 20–21	0.854	-0.991	0.339	0.611	0.049	-0.281	-0.668	1.121**
Aged 22–29	-0.198	0.077	0.063	0.288	-0.598*	-0.701*	-0.304	0.286
Aged 40–49	-0.152	-0.145	-0.034	0.163	-0.364*	-0.118*	-0.323	-0.185
Aged 50–59	-0.070	0.250	-0.095	0.618*	-0.073	0.784*	-0.101	-0.419
Aged 60–64	-0.637*	0.550	-0.063	0.833*	-1.289**	-0.331	0.002	0.505
Aged 65 or older	0.112	n/a	1.202	n/a	-2.036**	1.416*	1.472*	0.295
Tenure < 1 year	-0.539*	0.352	0.049	0.402	-0.499*	0.098	0.064	-0.380
Tenure 1 up to 2 years	-0.392*	0.014	0.012	-0.047	-0.429	0.136	0.138	-0.097
Tenure 5 up to 10 years	0.412*	0.116	0.003	-0.337	0.023	0.125	0.032	-0.012
Tenure 10 years or more	0.515**	-0.185	0.085	0.246	0.181	-0.240	-0.082	0.183
Paid 51–80 p.w.	1.549*	-1.349*	-0.288	-3.134**	-0.043	-0.603	-2.572	0.297
Paid 81–110 p.w.	-1.379	-0.976	-0.600	n/a	-0.984*	-0.271	-0.841	0.797
Paid 111–140 p.w.	-0.346	-0.054	-0.450	-0.544	-0.481	-0.042	-2.110*	0.194
Paid 141–180 p.w.	0.131	-0.267	-0.538	-1.547	-0.243	-0.390	-1.197	-1.137*
Paid 181–220 p.w.	0.930	-0.236	-0.918	-2.443*	0.190	-0.853	-1.472	-0.346
Paid 221–260 p.w.	0.921	0.151	-1.156	-3.932**	-0.358	-0.200	-1.367	0.257
Paid 261–310 p.w.	0.531	-0.237	-1.221*	-3.417**	-0.107	-0.656	-1.531	0.932
Paid 311–360 p.w.	0.337	-0.179	-0.651	-3.890**	-1.045	-0.859	-1.574*	1.154*
Paid 361–430 p.w.	0.246	-0.269	-1.265	-3.519**	-0.914	-1.097	-1.173	1.174*
Paid 431–540 p.w.	0.250	-0.255	-0.898	-4.080**	-0.913	1.196	-1.081	0.377
Paid 541–680 p.w.	0.165	-0.155	-0.993	-4.258**	-1.327	1.708	-0.229	0.748
Paid 681–870 p.w.	0.599	-0.433	0.552	-2.908**	2.549*	n/a	-0.500	n/a

Table 6.1 Continues

	Professional occupations	Associate Professional & Technical	Administrative & Secretarial	Skilled Trades	Personal Service	Sales & Customer Service	Process, Plant & Machine Operatives	Elementary
Paid more than 870 p.w.	0.625	0.303	-0.337	n/a	n/a	-0.914	-1.028	1.424
Any employees paid by PBR or merit pay	-0.217	-0.349*	0.481*	-0.058	0.409	0.047	-0.613**	0.006
If LOG entitled to employer pension scheme	-0.493*	-0.288	-0.553*	-0.219	0.380	-0.448*	-0.497	0.819*
If LOG entitled to car or car allowance	-0.129	0.221	-0.021	-0.202	-0.622	0.279	-0.487	-1.338**
If LOG entitled to private health insurance	-0.370*	-0.173	0.313	0.119	-1.638**	0.496**	0.350	-0.584
If LOG entitled to over 4 weeks' paid annual leave	0.691**	-0.204	0.655	0.197	-0.402	-0.167	0.207	0.101
If LOG entitled to sick pay in excess of statutory minimum	0.013	-0.049	-0.029	-0.106	0.712**	-0.112	-0.269	0.100
Establishment age under 5 years	-0.555*	-0.578	0.069	1.363**	1.014	-0.116	0.686	-0.131
Establishment age under 10 years	-0.182	-0.346	-0.204	0.817**	0.320	0.029	-0.187	-0.060
Establishment age under 15 years	-0.618**	-0.569*	-0.158	0.967*	0.015	0.598*	-0.523*	-0.379
Establishment age under 20 years	-0.173	-0.950**	-0.701*	0.442	-0.240	-0.434	-0.792*	-1.526**

Table 6.1 Continues

Table 6.1 Continued

	Professional occupations	Associate Professional & Technical	Administrative & Secretarial	Skilled Trades	Personal Service	Sales & Customer Service	Process, Plant & Machine Operatives	Elementary
Establishment age under 25 years	0.222	−0.476	−0.282	−0.141	0.146	0.749*	−0.773*	−0.690
EPQ Q1. Currently how many employees do you have on the payroll at this establishment?	0.000*	0.000	0.000	0.000	0.000	0.000	0.000**	−0.001**
Proportion of employees from a non-white ethnic group	0.000	0.003	−0.012	−0.001	−0.009	0.010	0.003	0.005
EO policy covering equality of treatment or discrimination	−0.034	−0.294	0.501*	−0.010	0.139	0.017	0.116	−0.707**
Proportion of employees with long-term disability	0.021	−0.036	0.056**	−0.093	−0.043	0.025	−0.027**	0.013
Proportion of employees aged 16 to 21	−0.015**	−0.024	−0.004	−0.002	−0.005	−0.010*	−0.011	−0.019*
Proportion of employees aged 50 or over	0.001	0.013*	−0.013*	0.005	−0.006	0.007	0.003	−0.016**
Female employees as a proportion of all employment	1.251*	−0.322	−0.165	−3.004**	−0.951	−1.488**	0.981	−0.592

	Professional occupations	Associate Professional & Technical	Administrative & Secretarial	Skilled Trades	Personal Service	Sales & Customer Service	Process, Plant & Machine Operatives	Elementary
Union density: banded	-0.176**	0.080	0.042	-0.049	-0.027	0.098	0.148*	0.163
Facing local market	0.149	0.620	-0.172	0.081	0.490**	-0.142	-0.071	-0.298
Facing regional market	1.062**	-0.106	-1.063**	-0.640*	0.153	0.146	0.191	0.429
Facing international market	0.431	-0.295	-0.127	0.560	1.856**	-0.050	0.181	0.550
Single establishment	-0.542**	0.734**	-0.230	-0.194	0.597*	0.483	-0.125	0.959**
UK-owned workplace	0.310	-0.322	0.764**	0.230	-0.455	0.463**	-0.176	0.573
Private charity	0.236	0.170	0.407	n/a	0.088	n/a	n/a	-1.813
Other private workplace	-0.280	1.672**	0.507	0.413	n/a	-0.825*	n/a	-2.428**
= 'Public ownership'	0.520	0.109	0.567	-0.496	-0.283	-0.672	0.334	0.432
Electricity, gas & water	n/a	0.050	-1.125	-0.387	n/a	-1.275	-0.188	n/a
Construction	-0.226	-0.913	-1.321	0.536*	n/a	n/a	0.108	-1.581*
Wholesale & retail	n/a	0.350	0.125	1.608**	n/a	-0.722	0.799**	-0.158
Hotels & restaurants	n/a	n/a	n/a	0.296	n/a	-0.892	n/a	-0.059
Transport & communication	-1.808**	-1.217	-1.084	2.426**	0.205	-0.208	-0.059	-1.534**
Financial services	-1.900**	-0.134	-1.672**	n/a	n/a	-0.792	n/a	n/a
Other business services	-0.536	0.099	-0.930	1.576**	3.970**	-1.782*	-0.035	-0.763
Public administration	-0.608	-0.484	-1.000	n/a	-0.770	n/a	n/a	n/a
Education	-0.247	0.431	-0.814	n/a	0.841	n/a	n/a	0.395
Health	-1.023*	-0.366	-0.850	0.057	0.387	n/a	n/a	n/a
Other community services	-0.357	0.320	-0.662	0.300	n/a	-0.807	-1.264*	-0.106

amount of autonomy or variety of work are connected to employee commitment. Pay satisfaction, however, is linked to the commitment of employees in three occupational groups: skilled trades, personal services and operatives.

There is consistent evidence that the commitment of employees is positively associated with the social support provided by managers, as discussed in Chapter 4. Employees who report trust in their managers are more committed to their organisations in all occupational groups with the exception of sales. For example, one nurse in the RUH case carried out as part of the People and Performance study commented,

> At the ward we have a new manager who is approachable – a good listener and gets to learn a lot … people go to her … she's very supportive. In six months the atmosphere is totally different in a good way. Communication in the ward is excellent now. Our manager is very approachable. She's in the coffee room with us now and so on.

In Jaguar one employee reported positively on recent changes to the role of the team leader:

> We put own views to the team leader and he always comes back with positive answers.

Managerial reports of the general quality of the relationship between management and employees are significant predictors of commitment levels in three of the eight occupational groups. There is a positive and significant relationship between this general climate variable and the commitment of administrative and secretarial employees, personal service workers and plant operatives. The connections between these measures of managerial support and commitment reinforce existing work on leader member exchange theory. Formal team structures have a positive and significant effect on commitment in the skilled trades and for those working in personal service occupations.

In summary, therefore, the most important variables are satisfaction with the work itself and support from managers. There is virtually no evidence to suggest a link between employee commitment and variables such as career opportunities, training and job involvement.

Employment subsystems

We now examine the findings of the analysis for five of the employee groups by effectively looking down the columns of Table 6.1.[4] We draw on our case-based research to provide examples to help our discussion of the links between HR practices and the commitment of different groups of employees. We begin with occupations requiring the least formal education (lower skill employees), then move on to the more skilled groups and finally examine professional and managerial employees. We do not attempt to discuss all the results and simply pick out the most distinctive and interesting findings. We have summarised our findings in Table 6.2 distinguishing between the variables which have a positive and negative association (shown in shaded rows) with employee commitment and ranking these by the size of their effect with those with the largest effect listed at the top. The results for each group are placed in a box in the text for ease of reference. Items in italics indicate a negative correlation.

Lower skill employees

The lower skill employee group (Boxes 1 and 2) includes process plant and machine operatives and elementary workers. Typically the work here has been subject to the division of labour where simple tasks are performed repetitively in an attempt to improve efficiency. Research in this area has been extensive particularly in the context of the debate over the extent of and limitations to the deskilling of work resulting from the implementation of mass production and especially lean manufacturing techniques (Braverman 1974).

In this study we find that social support and job satisfaction are particularly important for these lower skilled employees. Satisfaction with the sense of achievement from work is especially important along with satisfaction with work itself, the quality of relations with line managers and trust in managers. Looking again to the People and Performance data for an example of these phenomena, in Jaguar

---

Box 1   Lower skill employees: elementary
Satisfaction with work itself
Satisfaction with pay
Trust managers

Box 2   Lower skill employees: operatives
Expect long-term employment
Satisfaction with achievement
Relationships with managers
Job security
Satisfaction with work itself
Trust managers
Zero hours
Job sharing
PBR
Selection by performance tests

Table 6.2 Associations between employee and manager responses and organisational commitment[1] (negative associations in shaded rows)[2]

Professionals	Associated professionals	Administrative	Skilled workers	Personal service	Sales	Operatives	Elementary
Ability to change work patterns	Standard induction programme	Satisfaction with achievement	Zero hours contracts	Homeworking	Zero hours	Expect long-term employment	Satisfaction with work itself
Select via performance tests	Satisfaction with work itself	Relationships with managers	Satisfaction with achievement	Satisfaction with work itself	Satisfaction with work itself	Satisfaction with achievement	Satisfaction with pay
Satisfaction with work itself	Trust managers	Trust managers	Satisfaction with pay	Relationships with managers	Able to reduce FT to PT hours	Relationships with managers	Trust managers
Satisfaction scope to use initiative	Job challenge		Satisfaction with work itself	Satisfaction with pay	Job security guarantee	Job security	
Trust managers			Teamworking	Trust managers		Satisfaction with work itself	
			Job challenge	Teamworking		Trust managers	
			Trust managers				
Ability to work same hours		Ability to work same hours	Able to work term time only			Zero hours	
Zero hours contracts			5 days training			Job sharing	
			Satisfaction with job security			PBR	
			Employee unease			Selection by performance tests	

1 @ 99% respondents are in largest occupational group
2 ranked in order of importance

one assembly worker expressed his personal satisfaction in his achievements at work by saying:

> Being able to say 'I did that one' is a good feeling as a Jaguar goes by me on the road.

In addition there are other important results. Organisational commitment for these employees is strongly associated with expectations of long-term employment and satisfaction with job security. Pay satisfaction was not significant for the operatives group, although it was important for elementary employees along with trust in managers and the work itself. It is worth remarking on the negative associations with organisational commitment for the operatives group. We found that lower commitment was associated with the use of selection tests, the availability of job sharing and the use of zero hours contracts in the workplace. The last of these may be because the operatives see zero hours contracting as a threat to their job security which we know they value.

Sales and customer service employees

The work of sales and customer service employees has been widely researched in recent years because of the important role which they play in the service sector of developed economies. Korczynski (2002: 104) distinguishes between sales work which involves stimulating and satisfying consumer demand, whereas service work is more concerned with satisfying customer requests without necessarily encouraging a purchase, although he does note that in some environments, such as call centres, these distinctions are being eroded.

As the previous research has found (Frenkel *et al.* 1999) the pattern of results for these employees is quite unlike that of any of the other occupational groups (Box 3). The results are especially interesting, not only for the associations which exist, so much as for the associations which we have not found. This is the *only* group, for instance, where organisational commitment is not associated with social support from managers. This may be because, as Korczynski (2002: 106) found in the more extreme forms of sales work (such as commission-based sales of financial services and cars), the employees regarded themselves as quasi-independent contractors. He found something of a managerial vacuum in these cases – typically filled by commission payments.

Box 3   Sales
Zero hours
Satisfaction with work itself
Able to reduce FT to PT hours
Job security guarantee

This may well be because some sales staff are physically distant from their line managers as illustrated in the People and Performance case study of financial consultants in Nationwide. They may be working from home and interact with their managers quite infrequently, perhaps only one or two days a month. One of them said:

> My role is very independent within Nationwide, I control both the business and time management on a daily basis.

While another said:

> I have complete control over what I do on a daily basis. I am my own boss.

These employees are relatively independent of the normal supervisory arrangements and tend to have a close affinity with their job and their customers and clients. This point is well illustrated with the findings of a strong association between satisfaction with the work itself and organisational commitment. Korczynski (2002: 110) argues that satisfaction may come from direct interactions with customers. For example in the Brann call centre one employee said:

> If someone complains, it is really nice that we can solve their problem.

Three other findings are particularly interesting. Two strong findings relate to the association between the use of zero hours contracting and the ability to shift between full-time and part-time working. However, simultaneously, they value job security guarantees. This indicates that these employees value having control over their working time and job security.

The lack of association with pay satisfaction for this group is especially interesting since we might expect that employee commitment would be linked to the variable pay systems which often exist for sales staff. We believe that this absence of an association is because these employees have a high degree of control over their pay. Their actual level of pay is therefore often closely tied to their own efforts rather than anything the organisation is doing for them. Consequently, satisfaction with the amount of pay received is not reciprocated with organisational commitment. Indeed, Frenkel *et al.* (1999) suggested that sales staff resembled what they referred to as the entrepreneurial 'ideal type'. In this case sales workers have the autonomy to complete their tasks and achieve their targets. If they fail to reach these targets then their pay falls and their job security is weakened. In this instance, therefore, 'HRM plays a peripheral role' (Korczynski 2002: 109).

Browne (1973: 19) goes further and suggests that the challenge that their autonomy over their job gives them is itself a source of satisfaction. Sales staff take great pleasure from succeeding on the basis of their own ability and are willing to run the risk, in the form of job insecurity, if they fail to achieve their targets. Some authors also link this to ideologies of independence and masculinity (Collinson *et al.* 1990). Hodson and Sullivan (1995: 358) note the gender segmentation in sales in the US with women predominating in low value, low autonomy jobs while men dominate in the high value areas of motor vehicles and insurance sales.

Skilled workers

The impact of HR practices and work reorganisation on the commitment of skilled workers employed in the manufacturing sector has been the subject of extensive research (Arthur 1994; Appelbaum *et al.* 2000; Becker and Gerhart 1996; Huselid 1995; MacDuffie 1995). Much of this research has sought to establish links between high performance work systems and the performance of the organisation.

In our study the commitment of skilled workers follows the pattern seen elsewhere in respect of their relations with line managers and job satisfaction. However, there were also some distinctive features which deserve our attention (Box 4). The result for satisfaction with sense of achievement from work shows the importance of the ability to apply skills which have been acquired (Berg 1999; Boxall and Purcell 2003: 107). Satisfaction with pay and job challenge are also important for this group. Interestingly the presence of zero hours contracts is strongly associated with commitment perhaps because these employees may perceive this as providing indirect support to their own job security.

Distinctively we find that skilled workers are the only group where there is an association between the proportion of the largest occupational group working in a team and commitment. This has been the subject of extensive research (MacDuffie 1995; Boxall and Purcell 2003: 107) and may reflect the positive experience offered by teamworking in a variety of ways. This may be the result of a move

Box 4   Skilled workers
Zero hours contracts
Satisfaction with achievement
Satisfaction with pay
Satisfaction with work itself
Teamworking
Job challenge
Trust managers
Able to work term time only
5 days training
Satisfaction with job security
Employee unease

towards lean manufacturing which, it has been argued (Ramsey *et al.* 2000), has led to 'considerable strain on shop floor workers' (Delbridge 2007: 416). This was noted by some of our skilled workers:

> It's like a tug of war – if you don't pull together, you fall down.

> We cannot work alone so we have to work together.

Consequently, as Boxall and Purcell (2003: 107), have argued 'greater reliance is placed on employees to solve problems, and new skills obtained to take on a wider number of tasks and learn new ways of working, often discovered by the employees themselves'. In Jaguar we saw some of the benefits of teamworking in terms of:

> We all work in the same area, work and atmosphere, we are all in the same boat.

> It's a quality product and we are able to build on that. It's a brotherhood thing.

Some specifically referred to the ability to solve problems:

> If anyone is in trouble they've only got to shout and someone will come along to help.

While others drew attention to the ability to share knowledge

> Everyone knows what they are doing so everyone helps each other out. We all have each other so we stick together.

This combination of benefits associated with teamworking is likely to contribute towards the commitment of these employees.

Professionals

Professional knowledge workers play a key role in contemporary organisations but are often difficult to manage (Swart 2007: 450). The management of these intangible assets, however, is key to organisational success (Swart 2007: 461). These workers and the organisations which employ them have distinctive work processes, where 'outputs are intangible and encoded with complex knowledge and customised to the circumstances of each client' and 'professionals are employed as the primary carriers, interpreters and appliers of knowledge' (Greenwood *et al.* 2006: 6). These characteristics have major implications for the management of HR in these firms which we discuss in the next chapter. Our task at this point is simply to pick out some of the distinctive influences affecting the commitment of these employees.

In some ways these employees are like the other groups we have examined since their commitment is associated with managerial support and satisfaction with the work (Box 5). However, there are some findings which highlight the distinctive influences on their commitment. For example, their commitment is associated with reports of ability to change working patterns including shifts. This indicates that their ability to exercise autonomy over working hours is important.

This was illustrated in the software company AIT where, according to their employees,

> There is not a strict atmosphere, it's up to you when you do the job – they are flexible with hours.

> I like the way I can organise my time around what you want to – we have control over our working time. The team is very relaxed – as long as the work gets done it's up to you how you organise your own work.

This finding is further strengthened by their distinctive association with satisfaction with scope to use their initiative. Critically this refers to the ability of these employees to apply the knowledge and skills, usually referred to as 'know how' to practical, often poorly defined, ambiguous problems (Swart 2007: 452–3).

Again at AIT one employee said:

> We mostly have a free hand to make a success or failure of it, especially in a small team. It's up to me to do the job in the way I want to.

This is what we might expect given that knowledge workers have often invested heavily in their own education and are looking for opportunities to apply their knowledge and skills and to exercise their discretion (Swart and Kinnie 2004). This emphasis on professional knowledge is further reinforced by the association with selection via performance tests.

Interestingly, there is a lack of an association between commitment and career opportunities. As one nurse in the RUH said:

> My identity is with the team, the profession and the patients … not the Trust.

Box 5   Professionals
Ability to change work patterns
Select via performance tests
Satisfaction with work itself
Satisfaction with scope to use initiative
Trust managers
Ability to work same hours
Zero hours contracts

As has been discussed elsewhere, this may well be because professional workers look to the industry or sector to provide opportunities for career development rather than from inside the organisation because they have highly transferable skills (Swart 2007; Swart and Kinnie 2004). These career development opportunities exist because these employees often have to work across organisational boundaries, for example, with clients and intermediaries. In addition there may be strong external networks based on professional knowledge. This has major implications for the design of HR practices which have to take account of these pressures from outside the organisation as we discuss in Chapters 7 and 9.

Implications

This chapter began by remarking that much of strategic HRM research has assumed that HR practices influence the commitment of all employees in the same way. It also noted that this was in contrast to the available evidence which indicated that there are a number of occupational groups within the typical workplace. We have therefore asked in this chapter whether these different employee groups respond in the same way to HR practices.

Before examining this question we charted the emergence of internal labour markets and the development of heterogeneous workgroups within the organisation. We then discussed, referring to previous research, the types of employment subsystems which are applied to each group. These are the bundles of practices that are thought to be most appropriate for the characteristics of each of these employee groups. We then moved on to the more interesting and relatively novel area of examining the links between employees' experience of these practices and their organisational commitment. Our principal conclusion is that the emergence of these heterogeneous groups poses major doubts about the efficacy of the best practice approach: how can a consistent HR approach be effective when employees respond to practices in different ways?

This analysis established that there are some practices which seem to have a consistently positive influence on employee commitment across virtually all of the employee groups. These were satisfaction with the work itself and with the level of managerial support. However, there were other aspects of the work experience which were distinctively associated with particular work groups. Sales and customer service workers' commitment seemed to be closely tied to the flexibility of the job, whereas the role of line managers was unimportant. Pay satisfaction was important for skilled, personal service and elementary workers while teamwork was important only for the commitment of skilled and personal service employees. Quite notably, variables for job stress, career opportunities, job involvement and training were not associated with employee commitment.

The key role played by line managers for employees other than sales and customer service workers is especially important because this reinforces the HR causal chain model. Indeed, this demonstrates that for most employees the sheer presence of HR practices such as formal involvement mechanisms is not linked to their commitment whereas the day-to-day interaction with their line managers is very important (Purcell *et al.* 2003; Hutchinson and Purcell 2003). This strengthens our view that it is not simply a question of getting the 'correct' HR practice mix but that it is the implementation of these practices which is vital.

The theoretical implications of this are best understood in the context of the traditional distinction between the best practice and best fit views which we have already discussed. These results provide little evidence to support the best practice view. Indeed, they simply add to the contingent factors which other authors have said need to be taken into account when shaping HR strategy (Purcell 1999). After all, how can a universalistic approach be associated with success when a variety of practices are associated with the commitment of different occupational groups? More support is provided for the best fit view, only in this instance the key contingent factor is the need for fit to be related to employees' perceived organisational needs, rather than exclusively a 'fit' with business strategy as is normally argued. Guest (1997: 271) refers to this as 'fit as bundles' whereby there are distinctive patterns or configurations of HR practices and the task is to identify which of these is most effective. This is discussed further in Chapter 9.

The key finding, that commitment of employee groups is linked to satisfaction with different HR practices, has significant implications for managers. Indeed, the design of HR strategy becomes problematic as we have said because managers face a tension between the need for a consistent approach and one which takes account of the particular needs of different groups within their workforce (Lepak and Snell 2007: 211). On the one hand there is evidence of the effectiveness of consistent high commitment practices where the pursuit of employee discretionary behaviour and flexibility is often predicated on establishing an inclusive culture where all employees identify with and feel part of the organisation (Purcell *et al.* 2003). In addition there are important legal, ethical and moral imperatives to ensure consistency of treatment, what Boxall and Purcell (2003: 11–12) refer to as the pursuit of 'social legitimacy'. On the other hand our evidence shows that the commitment of employee groups is linked to satisfaction with different HR practices. This suggests that certain groups, for example professional employees, will respond to HR practices reflecting and responding to the particular forms of organisational support, such as opportunities to use their initiative, that are important to them.

This, in turn, may prompt managers to differentiate between their employees to pursue an efficient and cost effective approach. However, the ability of firms to offer practices meeting the specific needs of employees while satisfying the legal, ethical and moral imperatives identified by Boxall and Purcell (2003: 11–12) is decreasing in the heterogeneity of the workforce. Differences in treatment are unlikely to be in the areas of basic terms and conditions because many of the most obvious areas of unfairness have now been removed – at least symbolically (e.g. equal status canteens). Differences are more likely to arise in other areas concerned, for example, with opportunities for internal promotion, flexibility and involvement in decision making. These equity concerns and their associated costs are particularly likely to arise where differently treated groups work closely together (Lepak and Snell 2007: 216; Boxall 1998; Rubery *et al.* 2004).

Lepak and Snell (2007: 227) have noted that organisations overcome this tension by pursuing some practices which are internally consistent and others which are differentiated by employee occupational grouping. Another way of understanding this is to refer to the concept of 'table stakes', which we referred to earlier, discussed by Boxall (1996) in a slightly different context. There is likely to be a base of practices which need to be in place to generate commitment among all employees. In our discussion these included practices associated with job satisfaction and managerial relationships which were shown to be consistently important for virtually all groups of employees. These seek to ensure consistency of treatment, to satisfy legal and moral concerns and to improve employee attitudinal attachment to the firm. This suggests, in line with the best practice view, that there is an underpinning layer of generic HR practices that are needed for all types of employees associated with identity and recognition.

In addition to these basic table stakes there also has to be a tailoring of practices to meet the needs of different employee groupings while reflecting the business strategies of the firm which indicate what type of skill, knowledge and behaviour are particularly important and distinctive. Our discussion has pointed to the importance for example of teamworking for skilled workers, flexibility for sales staff and scope for initiative for professionals. The alignment between worker interests and firm needs is important since higher levels of organisational commitment are linked to meeting employee needs by the type of organisational support provided. It is commitment which is particularly important, as discussed, in influencing appropriate behaviour and thus the achievement of business goals.

This strongly implies that the design of strategic HRM needs to take account of both business strategy and employee interests. This has tended to be neglected in debates on best fit. The task, then, is one of knowing what to emphasise for each group. Effectively there is a need to identify the common and dedicated triggers of organisational commitment for different employee groups (Becker and Huselid 2006). This in turn raises cost issues for the employer: customising policy may be expensive and questions will be asked about the likely return on the investment. Moreover, this prompts the question of whether HR practices would be revised as the composition of the workforce changes because, as Lepak and Snell (2002: 537) note, once installed, HR practices are notoriously difficult to change.

Technical appendix

We have chosen to focus on the results for the largest occupational group within each workplace. So for example our data from professional employees will only apply to workplaces where they make up the largest occupational group, for example in consulting firms. This means we cannot address the issues surrounding professionals in other workplaces (e.g. engineers working in manufacturing plants) but it does give us more confidence in the information available about practices to which these employees are exposed. However, this does not work quite so well for the variables we build from the WERS 2004 survey of managers. In some instances the managerial respondents address questions specifically about the largest non-managerial occupational group. However, many of the questions asked of managers refer to HR practices within the workplace as a whole. In these cases we are assuming these practices apply to the largest occupational group. This is reasonable in most cases but in some this may not be true. For instance, a manager may say that a joint consultative committee exists in the workplace but this may only apply to a small group, perhaps operatives, while the largest group may be professionals who are not covered by this mechanism.[5]

We use the general linear model element of the complex samples feature of SPSS v. 14 in the generation of the regression results presented here. In doing so, we employ the weighting scheme suggested in the documentation of the WERS 2004 data for dealing with the complex sample design of the survey. The weighting approach involves accounting for the probability of being selected for interview in order to construct accurate population estimates of all summary and inferential statistics.[6] All regressions have been run in weighted and unweighted forms to assess the robustness of our results.

Independent variables

We have attempted to capture elements associated with each of the determinants of commitment indicated by our conceptual model (Figure 6.4). These include social support from peers and supervisors. The first is measured by the presence of teamworking in the largest occupational group in the workplace. The second is captured by a scale of employee trust in managers built from four questions. The inclusion of managerial support is consistent with the literature on leader–member exchange (LMX). For example, Epitropaki and Martin (2005) find that employee perceptions of the extent of supervisor sensitivity, dedication and intelligence are positively related to the degree of LMX and organisational commitment. The questions included in our measure of supervisor support ask for agreement with respect to statements about the behaviour of managers in the workplace. Typical statements are, 'Managers here can be relied upon to keep their promises' and, 'Managers here treat employees fairly'.

Job stress is captured using measures of role ambiguity, employee unease and workload. Communication is crucial to defining roles, and so we construct a measure of role ambiguity from four items in the employee questionnaire capturing the effectiveness of managers at keeping employees informed about, 'changes to the way the organisation is being run', 'changes in staffing', 'changes to the way you do your job', and 'financial matters, including budgets or profits'. Employee unease is codified as the inverse of the employee job-related well-being scale produced for the first findings from WERS 2004 (Kersley *et al.* 2006: 33). This is built from a series of six questions asking employees to reflect on the amount of time in the last few weeks that they have felt tense, calm, relaxed, worried, uneasy and content. Greater unease should typically diminish commitment, though employee self-selection into jobs offering differing degrees of uncertainty may also influence the answers to these questions. Lastly, we use employee reports of hours worked to examine any relationship between workload and commitment. We include this figure both in its level and as a squared value in order to allow for simple non-linearities in the relationship between workload and commitment.

We capture job involvement through measures of the presence of quality circles, the undertaking of employee attitude surveys and the presence of a joint consultative committee (JCC) in the workplace. All of these items come from the managerial questionnaire. We also include measures of various elements of job design including employee reports of their experience of autonomy, routinization, job challenge and flexible working arrangements.

Career opportunities are assessed in four ways: first, by manager indications of the extent to which vacancies are filled from within but also by other measures of the recruitment and retention system. In particular, we include variables capturing the use of personality or aptitude tests in recruiting and a variable measuring the proportion of non-managerial employees who are regularly appraised.

We assess the nature of training in the workplace using employee reports of the amount of off-the-job training they have received in the last year, as well as the degree of match between their skill set and the one needed to do the current job. We also include three dummy variables: one indicating whether the work-place gave five or more days of training to employees in the largest occupational group in the last year; a second indicating whether there is a standard induction programme for employees in the largest occupational group; and a third to indicate whether the workplace is accredited as an Investor in People. Our reliance on managerial reports of training in the largest occupational group is dictated by the survey design.

Job satisfaction is measured much more robustly in WERS 2004 than in WERS 98, as it consists of seven facet items and one overall measure of job satisfaction. Given the importance of job satisfaction as a correlate of organisational commitment and our interest in understanding the differences between occupational groups, we include all eight items of this scale separately. These include satisfaction with achievement from work, scope for using initiative, amount of influence over the job, training received, pay, job security, involvement in decision making at work and the work itself.

Employee demographic information is captured through the final section of the employee cross-section questionnaire. This allows us to ascertain self-reported levels of pay, age, tenure, education, nationality, marital status, union membership, contract status and whether or not the employee has dependent children. Workplace demographics are taken from the managerial cross-sectional questionnaire. This allows us to control for industry, workplace size, ownership structure, establishment age, average employee demographics, etc.

In our efforts to isolate any connections between these practice-related variables and commitment we need to control for the effect of other variables that have been shown in the past to influence organisational commitment. To this end, we include controls for many employee and workplace characteristics that might be thought to influence levels of commitment.[7]

7 People and performance in professional knowledge intensive organisations

Introduction

This chapter is the second in the series of three that seek to understand the application of the HR causal chain in specific contexts. Whereas Chapter 6 explored the impact of HR practices on different occupational groups we now turn our attention to how HR practices unfold in environments that employ professionals. In Chapter 6 our data indicated that different occupational groups would respond to different sets of HR practices. Here we illustrated that autonomy, for example, was more important to professionals, associated professionals and skilled workers than elementary workers. That chapter also indicated that different groups of employees should be managed in different ways. In this chapter we move on from this vantage point and we ask why specific HR practices have significant impact on the behaviour of professional knowledge workers. In summary, Chapter 6 identified *which* people management practices influenced the commitment of professionals and here we explore *why* these practices should have an impact on their affective commitment.

Structure of the chapter

It is important to emphasise the relevant sections of the text in relation to the management of professional knowledge workers. First, the process of management that we refer to here sits within the context of the HR–performance causal chain (see Figure 7.1). This is important in the context of the professional knowledge worker for a variety of reasons:

1   We are emphasising *experienced*, rather than intended HR practices. This is of particular significance in professional service organisations (PSOs) due to their dynamic and fluid nature. As we will discuss in the case study section, these (often very small organisations) may not have clearly articulated HR practices, however, their enactment has severe consequences for the firm. For example, the experience of insufficient professional skill development will cause an employee to leave the firm, most certainly to join a competitor, thereby depleting the PSO of its valuable human capital.

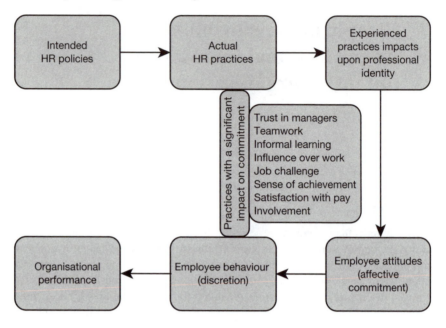

Figure 7.1 HR–performance causal chain for the PKW (adapted from Purcell *et al.*, chapter 2, 2007)

2   The model emphasises the importance of the *social context* for the enactment of HR practices. This is significant in the context of PSOs because, as LMX theory states, it is the relationship between the professional and the manager, during the enactment of HR practices, that will impact upon the *development of professional identity*.

3   We focus on the impact of experienced HR practices on affective commitment. As discussed in Chapter 6, it is the presence of this commitment that is likely to translate into discretionary effort and ultimately organisational performance. Small, dynamic PSOs are specifically reliant upon *discretionary behaviour* given their client demands and work organisation is often fluid thereby requiring client-focused work which stretches beyond narrow job descriptions.

In order to unpick the significant relationships between HR practices and professional knowledge workers' commitment we first need to establish the unique characteristics of this group of employees. The first section of this chapter takes a closer look at (a) the categorisation of professional knowledge workers and (b) their individual characteristics as well as (c) the nature of professional/knowledge working. Thereafter we turn our attention to the employing organisations and seek to understand how professional services organisations are structured and how they engage with their markets to deliver knowledge-rich services.

After a clear description of the professional knowledge worker (PKW) and their employing organisations we return to the WERS 2004 analysis of the HR practices that have an impact on this group of employees and we provide explanations for these findings drawing on qualitative case data collected between 2000 and 2006. Here we draw on case studies across research and technology organisations (RTOs), management consulting, law, marketing agencies and the health service (see Swart *et al.* (2003) and Kinnie *et al.* (2006) for further details).

This discussion will highlight certain challenges that PSOs are faced with when managing the careers of their professional knowledge workers. We discuss these challenges and possible ways to resolve them in the penultimate section. In the final section we summarise our findings and discuss these in the light of both HRM practice and theory building.

In summary, this chapter looks beyond the HR practice–commitment interactions by:

1   Understanding the characteristics of professional knowledge workers and their employing organisations (PSOs).
2   Drawing on these characteristics, we unpack the key HR–commitment links by through both quantitative data (WERS) and qualitative case data.
3   As we move from characteristics to practices that matter within the context of knowledge intensive environments, we become aware of some of the key challenges that the PSO needs to manage. We address these challenges by understanding how PSOs attract, develop and retain their knowledge workers.
4   The management of these challenges are discussed in the light of multiple identities that unfold between the PKW and the PSO. It is imperative that these identities are managed if the PKW is to remain with the organisation and if any of the HRM practices are to have their desired effects.
5   We link the practice areas back to the development of core knowledge assets because, ultimately, a PSO is focused on developing its human, social and

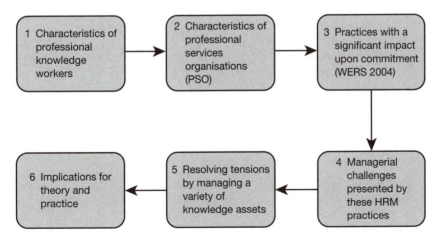

Figure 7.2 Structure of the chapter

organisational capital and its HR practices need to enable both the development and renewal of these core knowledge assets.

6   The concluding section of the chapter looks toward practical implications and areas for potential theory development.

The characteristics of professional knowledge workers

Professional knowledge workers (PKW) have been referred to as 'symbolic–analytic' workers (Blackler 1995) or gold collar workers (Kelley 1985; Zuboff 1988) who, on the whole, are highly paid, high-status employees (Reich 1991) and tend to work exceptionally long hours (Deetz 1995) with commitment related more to the nature of the work (consulting to a client, writing software code or solving a problem) rather than to the organisation. They have a strong sense of intrinsic motivation and are mostly interested in challenging work which requires considerable creativity and initiative (Alvesson 2000). These generalist descriptions of PKWs often lead to confusion as to how they should be managed and are characterised by debates that frequently end in the conclusion that it is easier to 'herd cats than it is to manage professionals' (Mintzberg 1998).

In order to unpack the HRM–performance link in knowledge intensive environments we aim to address the characteristics of PKWs by presenting a clear definition of a professional knowledge worker. This is focused upon three dimensions: the nature of professional knowledge, knowledge working and the knowledge intensive firms that employ them. The three-dimensional definition will enable us to explain the significant impact of particular sets of HR practices on commitment and performance.

It is important to recognise firstly that professional knowledge workers apply their specialised knowledge, or technical–scientific expertise, to high value-added problem solution processes. Scarbrough (1999: 7) asserts that knowledge workers are defined primarily by the work that they do, which is relatively unstructured and organisationally contingent, and which reflects the changing demands of organisations more than occupationally defined norms and practices. That is, having a particular set of knowledge is not enough to be recognised as a knowledge worker. It is the active application of the knowledge, through work, that is important. This systemic notion fits with the socially constructed nature of knowledge (Tsoukas 1996). To understand the individual professional knowledge worker we need to look toward the system within which the knowledge is embedded. We use the following three-dimensional definition, thereby paying attention to the *worker*, the *work* and the *organisation* (see also Swart (2007: 452)):

> Professional knowledge workers can be defined as employees who have clearly defined professional expertise and who apply their valuable knowledge and skills (developed through experience) to complex client-focused problems in environments that provide rich collective knowledge and relational resources.

Know-what (specific body of professional knowledge)

The 'possession' of a body of theoretical knowledge (developed through learning and experience) can best be described as 'human capital' (Bontis 1998; Davenport 1999; Lepak and Snell 1999) expressed through 'embrained' and 'embodied' knowledge (Collins 1993; Blackler 1995). Embrained knowledge represents technical–theoretical knowledge, otherwise referred to as 'know-what' (Ryle 1949) or 'knowledge about' (James 1950). Professionals are thought to have particularly deep sets of technical–theoretical or explicit knowledge (Polanyi 1966) that can clearly be linked to their profession. For example, a solicitor would study the theoretical knowledge of several sets of law, i.e. civil, criminal and possibly corporate law. This body of knowledge would have a deep history that is often based on case law or application of professional knowledge to practice. Knowledge workers can be seen to work from an in-depth knowledge base. However, 'knowledge of' will be of little use without experience of how to apply it.

Know-how (skilled professional)

The application of specialist knowledge refers to 'knowing how' to do something (Ryle 1949). This is illustrated by the lawyer who, with 25 years of experience, knows how to win a litigious case and how to apply case law to win an argument. This deeply specialist skill is often tacit, hence the notion of embodied knowledge: through application or action the knowledge worker does not focus on separate aspects or explicit parts of the skill. The domain of professional knowledge application is referred to here as skill, i.e. to be highly knowledgeable in a practical sense is to be a skilled professional. The practice-based skills create the foundation of knowledge *from* which the knowledge worker acts. They are part of the raw material in the knowledge conversion equation.

The client/customer/patient is seen as the focus of the know-how and is central to the development of professional skill. In other words, technical–theoretical knowledge is shaped around the needs of the client problem. High quality clients therefore provide challenging work and opportunities to develop cutting-edge skill (Maister 1993) which in turn provides the PSO with a superior human capital pool to draw from. Consequently, there would often be internal competition within the PSO to work on new and exciting work. This clearly presents a tension for the employing organisation as current clients need to be serviced but clearly talent will only remain with the organisation if they are exposed to challenging work. Many organisations respond to this challenge by rotating staff frequently between teams and managing multiple client team memberships. We explore this tension and the organisational responses further later on in the chapter.

The core skills that enable the conversion from know-what into know-how (Nonaka and Takeuchi 1995) include problem identification (marketing, advertising and customer consulting), problem solving (research, product design and fabrication) and brokerage (financing, searching and contracting) (Blackler 1995: 1027). Social skills and client relationships are also important to the process of knowledge work (Starbuck 1992) given the social nature of knowledge production. Knowledge workers therefore tend to develop their own social environments and professional networks within which they can enhance and enact their unique sets of expertise.

A further key characteristic of professional knowledge work, as opposed to knowledge work, is the capacity to apply the body of professional knowledge to both defined (familiar) and novel (unfamiliar) circumstances. It is therefore not the mere presence of human capital but also how it is applied that is important. Reed (1996: 585) argues that employees in this category 'specialise in complex task domains which are inherently resistant to incursions by the carriers of bureaucratic rational control'. He describes the application of the knowledge held by knowledge workers as esoteric, non-substitutable, global and analytical.

Link between know-what and know-how (professional identity)

The interaction between know-what and know-how is linked to the preferred training approach within the profession. The most frequently used training model is the apprenticeship model where the trainee professional can learn from the 'master' through shared practice in an action-learning environment. Professional institutions often play the role of guiding and monitoring this more informal work-based form of learning (Greenwood 2007). Hence, professional knowledge workers tend to identify with other like-minded professionals more than the organisation for which they work (Von Glinow 1988) and therefore develop strong professional networks that span organisational boundaries.

Know-how and know-who equals knowledge context

The conversion of human capital into intellectual capital is highly reliant upon the context for knowledge production. Professional knowledge workers interact with other professionals to produce knowledge-intensive outcomes. Knowledge workers work with knowledge: their own, certainly, but also the knowledge of others as communicated through information systems and artefacts, as well as the organisational and technical knowledge encoded in programmes, routines and managerial discourse (Scarbrough 1999). Here the 'encultured' knowledge (the process of achieving shared understandings through social relationships) and embedded knowledge (systemic organisational routines) influence the production of knowledge (Blackler 1995).

This process draws on 'what others know' as well as 'how easily that knowledge is shared', which, in turn, are influenced by the nature of the knowledge and the quality of the relationships. Smith *et al.* (2005), in their review of the knowledge management literature, identify three categories of organisational resources that impact on knowledge creation capability: stocks of individual knowledge, 'ego networks' and organisational routines. These routines comprise a firm's climate. Informally, and perhaps tacitly, they establish how the firm develops and uses knowledge (Smith *et al.* 2005: 347). The categories of resources that make the act of knowledge work possible are sometimes seen as different forms of capital. Ego networks refer to 'social capital' (Nahapiet and Ghoshal 1998; Leana and van Buren 1999) and organisational routines are attributes of 'organisational capital'. Both social and organisational capital impact on the knowledge creation capability of an organisation and the ability to conduct knowledge work.

If we look at the managerial implications of the knowledge production process, it is clear that we cannot manage professional knowledge workers without managing the knowledge environment within which they operate. An organisation cannot logically lay claim to be a knowledge intensive firm if it does not employ individuals who are actively engaging in knowledge work. Hence, it is critically important to manage the knowledge environment to ensure that knowledge work is possible. This depends greatly on the quality of the relationships that the firm has in its network of clients and collaborating producers. Challenging and committed clients make for challenging and exciting work, which allows for the co-production of knowledge. To understand this systemic process better, it is important to be aware of the characteristics of the professional services organisations.

The characteristics of professional services organisations

Organisations that facilitate knowledge production have a number of distinctive characteristics which are critical to the performance of the business. They operate in a 'pressure cooker' type of environment where product and labour markets are often unstable and technology is changing quickly. They tend to develop complex and innovative internal and external structures and forms (Frenkel *et al.* 1999; May *et al.* 2002) in comparison to other more traditional, slow growing and relatively bureaucratic organisations.

These organisational and environmental characteristics challenge traditional ways of organising based on hierarchy and specialisation and pose a whole series of questions about the people management practices most appropriate in these contexts. Ghoshal and Bartlett (1995: 96) suggest this may require a shift from what they term the 'strategy–structure–systems' paradigm, where the managerial task is largely concerned with allocating resources, assigning responsibilities and then controlling the outcomes, to one based more on 'purpose–process–people'. This is where the task is to 'shape the behaviors of people and create an environment that enables them to take initiative, to co-operate and to learn'. The management of professionals has been compared to conducting a symphony orchestra (Mintzberg 1998) where the key role of the manager is creating an environment for the harmonious flow of knowledge.

In many employment situations, the management of the professional knowledge worker is loosely structured with fluid project teams, rotation of leadership positions and low degrees of monitoring and control being present (Alvesson 1995). This often fits with employee needs for autonomy and self-directed development (Morris 2000). May *et al.* (2002) argue that this need for autonomy and cutting-edge skill development can best be met by creating an 'enclave' organisational form: an independent section of experts within a larger organisation. Inside the enclave, a high degree of interdependence between professional knowledge workers with complementary forms of knowledge is likely to prevail. The authors warn that this enclave should not have absolute autonomy but managerial control and market-based mechanisms such as performance-based reward systems should be used to focus professional knowledge workers' efforts on organisational and strategic objectives.

Given the fluid nature of professional knowledge *working* (transforming know-what to know-how) as well as the *organising* of this work, managers often seek to use ideological controls and strive to create a strong sense of belonging or a strong culture (Alvesson 1993). A process of establishing an organisational identity (Mael and Ashforth 1995) helps an organisation to erect mobility barriers and goes some way toward tying valuable knowledge workers to the organisation. Small to medium-sized knowledge-based firms often benefit from a strong sense of shared identity at the firm level. This is often because the owner-manager is still present in the firm and/or the majority of the original workforce is still part of the organisation. In larger firms, however, this sense of belonging needs to be 'manufactured' by using individual performance and/or organisational rewards (Alvesson 1993), establishing a variety of community-based activities (Swart *et al.* 2003) and engaging in some cultural manipulation to influence how knowledge workers view themselves and their relationship to the firm.

Project-based work has become the dominant form of organising professional and innovative knowledge work (Lam 2005, 2007) and a key organisational characteristic. However, project-based working presents a danger because it is often the case that knowledge workers build a strong sense of identification with their project team, which may replace their identification with their organisation. Furthermore, if the team is client-focused and client-based, there is a strong possibility that valuable competitive knowledge may leak out to the client and remain outside the boundaries of the firm.

It is therefore important to think relationally when seeking to understand the management of knowledge workers (Gulati *et al.* 2000: 203; Granovetter 1973). Knowledge-based firms frequently operate within larger networks where they have frequent interaction with clients, partners, educators and suppliers at many levels of organisation and knowledge tends to flow relatively freely across these boundaries (Grimshaw *et al.* 2005; Swart and Kinnie 2003). These knowledge flows are regarded as a key part of the knowledge production process. It is important to note that knowledge workers work with knowledge at an *inter*-organisational level.

This phenomenon is often to the advantage of smaller firms who may be able to exploit knowledge outside the permanent employment relationship or, indeed, any employment relationship. A cluster of small biotechnology, life-science research and law firms may work together on a larger process of knowledge production. Similarly, three or four law firms may work together on a management buy-out and a life-science research firm may work closely with a pharmaceutical firm to produce compounds for further research. Such co-production of knowledge outputs focuses our attention on the quality of the knowledge network within which the firm operates.

The management of knowledge workers is influenced, and sometimes controlled, by relationships with organisations in these networks (Grimshaw *et al.* 2005; Grimshaw and Miozzo 2006; Rubery *et al.* 2002, 2004). Where firms have fewer and longer-term business-to-business relationships, we need to consider how suppliers, partners, clients and customers influence the way in which people are managed in the focal firm.

In summary, knowledge-based firms often operate in volatile, fast-changing environments. Within this context they need to manage ambiguous work through fluid structures. Internal (knowledge work and professional knowledge workers) and external (knowledge environment) forms of fluidity are put under pressure by the nature of network relationships. Networks determine the opportunities for challenging knowledge work within the firm, such as working on exciting projects, as well as the quality of knowledge outputs at the network level.

The characteristics of both professional knowledge workers and their employing organisations have been discussed. These characteristics and the interplay between the individual and organisational levels are summarised in Table 7.1. We now turn our attention to the HR practices that have an impact in these environments.

Explanation of HR practices which are significant

The previous sections have drawn from previous research to give an indication of the types of people management practices that will be important to professional knowledge workers. In this section we turn to empirical research to draw a series of conclusions.

We draw on quantitative data from the employee and managerial cross-sectional questionnaires of the WERS 2004 data set. As described in Chapter 6, the precise details of the design and execution of this study are recorded elsewhere (Kersley *et al.* 2006). Fitting with the focus of the chapter, our unit of analysis is the employee and we merge information on each workplace (e.g. industry, size, HR practices, etc.) into this employee information.

We continue to use the Standard Occupational Classification system of 2000 (SOC 2000) to identify groups of professionals within the data set. We include both professional and associate professional and technical occupations in our analysis here. The reason for this is that we are interested in the implementation of HR practices within professional services organisations and although one can assume that in most cases the professionals will be the largest occupational group, there are some examples (for example nursing) where associate professionals will be the largest occupational group. The impacts of HR practices on these two occupational groups are listed separately in Table 7.2 and discussed together in the section that follows.

Affective commitment remains our dependent variable within the quantitative analysis (e.g. Kacmar *et al.* 1999; Balfour and Wechsler 1996; Mowday *et al.*

Table 7.1 Links between professional knowledge worker, professional services organisation characteristics and HRM practices

PKW	HR practices	PSO
	Know-what	
Clearly identifiable body of knowledge. Established through historical practice and regarded as scientific within the community of professionals – embrained knowledge (Blackler 1995); explicit, theoretical, know-what (Reich 1991).	• Recruitment and selection • Performance-based selection.	• Market advantage due to base of professional knowledge (this is what they 'sell' to clients). Human capital is therefore critically important to survival
	Know-how	
Body of professional knowledge is intertwined with practice, i.e. know-what is linked to know-how. Embodied knowledge (Blackler 1995; Tsoukas 1996; Scarbrough 1999; Morris *et al.* 2007)	• Informal learning through shared practice rather than formal training (mentoring systems) • Performance management (teaching others becomes a key focus) • Work organisation – organisational structure (skill development will be linked to the way in which the firm is organised, e.g. if the law firm is organised along industry lines rather than traditional practice groups it will impact upon the partner which you learn from) • Allocation of staff to projects – as contracts conclude or start up the development of professional skill needs to be taken into account during staff allocation	• Builds deep know-how through staff retention and shares the know-how from more experienced staff with new PKWs
	Conditions needed to develop know-how	
Client-focused know-how Application of professional knowledge is mostly client/patient-focused	• Develop client capital • Work organisation • Job design	• Organisation around client-based project teams Highly fluid networked way of working (the closer you can get to understanding the client needs the better)
Challenging work is important to apply the technical professional knowledge	• Job challenge • Work organisation • Client relationship management skills	• Need to attract clients or engage in work that provides the appropriate challenge

PKW	HR practices	PSO
Skills that take you from know-what to know-how Problem-solving, problem-identification, brokerage, social skills and client relationships (Blackler, 1995; Starbuck, 1992) *Know-who – social networks* Know-what and know-how are linked (wider resources in the network) Professional identity	• Formal training • Informal learning • Staff allocation • Work design • Sharing of best practice through post-project reviews • Work design (permeable boundaries) • Multiple teams • Community of practice	• These skills are what would provide the competitive advantage – it is in the PSOs' interest to develop them – but this could only be done through good external (client) relationships and internal (experienced PKWs) resources. • Professional networks • Multiple teams • Challenging clients
	Individual characteristics	
Work exceptionally long hours (discretionary behaviour) but also commitment to profession and organisation Intrinsic motivation	• Balance loyalty between profession and organisation • Design value-driven HRM practices • Attract motivated PKWs	• The PSO competes on the basis of this discretionary behaviour • It is important to establish a strong culture organisation which generates commitment • Populated with highly motivated individuals – part of client proposition and in some ways could have a negative impact on social capital • Part of wider professional network • Establishment of communities of practice • Build relationships (trust, loyalty) and ensure that knowledge sets overlap
Continuous development of transferable professional skills important to career satisfaction	• Job challenge • Vocational/professional development • Need to work with other professionals to build skills (good colleagues who are willing to share knowledge and whose knowledge can be shared)	
Identify with the profession, develop strong professional networks (also required through professional associations)	• Balance loyalty between profession and organisation • Design value-driven HRM practices	• Embedded within wider network and links to professional associations is a valuable way to update knowledge and move within the knowledge network. Need to erect resource mobility barriers so as not to lose valuable employees through these networks.

Table 7.2 Significant relationships between enacted HR practices and professional knowledge workers' commitment[1]

Practice	Professionals	Associate Professionals
Social support		
Trust in managers	0.162**	0.173**
Training		
Employee report of own training in last year		0.095**
Job design		
Job challenge	0.116**	0.104**
Ability to change working patterns	0.567**	
Job satisfaction		
Satisfaction with sense of achievement	0.240**	0.333**
Satisfaction with amount of pay received	0.116*	0.244**
Satisfaction with the work itself	0.436**	0.537**
Satisfaction with involvement in decision-making	0.158*	0.273**

[1] Regression results from analysis of the organisational commitment of employees using the WERS 2004 data. Estimates calculated using the SPSS complex sample general linear model. Estimates weighted using the employee weights. Cells report regression coefficients. Significance levels flagged at the 95 per cent (*) and 99 per cent (**) levels. All regressions include unreported intercepts, employee controls and workplace controls.

1979). The interaction between affective commitment and discretionary behaviours or organisational citizenship behaviour (Meyer *et al.* 2002) is particularly relevant within the context of managing professional knowledge workers given that their commitment extends beyond the organisation to their profession and their clients (Alvesson and Willmott 2002; Empson 2007). We measure affective commitment using the same three-item scale from the employee questionnaire that appeared in WERS 1998. This captures affective commitment through questions asking employee respondents to express their degree of agreement with statements like 'I am proud to tell people who I work for'. Evaluated on a five-point Likert scale anchored by 'strongly agree' and 'strongly disagree', this measure provides an internally reliable and externally valid measure of commitment.

We also draw on qualitative case-based analysis as another key data source to unpack some of the reasons as to why there are significant relationships between sets of HR practices and professional knowledge workers' commitment. The data were gathered between 2001 and 2006 from research and technology organisations (RTOs), management consulting, law, marketing agencies and the health service. In total we draw from 21 case-study firms. In each firm we collected data via semi-structured interviews from a cross section within the organisation. We paid attention to the variation between experienced HR practices (by employees) as implemented by line managers and intended HR practices (as expressed in policy documents). In each of the cases we were able to study secondary data in the form of employee handbooks as well.

The analysis of the data will now be presented in sections as shown in the

WERS 2004 data set. The practice implications are also discussed in each section. Thereafter we turn our attention to the tensions that may arise from the implementation of these practices.

Social support

The conversion of theoretical knowledge (know-what) into professional skill (know-how) is highly dependent upon the environment within which the professional knowledge worker operates and the managers they work with. It is therefore not surprising that *trust in managers* has a significant correlation with these employees' commitment (b = 0.162** for professionals and b = 0.173** for associate professionals).

Using the work of Leana and van Buren (1999) which divides trust into generalised and dyadic trust it is clear from our data that dyadic exchanges are important within the professional context. That is, the trust requires knowledge of and contact with another actor which is different from generalised trust which pertains to the social unit as a whole rather than specific actors. The professional knowledge workers often identify who it is that they would want to work with before they join the firm. Trust in the PSO context is therefore intertwined with professional respect. As one of the research scientists in a life-science research organisation said:

> I wanted to come and work at X because it is known as the best post-doc training ground. Also Professor Y is a walking library of tacit knowledge. He knows everything there is to know and I would not be able to get this knowledge at any other company. It really is an honour to work with him.

Managerial trust was also closely associated with career progression, which is also very important to highly motivated knowledge workers. It is interesting to note that in this context it was more than just the technical competence of the manager that was important. The ability to manage people, to delegate and to inspire others to reach their goals was also seen as central to managerial competence within the career progression context. This was described well by a software consultant who said that 'progression depends a lot on who you have as a manager. Some are very good at the task but very poor at man-management but most have to do both.'

It is interesting to note that when the issue of managing the careers of others was explored in our line manager interviews, most managers found the transition from technical competence to managerial competence very difficult and commented on the notion that most front line managers in professional environments tended to micro-manage where they focused more on 'doing the task themselves' rather than 'teaching others how to do it'. Some of the fast growing medium-sized organisations, particularly in the software and marketing sectors, became aware of the importance of investing in front-line managerial skill development and therefore made considerable investments in these training programmes, given their size and resources. These case organisations tended to have higher degrees of career satisfaction amongst their knowledge workers than organisations that had not made such investments.

The ability of managers to lead and facilitate learning amongst professional staff was also closely associated with the preferred method of learning in professional services organisations.

Training

I have gained experience and I feel that training is not that important.

The WERS 2004 data analysis shows no significant links between the availability and reports on formal training and commitment. This is not surprising and fits well with the qualitative data that we gathered. Our data indicate that professionals found it most valuable to learn informally from others. As one of the software engineers, that they enjoyed the challenge of being thrown into the deep end. This form of learning is of course also interlinked with the PKW's need for job challenge.

Hutchinson and Purcell (2003) also found statistically significant positive associations between managers who provided guidance, coaching and staff commitment motivation, job satisfaction, career satisfaction and satisfaction with the performance appraisal system.

The apprenticeship model of learning rather than training was therefore seen as the preferred approach to the conversion of explicit knowledge into tacit skill (Polanyi 1966; Nonaka and Takeuchi 1995) and it was regarded as a powerful form of new knowledge generation in the organisation. This is because the learning model (as opposed to the training model) was not always hierarchically driven. For example, a small software house ensured that they constantly updated their 'yellow-pages' and skill maps and it was the most competent individual who would lead the skill development. As one director explained: 'If a student software programmer knows the code and the processes he would teach me how to do it. We have to learn from the person that knows.'

The focus of the learning-by-doing model was also important. The professional knowledge worker was less interested in acquiring organisation specific skills (as taught by more senior members in the hierarchy) and they often associate their organisational commitment with the extent to which they are able to develop transferable skills (May *et al.* 2002). Hence the example above where a student engineer will teach a director these more 'transferable' skills. However, in the law firms that we studied we observed a further willingness to learn from the more experienced partner in the firm. These skills, such as drafting contracts, are of course also associated with transferable skills rather than practice or firm specific skills.

Given that many of the PSOs sell cutting-edge skills to their clients, the knowledge workers often regarded it as a demotivator if they could attend formal training. They felt very strongly that their skills needed to be cutting-edge and although they may acquire soft skills through formal training, they needed to be technically ahead of the game.

Job design

The particular aspects of job design that show significant results here include job challenge and autonomy. As can be expected, we found statistically significant relationships between *job challenge* and commitment at the 99 per cent confidence level (b = 0.116** professionals and b = 0.104** for associate professionals).

Knowledge in and of itself naturally becomes the focal point for the knowledge worker's activities. The factors that drive knowledge workers to choose some projects over others are often related to the feedback received on their knowledge outputs (often through performance management systems or client relationships) and the desire to deepen technical expertise by taking on challenging projects.

Importantly, our qualitative data shows that one of the key causes associated with low levels of career satisfaction is lack of job challenge. One of the software engineers in the case study with the lowest career satisfaction scores said that 'a career in McDonald's will be slightly more satisfying than working here', and another said 'From a developer's point of view the morale can be low, we are expected to work very hard and to be quite honest the work is not that exciting'.

As indicated in the section that discussed the characteristics of professional knowledge workers, the quality of the tacit skills which they developed will be directly related to the degree of job challenge that they are exposed to. That is, difficult, stretching work is not only likely to develop commitment and motivation but it is also likely to increase the quality of the available human capital pool.

This is of course where the positive spiral or set of relationships between the client, the PSO and the professional knowledge worker develops. The PSO will not be able to offer challenging work without clients who provide challenging problems and are willing to explore innovative solutions. The quality of the client relationship is therefore intimately linked to the degree of job challenge that can be experienced. Of course, the PSOs would need to balance their ability to retain current clients to whom they offer more standardised solutions or services which they are known for with more innovative and exciting work.

The most significant relationship that we found was between *autonomy* and commitment (b = 0.567** for professionals). This finding supports that of Alvesson (1995) who speaks clearly of the need for a high degree of autonomy. Morris' (2000) notion of the employee's need for autonomy and self-directed development further supports this statistically significant link. Our case studies were characterised by several expressions of the need for and the presence of autonomy. We include examples from the research and technology organisations here:

Free to organise time and long term planning.

We have a lot of responsibility.

You are given an objective and then you have the scope to do it your own way.

We work autonomously and can change things within the research.

We control our own work pace and pattern.

In the day-to-day planning of things we have a lot of control. We also have team meetings when we want to discuss larger issues.

No one else can do my job so I can do as I see fit.

A close analysis of the data indicates that not only do professional knowledge workers prefer to work independently of a routine or tightly scripted work practices but they also need to work with complex, often ill-defined client problems (Alvesson 2000). In other words, they not only want influence over *how* they apply their skills (processes, shift patterns, etc.) but they also want to have autonomy in *what* they do (i.e. the interpretation of the client problem).

This need for autonomy is often well matched with the client needs and demands in that the client looks to the PSO for solutions. If they were in a position to define and describe to the knowledge workers what to do they certainly would not be buying the service. However, the freedom in interpretation and work patterns often makes the professional knowledge workers very difficult to manage. This puts the organisation in a vulnerable position particularly given the interdependence of knowledge processes or knowledge sets in the firms' offering to its clients.

Due to the strong presence of professional bodies and personal links across their profession, knowledge workers are often in control of the networks that they develop and the skills that they acquire (May *et al.* 2002). This adds to the ability to work in an autonomous manner or in extreme examples to work in a self-employed manner.

The ability and desire to work with high degrees of job discretion were also associated with the level of experience. This brings us back to the discussion on the preferred learning model. It was clear that in our law firms and management consulting firms the newly qualified professionals wanted to have guidance and structure to develop their deeply rooted tacit knowledge. Many of the knowledge workers had an ambition to 'move on from the training ground' and work independently once experienced.

Job satisfaction

In this section we give attention to satisfaction with amount of pay received, satisfaction with the work itself and satisfaction with involvement in decision-making.

We found significant and positive links between satisfaction with amount of pay received and affective commitment for professionals ($b = 0.116^*$) and associate professionals ($b = 2.444^{**}$). This finding is consistent with that of May *et al.* (2002), who in their research on the job expectations of 134 knowledge workers in Australia, Japan and the USA, found that pay was regarded as the first or second most important aspect of the job. One of the reasons why pay and rewards were so important to the knowledge workers in this study was that in many of the new professions (e.g. software and marketing), status was less hierarchy- or tenure-based. However, the abstract nature of the knowledge worker's skills was priced on a perceptual basis: 'my client cannot do what I do (they may not even know how I do this) and because they think I'm invaluable, they'll pay a lot for my services'. This spiral of reward (perception–high reward–positive perception) is also the mechanism through which knowledge workers tend to determine their status and their 'next big career move'.

The professional knowledge worker also tends to command high rewards because their know-what, know-how and know-who is valuable and difficult to replace or imitate (Barney 1991). They know that their organisations cannot sell their services without them and this places them in a strong bargaining position.

Interestingly, the satisfaction with the level of pay received was seen as a table stake (Boxall and Purcell 2003) and it did not serve as a motivator. This fact gave the firms that we were studying a real opportunity to create loyalty to the firm through other practices that created a sense of belonging. Here the firms which had strongly articulated value statements and values-driven HR practices (as mirrored in the recruitment and performance management systems) could benefit from increased organisational commitment without having to compete on the basis of pay. As one of the software developers in a small firm said:

> I could get more elsewhere but I enjoy the non-monetary aspects of the work, i.e. the people that I work with and the social aspects of the work. I really feel a sense of belonging and that's what keeps me here.

Not only were the organisational culture and values important in motivating and retaining professional knowledge workers but the *satisfaction with the work itself* was statistically significantly related to commitment for professionals (b = 0.436**) and associate professionals (b = 0.537**). The satisfaction that derives from doing professional work is closely associated with the development of professional identity (Alvesson 2000; Alvesson and Willmott 2002; Brown and Starkey 2000; Hatch and Schultz 2002; Scott and Lane 2000). A professional's identity development is closely associated with the development of tacit skills, or learning how to do the work. Once again there is a strong link between job challenge and job satisfaction. That is, professionals expect to have challenging work but they also expect of themselves to enjoy what they do.

> It is nice to see the result of your work in people's homes.

> I believe in the cause. Seriously, I believe in what the company stands for and that is satisfying.

> I get a real buzz from doing the work.

This satisfaction with the work itself has often been discussed in the light of the differences between jobs and vocations. Communities expect professionals to hold strong values about their 'vocations' and to believe in what they do. Similarly a substantial part of professional training is often dedicated to the ethics involved in professional working and the values that should be upheld in acting professionally. Greenwood (2007) argues that 'modern' professionals often experience tensions between satisfaction that derives from the job itself (doing something because you enjoy it) and a commercial obligation to manage, for example a law firm, in a commercially viable manner. He states that 'the professions are highly privileged. It is time, once again, to scrutinise more carefully the forces determining the relative priorities which lawyers give to professional and commercial values and to consider whose interests they serve' (2007: 196).

Finally we found significant links between satisfaction with *involvement in decision-making* and commitment for both the professionals (b = 0.158*) and the associate professionals (b = 0.273**). This finding supports that of May *et al.* (2002: 791) who found that professional knowledge workers expected to be involved in decisions that will influence their developmental opportunities and careers (more so than organisation-wide decisions).

In our case studies we found clear coexistence between involvement in decision-making and employee and client retention. Put simply, knowledge workers tend to stay with organisations that take their views into account and these organisations are also more likely to keep their clients.

As several of our interviewees commented:

> There is a general openness and exchange of ideas and issues: you don't feel as if anything is done behind your back.

> You have an influence and your views are taken into account. I am satisfied just knowing this.

> Our manager always takes our views very seriously and takes it up to management.

A key area in which we saw the need of the professional knowledge worker to be involved in organisational decision-making was in the adoption of performance management practices and systems. The process of performance management on both individual and team level is characterised by a tension: knowledge intensive outcomes tend to be highly ambiguous yet professional knowledge workers have a particularly high need for recognition. This tension resulted in the performance management policies and systems being a particularly sensitive issue in all the cases in our sample. Distinctive issues that intensify this tension include:

1   the commitment to the performance management system, in particular how the outcomes within the system are determined;
2   the ownership of the system, including its origin;
3   chargeable time devoted to the system;
4   the links of the performance outcome to either reward and development;
5   the role of the performance management system in building social capital.

The professional knowledge workers in our sample were sensitive about their professional identity: how fellow workers regard their levels of competence. According to our participants, one of the most formal ways in which this identity is established is through the discussion of performance outcomes/achievements. There was acknowledgement that informal conversations and 'learning transactions' contributed to the professional respect. However, the record keeping and in some cases 'public display' of performance achievements meant that the performance management system was laden with emotions. It could be argued that this is true in many other organisations but we found that it has even greater impact in PSOs because the performance management system was often the only formalised people management system in the small to medium PSOs.

The extent to which the performance management system was embedded in the PSO was related to its origin. Knowledge workers themselves often took ownership of the development and implementation of the performance management system. There was a sense that because performance outcomes are ambiguous it was best left to the knowledge workers themselves to devise a system (often competency- or points-based) that could differentiate between levels of performance. This emphasises the socially constructed nature of these performance outcomes. How competent you are as a knowledge worker, how 'much' you knew and the value you added to your clients are determined through a negotiation process. It was the working together in project teams, learning from the 'master', constantly judging your own and others' competence that established the performance negotiation process. Being able to judge performance was therefore situated in your own experience as a knowledge worker: tacit knowledge and tacit skill were the backbone of performance management.

The illusive quality of the performance measured or judged, together with a rather illusive process of judging performance and the sensitivity surrounding the outcome of this process, meant that knowledge workers would devote a great deal of their time to this system. In the successful KIFs this process went through several iterations without any sign of demotivation. The strong sense of ownership together with involvement in the design of the process established this sense of commitment.

For example, in a software consultancy organisation, senior and principal members of staff dedicated some of their chargeable time to the running of the performance management system. Employees are assigned reviewers that 'fit' their employment profile. The consultancy manager managed the process of assigning reviewers. Performance reviewers would also follow their appraisees on client visits. These observations would then be followed by developmental discussions and the completion of a detailed project assessment form. Further performance data were gathered from project managers, peers on the same project and the client. Prior to the performance discussion the employee had the opportunity for self-assessment. Detailed comparisons of the 360-degree review are then recorded for future developmental and reward purposes

When we questioned the performance reviewers in the above case about the sacrifice of their chargeable time, the perception was that they were not reducing their fee-earning potential but that they were strengthening the organisation by developing employees and by building networks for performance feedback. This theme was confirmed in several of our other successful organisations: performance management was regarded as a tool to build social capital. Latham and Wexley (1981) also found that performance appraisals could be used to outline and reinforce behavioural norms and build social capital.

Performance reviews were the key system that enabled professional knowledge workers to bridge several boundaries:

1   An employee outside the core project team conducted performance reviews.
2   Clients were often involved in performance evaluation.
3   Teams of performance reviewers would often meet to discuss the process of evaluation as well as the subsequent developmental options, thereby establishing another community of practice.
4   The outcome of a performance discussion would often be linked to further development, which in these KIFs translated into workplace learning. This strengthened the organisation specific skill acquisition and accounted for the culturally driven nature of development.
5   During performance discussions, knowledge workers were often made aware of 'experts' whom they could approach when working on a specific project. This strengthened the knowledge network and answered the all-important *'knowing who to ask?'* question.

Professional knowledge workers are eager to influence decisions that will have an impact on their experience of work. The example of the detailed involvement in the establishment and implementation of the performance management system indicates the desire to have an influence over their own work experience. Clearly the particular example of the performance management system also shows that these knowledge workers feel that they want to judge their own knowledge-based outputs, and possibly that they do not want to have in 'imported' HRM system to influence their professional careers. This fits well with the first finding presented here, i.e. the impact of trust in managers, and the professionalism associated with this, on affective commitment. However, the professionals' desire to be involved in people management practices also points to further challenges that are experienced when managing professionals. That is, their loyalty lies primarily with their profession, their individual networks and with the act of professional working, rather than with the organisation within which they work (Empson 2007; Gardner *et al.* 2007).

In summary, given that professional knowledge workers work autonomously in their own networks and want to have control over their own careers it is not always easy to establish a sense of commitment amongst this group of employees. Our data indicated that the most significant links between HR practices and affective commitment were in the areas of autonomy and satisfaction with the work itself. Other important practice areas include social support through the managerial system, learning from others, satisfaction with pay and involvement in decision-making.

The next section briefly explores these challenges through the theoretical lens of content (the professional knowledge worker), context (the network-based way of organising) and process (the ambiguity of knowledge-based outcomes and the ownership over knowledge processes).

Three-tiered managerial challenges presented by the PKW

In prior sections we discussed the characteristics of professional knowledge workers, their employing organisations and the types of practices that make a difference to these employees' affective commitment. However, it is clear that many of these practice areas will represent further managerial challenges to the organisations that employ them. These challenges can be summarised by (a) understanding the very nature of the HR practices that could impact upon the PKWs' commitment (i.e. the content), (b) examining the context of professional working and (c) appreciating the ambiguity involved in the process of knowledge-based work and its outcomes. Figure 7.3 summarises these three-tiered challenges which are discussed in this section of the chapter.

First, we need to understand the very nature of these managerial challenges, i.e. what are we seeking to manage. It is important to understand that we have moved on from purely seeking to understand how we manage professional knowledge workers and our focus is here on the practices that matter to the commitment of these employees. That is, when we speak about the *content* in Figure 7.3 we are referring to the analysis of our data presented in section 5 in this chapter. Our findings indicate that *autonomy* and *satisfaction that derives from the work itself* have the most significant impact on the professional knowledge workers' affective commitment. However, one could argue that neither autonomy nor the nature of the work will be derived from or controlled by the organisation and that both will be associated with the act of *professional working* which is output-driven (what

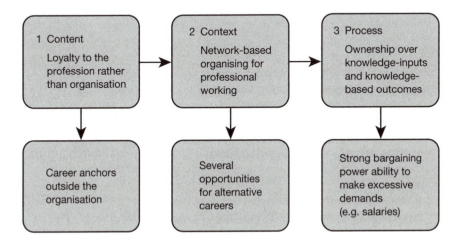

Figure 7.3 Three-tiered challenges for managing PKWs

we achieve not how long we spend at work) and characterised by values which are anchored in the profession (Gardner *et al.* 2007). An organisation which therefore seeks to implement HR practices that facilitate these outcomes may run the risk of investing in their employment practices only to have the employees leave the organisation for another employer or to work independently.

The desire to achieve satisfaction from the work itself is also associated with a loyalty to the client/patient rather than the organisation. Here the client/patient becomes the focal point of professional working and it is through the feedback from this focal point (e.g. a satisfied client) that the professional feels a sense of satisfaction that is derived from the work itself. However, the organisation may have very little control over this sense of satisfaction. Here we see that the locus of control of the management of the professional seems to be outside the organisation with the work itself and with the client/patient relationship rather than with the organisation. The very content of the management of the professional therefore presents the organisation with a set of managerial challenges. For example, how can loyalty and identification be created with the organisation within this very strong drive to identify with the profession and the outputs of professional working.

The emphasis on loyalty to the profession, rather than the organisation (as expressed here in the need for autonomy and satisfaction that derives from the work itself), presents further challenges to the management of these employees when we look at the *context of professional working* or the way in which professionals organise themselves. These knowledge workers are often found not only *inside* organisations but *across* them, drawing on their personal, professional and expertise networks (Empson 2001; Karamanos 2003; Maister 1993; Uzzi *et al.* 2007). Professionals are therefore frequently working with multiple stakeholders across organisational boundaries as knowledge and skills are exchanged between members of the network. This cross-boundary working also provides the opportunities for them to move between employers. However, at the same time it is essential that the firm retains the individual and collective knowledge and skills if it is to be successful; but because of the prominence of these individually controlled networks, the organisation has less control over how it manages 'its' professional knowledge workers. Non-standard forms of employment such as contracts for services and fixed-term employment can therefore be more suitable and are frequently found across knowledge-based organisations. This approach to organising lends itself to organic or network-based organisational forms characterised by decentralised flexibility and autonomy (May *et al.* 2002: 777).

Furthermore, the *process*, and therefore the output of the professional working process, is often intangible (for example, consulting advice) and its quality is difficult to determine. In most professional work, the criteria for evaluating work are unreliable or entirely absent (Alvesson 2001: 867). Whether a solution is 'good' or 'no good' is often determined by factors external to the solution itself, such as changing market forces, the interpretation of the clients buying the solution and the degree of trust that the sellers of the solution inspire.

This intangibility of output is further complicated by the fact that there is a very direct relationship between 'knowledge inputs' and 'professional services'. There is therefore ambiguity over who 'owns' knowledge within the firm. Professional knowledge workers have a high sense of ownership over their knowledge and will lay claim to the outputs they 'sell' directly to clients. Concurrently, the firm needs to extract high value or rents from this knowledge which is at the core of the business if they are to satisfy their clients. This creates the managerial tension of *value appropriation* which is often expressed through the bargaining for high salaries or share ownership schemes which acknowledge the firm's dependence on the individual's knowledge and skills. Often the firm is subject to industry practice and the bargaining power of the individual knowledge worker to reward exceptionally well in order to develop and retain its professionals.

In summary, the challenges to the employing organisations are presented on three different layers. First, the emphasis on loyalty with the profession which is captured here through the quantitative (WERS 2004) results. Second, the way of organising professional work through networks which leverage individual professional control. Finally, knowledge outputs are ambiguous and difficult to control or manage, which once again provides the individual knowledge workers with tremendous power within the employment relationship. That is, professional knowledge workers often reject an organisation's performance management system for a professionally owned and controlled performance management system.

Given these three-tiered challenges (content, context and process), we ask how the organisation can erect appropriate mobility barriers (Mueller 1996; Boxall and Purcell 2003) to create loyalty to the organisation in order to manage the careers of its professional knowledge workers. We explore these processes in the next section through the theoretical lens of social identity.

HRM practices that address these PKW challenges

It could be argued that each of the three-tiered managerial challenges (content, context and process) can be resolved by establishing a strong identification with the organisation (Empson 2004). Here a strong loyalty to the organisation may create a willingness to remain with the firm even in the face of attractive alternative career offers. This organisational identification and loyalty may also translate into a willingness of the professional knowledge worker to negotiate over the appropriation of rent from the knowledge-based services and outputs delivered to clients. Ultimately, it may seem that the development and management of a strong organisational identity could act as a key mobility barrier (Mueller 1996) and anchor the professional knowledge worker's career within the firm, thereby ensuring that valuable human capital remains within the professional services organisation.

Much of the recent interest in the concept of identity has focused on organisational identity, especially the attempts to shape the extent to which employees identify strongly with their employing organisation (Alvesson 2000; Alvesson and Willmott 2002; Brown and Starkey 2000; Hatch and Schultz 2002; Scott and Lane 2000). Organisational identity has also been researched in the light of firm performance where it is thought that firm performance is directly dependent upon the professionals' ability to sell their services to clients whilst embodying the firm's identity (Ibarra 1999). This is because of the ambiguity of client problems and the intangible nature of the client offerings. The brand and identity of the firm therefore become strong indicators of the quality of the client solution. However, the sole development of an organisational identity, perhaps at the cost of other competing identities, may not resolve these three-tiered managerial challenges.

Identity is seen as emerging from a complex interplay between various stakeholders (Alvesson and Willmott 2002; Albert and Whetten 1985; Hatch and Schultz 2002; Scott and Lane 2000). The extent of permeability of the boundaries between firms and their clients (Hatch and Schultz 2002) intensifies with the extent to which various sources of identity compete. Previous research also indicates that professionals will not always identify strongly with their organisation (Heinz and Laumann 1978) and often face multiple sources of identity through their networked way of working. It is the multiplicity of identities as well as the management of these identities that are central to our understanding of the ability of firms to develop and retain their professionals.

Researchers have previously noted the links between identity formation and career choices (Ibarra 1999; Pratt and Foreman 2000). This is because identity/identification can provide a career path which may challenge the ability of the organisation to retain the professional knowledge worker. For example, a strong client identity may translate into a career with the client, thereby causing irreplaceable loss of tacit knowledge and skill within the PSO. Cross-boundary working within the PSO network presents the professional knowledge worker with several opportunities but these will only translate into career alternatives if there is a strong social identification. Professional knowledge workers therefore choose careers based on their identity construction (Albert *et al.* 2000).

Identity plays a more 'directive' role in PSOs given the unstructured and dynamic way of professional working (Alvesson 2000) and the often unstructured client demands (Morris 2000; Swart 2007). The development of an identity or multiple identities is therefore highly significant for professionals. A professional's identity is developed through interaction with various sources of identity (Ashforth and Mael 1989; Brown and Starkey 2000). There are several competing groups with whom they can potentially identify as Ashforth and Mael (1989) have argued, 'the individual's social identity may be derived not only from the organisation, but also from his or her work group, department, union, lunch group, age cohort, fast-track group and so on'. We highlight four sources of identity (professional, organisational, team and client) that could compete as career anchors and trajectories. These four identities are developed through the knowledge sets, continued interactions and client focus that are so central to knowledge work.

Organisational identity is concerned with the loyalty and commitment which employees display towards the organisation. This may take various forms including strong shared values, trust and knowledge of and agreement with the goals of the organisation. Evidence of this usually takes the form of a willingness to engage in discretionary activity, to participate in activities not directly related to their job and to share their knowledge. Employees with strong organisational identity are likely to see their career focus as lying within the organisation. The notion of identification with an employer, workgroup, or occupation may seem quaint, even naïve in times of large-scale continuous change, mergers and acquisitions (Hogg and Terry 2000) and the move from long-term relational contracts to shorter-term transactional ones. However, it is partly because of the loss of organisational moorings that identity and identification have become such critical issues (Albert *et al.* 2000: 14).

Team identity develops because employees spend much of their time working in project teams which may be the principal way in which they experience the organisation. They will have frequent contact with their team leader and other team members and often much less contact with other members of the organisation. Employees come to know one another especially well if they are working for a small team for several months or years. This identity can become even stronger when the team works away from their employer's own place of work. This is often evidenced by a strong sense of teamworking and a willingness to help one another. In our qualitative case data we found an overwhelming sense of the importance and identification with the team. Professionals often expressed that they experienced the organisation through their team and certainly that career progression was dependent upon the team that you worked with. This was also strongly linked to managerial respect and the wider organisation of work.

Professional identity can be defined as the relatively stable and enduring constellation of attributes, values, motives and experiences in terms of which people define themselves in a professional role (Schein 1978). It is built upon professional training, membership of professional bodies and participation in various networks. These range from formal professional institutions to much looser arrangements perhaps based on virtual networks reliant on common interests. These can often have a strong pull on employees' career interests because they provide not only an opportunity to improve knowledge and skills but are also a source of job opportunities.

Finally, client identity develops because much of an employee's working time is spent on developing services for a specific client. Employees often have to develop a very close knowledge of the client and its products and processes because they are under operational pressure to deliver to the client, whereas their employing organisation can seem somewhat more distant. Indeed, over time they often internalise the values and ways of working of the client – in common language they 'go native'.

These four identities exert competing pulls on the career of the professional knowledge worker. Professional knowledge workers have frequent and prolonged contact with clients; their project teams may establish their own identity, a strong organisational culture may give rise to an organisational identity (Orlikowski 2002) and a professional network outside the organisation may be a strong focus of interest. Perhaps the most likely tension is between serving the interests of

Table 7.3 Theoretical links between HRM practices and the management of professional knowledge workers' identities

Identity	Desired outcome	HRM practices
Organisation	• Increased loyalty leading to improved retention • Career anchor within the organisation • Shared values, language and frameworks	• Strategic view of contribution of human capital to the business • Value and culturally driven recruitment • Values-based induction • Opportunities for involvement in decision making
Team	• Good teamworking to maximise the team's potential • Permeable team boundaries to ensure that team identity is not stronger than the organisational identity • Improved internal flows of knowledge	• Work design • Project/client team design and allocation of staff to teams • Development of teamworking skills and line management skills where needed • Multiple team membership to improve versatility and flexibility
Professional	• It is mainly the professional development needs of the individual employee that drive this identity formation • Development of professional skills in a way that is related to the firm, i.e. being a good creative because of the opportunities provided by the firm (rather than professional bodies or external networks) • Link development of in-depth professional ability with the opportunity to work across professional disciplines thereby avoiding silo professions within the organisation • Allow and encourage external connections and networking	• Opportunities to learn new skills on the job • Job rotation to improve skills and knowledge • Opportunities for external professional development • Clear but flexible career paths • Mentoring, feedback and general management training • Pay linked to skills and performance not tenure • Focus on performance targets as linked to values-driven behaviour (not just results)
Client	• Focus on client's needs but not at the cost of the firm • Improved ability to understand client's needs and their customers as expressed through analysis of client briefs and writing of creative briefs • Maintain client relationships and retain client's business and look for new business	• Research and education about client, their market and consumers in client's market • Development and provision of client specific knowledge and skills • Coaching and support provided for working with clients • Improved client brief and creative brief writing skills • Staff allocation policies

the client and those of the employing organisation (Alvesson 2000). Professional knowledge workers are required to pay close attention to the needs of their clients and often form close relationships with key members of their staff. However, they also need to keep the interests of their employing organisation in mind – for example to keep costs low and maximise opportunities for new business. Competing interests might also exist inside the PSO. Team identity may be strong making it difficult to contact staff in other teams leading to problems with sharing knowledge. There may also be a clash between an individual's professional career interests and the needs of the firm. Some employees who are looking to improve their employability (Valcour and Snell 2002) will be reluctant to take on work they regard as mundane or low level. Others will try to refuse to work on off-site locations or will be unwilling to carry out internal administrative tasks which take time away from pursuing their own self-interests.

These sources of competing identity represent different career routes for the professional knowledge worker (Albert *et al.* 2000; Pratt and Foreman 2000). Several opportunities may arise because of the very nature of professional work, however, it is the strength of the socially constructed identity that will translate into career choices (Ibarra 1999). Clients seeking to recruit highly competent people will often find a ready source in the agencies and suppliers who work for them. The professional knowledge worker with a weak organisational identity may be attracted by such an offer, especially if it seems there are better opportunities for career development. Close-knit teams may tire of the constraints imposed on them by their employer and decide to set up their own business, perhaps taking some of their best clients with them (Alvesson 2000: 1103).

PSOs are well aware of these competing sources of identity and may take a series of measures in an effort to retain and develop their staff. We believe that the formation and maintenance of these identities is manageable (Pratt and Foreman 2000). Firms often use various strategies and practices to strengthen organisational identity and thereby erect mobility barriers (Mueller 1996). This is where our focus turns to the management of human capital within the firm in the establishment and maintenance of the various identities. Table 7.3 shows the theoretical contribution that HRM practices might make to the four identities.

Organisational identity is best strengthened by means of developing a strategy which establishes a link between human capital management and the culture of the firm. This will be supported by the development of a values-based recruitment and promotion policy. Opportunities for staff to participate in organisational decision making are also likely to stimulate loyalty and commitment (Purcell *et al.* 2003).

Team identity will be influenced by work and project team design as well as staff allocation policies. Teams which stay in place for a long time working together for the same client are likely to develop a clearer sense of identity. Similarly, practice groups in law firms which have little or no interaction are likely to have a strong sense of identification with their work team (Sherer 1995). This will also be established when there is limited rotation of staff between teams (Swart and Kinnie 2004).

Professional identity is likely to be influenced by the opportunities internally and externally to develop professional skills as well as the opportunity to develop professional communities of practice (Wenger 2000) inside and outside the organisation. This is likely to be influenced by various mentoring and performance management systems which give feedback and training activities which are available (May *et al.* 2002; Swart and Kinnie 2004). The breadth of jobs will influence the opportunity to develop new skills as will the extent to which career paths internally are fixed or flexible. Pay systems which are linked to skills as well as performance are also likely to be important.

Client identity will be influenced by the type of work conducted and the frequency of interactions with the client. Highly specialised work, especially work which requires in-depth research-based knowledge, is more likely to develop a sense of identity with the client. Training programmes which improve the ability to understand the client's needs are likely to be influential in stimulating this identity as will working closely with the client, especially when this is on their own location.

In summary, specific human capital foci can be used, not only to establish a particular identity, but also to manage the strength of the identity. For example, the strength of the client identity will be directly influenced through the nature of interactions with them and the way work design is managed within the firm. Many PSOs therefore choose not to conduct on-site services for clients and rotate professionals frequently across client teams. They want to protect their organisational identity through their job design and rotation policies.

Managing knowledge assets within the employment relationship

In previous sections we discussed how the organisation can overcome some of the key challenges presented by the management of professional knowledge workers. However, the focus of this discussion was limited to the career of the professional knowledge worker with the aim of developing and retaining these valuable employees. In this section we aim to explore how the organisation can ensure that all its knowledge assets are managed.

The *raison d'être* of the employment relationship, the professional networks and indeed the client relationships can be seen as the development and application of knowledge. In order to apply the valuable tacit skill that we discussed in the first section of this chapter it is important to draw on knowledge assets beyond purely this individual human capital.

The process of knowledge conversion, from individual human capital to knowledge-based outcomes[1] that have value in the marketplace, will be reliant upon social capital (relationships) and organisational (structures, processes and technologies) capital. This is one area where interdependence (Bowman and Swart 2007) between the firm and the knowledge worker can be identified. Individuals are often dependent on the organisation for access to other knowledge workers, including those with complementary skills. They also rely on the physical and financial capital in research laboratories or technology to develop their core skills. The organisation, on the other hand, relies increasingly on the knowledge and skills of its human capital to create a competitive advantage.

Individuals therefore rely upon the professional service organisation for their social and organisational capital and organisations rely on professional knowledge workers for their human capital which they 'sell' to their client base. It is useful to frame this interdependence between the organisation and the individual within the process of knowledge trading because it highlights the need to focus not only on the development of human capital in the employment relationships but it speaks further to the importance of developing social and organisational capital.

Developing human capital

Knowledge trading between knowledge workers and organisations has an impact on recruitment, development, work organisation, and pay and reward. First, managers need to take a human capital focus in employee resourcing activities by specifying the nature of knowledge inputs that are needed within the organisation: which skills need to be developed to ensure effective knowledge trading.

A human capital focus also has an impact on resource allocation. For example, if a particular skill is in demand by a client group, it is often the case that key skilled employees will be placed across project teams to allow for dispersion of the particular skill-set across the organisation. Here the organisation needs to create tacit learning environments to ensure cost-effective skill development.

Finally, the nature of knowledge trading may have an impact on pay and reward by putting the employer in a stronger bargaining position. Knowledge workers often claim high rewards given the complexity and uniqueness of their skill, but if the interdependency of knowledge trading is emphasised, the employer can argue that knowledge production would not be possible without access to organisational resources, networks, physical and financial capital, thereby undermining claims for excessive remuneration.

The knowledge trading presents a specific challenge with regard to the development of knowledge workers who are interested in knowledge trading because they are highly focused on employability (Cappelli 1999). This enables them to move on to a career opportunity that will enable them to develop further unique skills that are attractive to other employers. The interest of the employing firm, however, is focused on retaining core skills that enable value generation and competitive advantage. The tension between employees wanting to move between organisations and the organisation needing to hold on to key talent can be termed the '*retention-employability*' dilemma (Swart and Kinnie 2004). We argue here that insight into the interdependence of knowledge trading can help address this challenge.

Developing social capital

Professional knowledge workers rely most strongly on the process of informal learning to develop their tacit skills. The learning-by-doing is closely associated with the degree of job challenge, i.e. having exposure to challenging client work in order to apply explicit knowledge. However, it is also clearly linked to the social capital or strength of relationships within the organisation. Many of our respondents in our case studies expressed the need to '*know-who to ask*' when faced with challenging work.

The creation of this glue that helps learning was often mentioned as a key reason why employees would remain with the organisation. That is, they worked with bright and ambitious people with whom they got on well and from whom they could learn a great deal in order to develop their own employability (Cappelli 1999). How then did our successful organisations go about the creation of social capital?

One of the first themes that emerges very strongly when answering this question is the implementation of values-driven HRM practices. Our organisations with strong social capital tended to use values-driven recruitment practices. Here they sought to attract not only competent individuals but also like-minded people who would get on well. In the cases where professional knowledge workers became friends, they were also more likely to share knowledge with one another. These organisations tended to use the same values in their performance management systems, i.e. they were not only interested in the level of output of their employees but the *process* or way in which this was achieved was also important. Interestingly, they often developed these values and processes from the ground up and therefore the value systems were owned by the individual knowledge workers, rather than forced down from top management.

In summary, it was the strong culture organisations that had cohesive relationships or high degrees of social capital and it was also these organisations where employees felt most satisfied with their career opportunities and where knowledge was shared.

Developing organisational capital

Our conceptualization of organisational capital includes structures, processes and technologies.

Successful PSOs relied upon the fluidity of their structures to facilitate knowledge sharing and to build social capital. For example, in many of our case studies we observed an active strategy to establish multiple teams in order to avoid impermeable team boundaries. Some of the teams were client-focused but others focused on the activities of the organisation, such as policy design teams, or they were vocationally based communities of practice (Wenger 2000). These PSOs also ensured frequent rotation between project teams to facilitate the development of human capital. For example, in our marketing agencies a specific employee would work on several client teams to build a variety of skills.

These organisations did not only pay attention to meta-physical structures such as team boundaries but the actual physical structures were also important in knowledge trading. For example, law firms tended to move more toward an open plan way of designing workspace in order to facilitate the flow of knowledge across practice groups within one industry or client account. This did have an impact on client satisfaction and skill development. Likewise, marketing agencies tended to arrange physical office space creatively to enable active working on client accounts across professional skill boundaries. For example, several spaces such as games rooms, bistros and comfortable sofa areas were created in these agencies to enable account handlers, creatives, copywriters and clients to come together around a specific problem.

The inspirational PSOs also designed their processes and technologies in specific ways thereby adding to their comparative advantage. They took great care to use an evolutionary approach to capture their core client interface processes or indeed their people management processes. We have given earlier examples in this chapter of how performance management systems evolved in a research and technology organisation. In a similar manner our marketing agencies established their creative briefing documents by observing how they actually went about meeting client demands and then by trying to systematise how this process was implemented across several client accounts.

This particular approach to managing organisational capital allows for an integration of valuable tacit knowledge into the more explicit knowledge that is housed within the firm. It also differentiates the firm from its competitors by embedding valuable know-how into organisational processes. This is a way of creating embedded capital (Bowman and Swart 2007) which further ties the loyalty of the professional knowledge worker into the organisation.

Finally, successful PSOs also ensured that the lessons learnt through post-project reviews became part of the organisational capital. This is an active example where learning-by-doing is captured in the organisational processes and used to provide a human capital advantage. It is also another example of the evolutionary nature of organisational capital. That is, in order to meet the ever-evolving nature of client demands and to stay ahead of its competitors the PSO continually had to evolve its organisational capital.

Conclusion

This chapter focused on the unfolding of the HR–performance causal chain in the specific context of professional knowledge intensive environments. In order to understand the specific challenges involved in the management of professional knowledge workers we sought to understand the characteristics of these knowledge workers as well as their employing organisations.

On the one hand we expressed that the very nature of professional knowledge, professional working and knowledge-based outputs placed the employee in a position of considerable bargaining power. They could sell their knowledge directly to their clients/patients and on the whole they are more loyal to their profession than to their employing organisations (Empson 2007; Alvesson 2002).

One main connecting point between the professional and their organisation came into focus through the need to do challenging work, i.e. job challenge has a significant impact upon the professional knowledge workers' affective commitment.

Here the employing organisation is somewhat at the mercy of its clients. If it is able to attract and retain high quality clients, who are not risk averse, it is likely to offer substantial job challenge and is therefore likely to attract and retain its professional employees (Maister 1993).

Here we were able to take a closer look at the characteristics of PSOs and summarised that they are organised *internally* along client–project teams and *externally* they operate in complex knowledge networks. The dominant organisational form that we find in these contexts is consequently a network-based organisation (Lam 2005). However, these internal and external networks are often controlled by individual knowledge workers or their clients. In other words, PSOs can experience employment challenges from both their employees and their valuable clients.

In the section that followed we argued that if PSOs are to attract and retain their human capital they would need to generate affective commitment. That is, they need to tie the careers of their knowledge workers into the organisation. Here our findings indicated that the establishment of *autonomy* as well as *satisfaction that derives from professional working* are most likely to be associated with affective commitment (statistically significant results at the 99 per cent confidence level). However, these outcomes can be associated with the profession rather than with the organisation which means the organisation could risk a loss on the investment in its HR practices and still have the professional knowledge workers exit from the organisation.

We argued here that a possible way in which the PSO could attract and retain its key knowledge workers would be to manage the competing identities which resemble career anchors for the professional. The key message here is that the PSO needs to anchor the career of its employees into the organisation whilst meeting their professional wider career demands. That is, client, team and professional identity need to be anchored into the organisation.

The managerial and theoretical implications of this approach highlight the need to emphasise the interdependence in the process of knowledge trading. In other words, the PSO is dependent upon its human capital to compete; however, the professional is reliant upon the organisation for its social and organisational capital. Managerially, the PSO therefore needs to manage all its knowledge assets in its employment relationship. The focus needs to stretch beyond the management of people to the management of relationships and processes upon which its human capital relies to convert knowledge into services and products.

Likewise, our HRM theoretical models need to take into account the multiplicity of knowledge assets when we seek to understand the successful management of human capital. We need to be clear on how the HRM practitioner can develop social capital as well as organisational capital. As discussed here and in Chapter 3, the establishment of a strong culture and values-driven HR practices play a key role in this. Furthermore, an appreciation of the evolutionary approach to the development of organisational capital facilitates the interdependence between tacit (skills) and explicit (processes) which the organisation uses in its process of knowledge trading.

The need to understand the management of the multiplicity of knowledge assets points to a further implication highlighted in this chapter, i.e. the importance of a network-based approach to HRM. We indicated here that individual knowledge work tends to happen within the networked environment. Likewise, the organisation operates within a wider web of organisational networks. We therefore cannot ignore the impact of the network-based organisational form if we are to understand the success of HRM within the professional knowledge intensive environment. We explore these practical and theoretical implications further in Chapter 9.

In summary this chapter looked beyond the HR practice–commitment interactions by:

1   understanding the characteristics of professional knowledge workers and their employing organisations;
2   drawing on these characteristics to unpack the key HR–commitment links as found in both quantitative data (WERS) and qualitative case data;
3   linking the practice areas to the challenges that PSOs are faced with when they seek to manage their knowledge workers (we point to these challenges by referring to the content, context and processes framework within which the PSO operates);
4   resolving these challenges through the management of multiple identities that unfold between the knowledge workers' careers and the PSO;
5   exploring the importance of interdependence in the knowledge trading process which is linked to the management of the multiplicity of knowledge assets because, ultimately, a PSO is focused on developing its human, social and organisational capital and its HRM practices need to enable both the development and renewal of these core knowledge assets;
6   concluding with managerial and theoretical implications of the management of these varieties of knowledge assets.

8 Analysing the links between people management and organisational performance

The case of Nationwide Building Society

Introduction

This chapter attempts to apply much of what has been developed in the preceding chapters in the context of a specific organisation: Nationwide Building Society. Chapter 6 illustrated the importance of employee and occupational context in understanding the response of employees to HR practices and here we examine how the responses of employees drive performance in a particular company context. As we will see, the search for links between people and performance in any particular organisation requires a series of integrated choices that must all support the ultimate aim of the analysis. Key among these choices is the selection of an appropriate performance benchmark for the business unit under consideration. Indeed, the problem in organisations tends not to be finding performance measures but selecting among them. The results in this chapter, which focus on corporate social responsibility, employee commitment, turnover and mortgages, are specific to Nationwide. Other companies in other industries with different business strategies may well find that other things matter. Employees in various occupations may respond in a variety of ways, as suggested in Chapter 6. This chapter illustrates how internal data can be used in conjunction with academic theory to identify important linkages between HR and performance. These results serve as an illustration of the HR–performance link, and they extend the work of Chapter 7, which examined precisely how this causal chain was initiated for professional knowledge workers.

We begin this chapter with some facts about Nationwide.[1] This is followed by a brief review of the literature focusing on links between people management–performance in financial services that highlights the importance of employee turnover for the performance of these organisations. This review leads us to focus on the determinants of organisational commitment in the fourth section because of the well-established connections between commitment and turnover in the literature (e.g. Meyer *et al.* 2002). The fifth section then illustrates the importance of employee commitment in Nationwide through a service–profit chain analysis that includes employee turnover. The sixth section concludes.

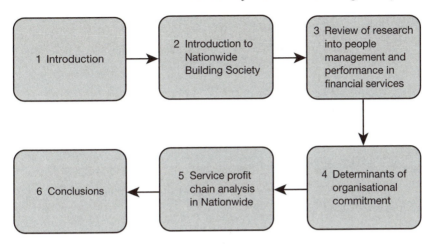

Figure 8.1 Structure of the chapter

Some facts about Nationwide Building Society

Nationwide is one of the UK's largest financial service organisations and provides a broad range of retail financial products and services to approximately 11 million members including mortgages, savings, current accounts, life assurance, personal loans and household insurance. It is the largest building society in the world and employs around 16,500 staff (13,850 FTEs) with the bulk (circa 7,500) working in the network of 681 branches across the country. The remainder are employed in two major offices in Swindon and Northampton and in seven administrative centres.

Nationwide is committed to its status as a mutual organisation, whereby it is owned by its membership rather than shareholders. As other building societies have converted to plc status this form of ownership has come to distinguish them from their competitors and it is translated into a set of values which are applied to members and employees alike. Nationwide's public stance on mutuality began back in 1995 and this resulted in the development of a new business strategy to improve customer services and streamline operations by reducing margins. Various initiatives have emphasised the difference between Nationwide and the banks, and have also promoted its image as champion of the consumer in the personal financial market. The Society has attempted to protect its mutual status through the creation of the Nationwide Foundation, through which all new members assign any windfall gains associated with conversion from mutual status to the Foundation. This provides a source of income to fund various charitable activities associated with Nationwide. The Foundation's annual report for 2007 reveals over £2 million in charitable activities, including a small grants programme open to registered charities, as well as specific schemes focused on young offenders, domestic violence, etc.

The benefits and obligations of mutuality are stressed for employees. Nationwide seeks to generate a positive set of values and attitudes among its employees that are designed to distinguish them from their competitors and should be reflected in better performance relative to other financial service companies. These values have been summarised in recent years by the PRIDE initiative:

- Put members first
- Rise to the challenge
- Inspire confidence
- Deliver best value
- Exceed expectation

Each year emphasis is placed on one aspect of PRIDE with extensive communications led by the Chief Executive.

What do we mean by performance in Nationwide?

Chapter 1 described some of the challenges associated with performance measurement, and these are worth considering carefully in the context of this particular example. Our difficulty in this case, as in all cases, is one of deciding which of the array of available performance measures is appropriate to the task at hand. We discuss these issues in this section.

Nationwide is the UK's fourth-largest mortgage lender and residential mortgages are the core of the business. Total assets of Nationwide Building Society were valued at £118.2 billion in 2006; £92.6 billion of this total were loans and advances to customers and £82.8 billion of these were fully secured on residential property (Annual Report and Accounts 2006: 40). This means that approximately 70 per cent of Nationwide's assets are linked to residential mortgage lending. This makes mortgage markets the key market in which to measure performance of the retail branch network.

One of Nationwide's early initiatives in translating 'mutuality' into operational management and associated measures was the use of a form of key performance indicators (KPIs) which are used to measure performance against three key areas. In 1999 these were expressed as:

- Nationwide is my first choice
- Nationwide has the best ratings
- Nationwide is where I want to work

Ten KPIs, which all have equal value, are set annually to measure performance against these criteria. Employee satisfaction, for example, (based on the annual employee attitude survey) and competence are used as indicators of 'Nationwide is where I want to work'; mortgage share and complaints are included in measures of 'Nationwide is my first choice'; capital ratios, costs and controls reflect the statement 'Nationwide has the best ratings'. Initially set at corporate level these measures cascade down into divisional, departmental, team and finally individual plans. The KPIs therefore act as a means of communicating the society's values and individuals can see clearly how they influence the corporate objectives. The whole planning process is managed by the Group Planning department who develop the corporate plan (which runs from April to March) after consultation with all divisional directors and the board. Each division then develops their own plan, with a steer from the Planning department. A traffic light system is used to monitor performance on a monthly basis and progress can be monitored via the intranet site. All employees receive an annual corporate bonus, which is based on some of the KPIs, and this again can be tracked on the intranet which provides a quarterly update on the scheme including examples of how performance has improved and suggestions as to how improvements can be made. This is perceived to be a strong motivational tool.

In the branches targets are set by the divisional director of the branch network based on targets in the corporate plan. A team bonus is payable based on performance targets, which takes the form of reward vouchers rather than cash. This method is felt to be cost effective and, according to research, the most popular form of rewarding teams (as one ex-branch manager explained 'the idea is that you can spend it on yourself rather than just using it to pay off a credit card account'). High performance league-based competitions are also run under the title of the 'Diamond Club' scheme, rewarding top performing branches, areas, and individuals on a monthly and annual basis. Branches, for example, compete within the same grade (a branch grading model was introduced in 1995 which is updated every six months – there are currently five grades) and winners receive a visit from the executive or divisional director who presents a team plaque or individual award certificate and pin badge. The annual award winning team also receives some money to pay for a team event of their choosing whilst individual winners receive a small prize such as a weekend theatre break. Details of all the league tables are readily available through a range of media including the intranet, staff newsletter, videos/cassettes and notice boards. Recognition therefore, rather than financial reward, is clearly a preferred means of motivating staff and more in keeping with the values of the society.

Nationwide has been collecting performance data for many years covering all aspects of the business in line with KPIs. Data comes from operational finance targets such as mortgage conversions and savings, customers are regularly surveyed on the quality of service provision and annual employee surveys are undertaken covering over 120 questions. Response rates are high. In addition, the usual employment data are collected on staff turnover and absence for example. Using this range of data it is possible to explore the interconnection between employee and customer attitudes and performance.

Performance outcomes have been positive in recent years, as seen in regular awards in the financial press, as well as in increased market share and benefits passed back to members. Nationwide was rated amongst the best companies to work for in the *Sunday Times*' 'Best Companies to Work For' list from 2001 through 2007, topping the list of big companies in 2005. In a survey of 1,000 organisations by the European Commission, they were rated as one of the top 100 best workplaces in the European Union in 2003. They were also rated 11th in the *Financial Times'* 50 Best Workplaces in the UK in 2003. Behind these awards is a wide range of sophisticated HR policies covering all aspects of the employment relationship. These are centrally determined and applied across all parts of Nationwide, as is common in retail and financial organisations.

There is clear evidence of a high level of organisational success in Nationwide. The most important measure of financial performance (the percentage value of mortgages sold compared with the target set) is approximately 108 per cent of the target set, although there is quite a high degree of variation around this mean (s.d. = 30.8%). For the purposes of this chapter we measure customer service as a composite approval rating across three relevant measures yielding an average level of customer satisfaction of 80.67 per cent. Variations around this mean are low (s.d. = 3.3%) indicating the high levels of consistency typical of strong value companies. The chosen HR measures are also good with low levels of labour turnover (mean = 10.14%) and absence (mean = 3.56%).

In summary, at the general level there is clear evidence that emphasis on culture and values, seen in the mnemonic PRIDE with each letter representing a particular aspect of Nationwide values and 'mutuality', is reflected in high levels of organisation commitment. This, in turn, is strongly related to low rates of labour turnover, customers having positive views on service quality and in better financial performance seen in mortgage values against target. Our understanding of the relationships identified in this examination of the aggregate picture from Nationwide can be verified and quantified by examination of data from various pieces of the retail branch network, which we undertake in the fourth and fifth sections, but first we examine other work on people and performance in financial services organisations.

People and performance in financial services

Links between people and performance in financial services have been the subject of a reasonably large literature in human resource management. Perhaps this is because in financial service organisations it is relatively easy to judge performance, as output is typically measured directly in monetary units, and also because the multi-site nature of many financial service organisations allows researchers to capture substantial variety in HR practices within a single HR policy environment.

Much of the work in this area relies on a service–profit chain framework (Heskett *et al.* 1994) or on a SERVQUAL framework (Parasuraman *et al.* 1985), both of which emphasise the role of employee attitudes in delivering customer satisfaction and profits. These relationships are perhaps most vividly illustrated by the Sears case presented in Rucci *et al.*(1998), but work in financial services also demonstrates connections between employee attitudes and customer satisfaction (e.g. Maddern *et al.* 2007; Newman 2001). Some of this work focuses on links between employee attitudes, customer satisfaction and employee turnover as the delivery mechanism for financial performance. This is because employee turnover creates vacancies that create direct costs associated with recruitment, induction and training. Unless vacancies are immediately filled, employee turnover also generates staffing shortages that can impair customer service. Even if vacancies are immediately filled they may involve the loss of substantial amounts of skills and knowledge that impair the delivery of customer service even though the head-count has not changed. Dissatisfied customers may take their business elsewhere or fail to recommend the company to others. We discuss some of this literature in more detail below.

Gelade and Ivery (2003) examine the impact of people management on performance through inspection of area level data from the retail branch network of a bank in the UK. They limit their focus to a small number of HR practices (staffing levels, overtime and professional development) and they construct seven barometers of work climate from a 155-item employee survey. They averaged these seven scores to produce an overall measure of 'general climate' and find clear support for the role of work climate as a partial mediator between HR practices and business unit performance.

Mediation is a statistical concept that, instead of hypothesising a direct causal relationship between the independent variable and the dependent variable, hypoth-esises that the independent variable causes the mediator variable, which in turn causes the dependent variable. Partial mediation suggests that although there is some effect through the mediating variable there is also a direct effect of the inde-pendent variable on the dependent variable.

Gelade and Young (2005: 15) extend the work of Gelade and Ivery (2003) through a cross-sectional analysis of data from the branch networks of three other banks and find employee attitudes and customer satisfaction account for about 10 per cent of the variance in branch sales performance. They find evidence for the role of customer satisfaction as a partial mediator in the relationship between employee attitudes and financial performance, but the authors recognise that the omission of employee turnover from their model could account for the weakness of their mediation results. Despite these issues surrounding the nature of the rela-tionship Gelade and Young identify, the magnitude of the link between employee commitment and performance is meaningful. They report that an increase of one standard deviation in commitment is associated with a 0.31 standard deviation increase in sales achievement. The standard deviation of sales achievement is 19.5 per cent of its mean in their sample, so a one standard deviation change in commitment is equivalent to a 6 per cent increase in average sales. They recognise that such a large change in employee attitudes would probably be impractical in aggregate, but their evidence is consistent with a meaningful link between employee commitment and business performance.

Bartel (2004) examines the role of HR practices on the performance of the retail branches of a Canadian bank using data from 160 branches, most of which provide data from two of the three years from 1995 through 1997. Bartel finds that 'performance and reward' is the most important correlate of branch-level performance in this environment, though again the model employed omits employee turnover from the specification.

Nalbantian and Szostak (2004) report on their work for Mercer within Fleet Bank in the USA. Fleet's business strategy was customer-focused and according to Nalbantian and Szostak (2004: 117) Fleet recognised in the late 1990s that the 'most pressing human resource issue' was high and rising employee turnover. Turnover had reached 25 per cent annually and exceeded 40 per cent in some areas of the business. Nalbantian and Szostak modelled turnover directly with an internal labour markets approach using personnel data. They identified several key drivers for Fleet and helped devise and implement policies to address these issues. They report that within 8 months employee turnover had fallen by 40 per cent among salaried employees and 25 per cent among hourly employees. Nalbantian and Szostak's presentation leaves much of the detail beyond the inspection of the reader, but it still provides useful anecdotal evidence of the value of turnover-focused HR practices in financial services.

This literature suggests that employee turnover is an important driver of business performance for companies like Nationwide, and this leads us naturally back to the academic literature on organisational commitment because of its established links to employee turnover (Meyer *et al.* 2002), and also because understanding the determinants of commitment in Nationwide provide evidence that could be used to manage the employee attitudes that feed performance.

Determinants of organisational commitment

In this section we investigate the determinants of organisational commitment with a particular focus on Nationwide. We use data from within Nationwide to build a model of employee commitment which draws on social identity theory and which examines the role of corporate social responsibility (CSR) as a driver of commitment. Examining the role of CSR in determining commitment is particularly relevant within Nationwide as the company has a well-documented focus on non-financial performance as evidenced by its stance on mutuality and the charitable activities of the Nationwide Foundation.

Allen and Meyer (1990) distinguish between three forms of organisational commitment: affective commitment which denotes 'an emotional attachment to, identification with, and involvement in the organisation', continuance commitment which reflects 'the perceived costs associated with leaving the organisation' and normative commitment 'which reflects a perceived obligation to remain in the organisation' (Allen and Meyer 1990: 21). Recent meta-analytic studies show that each of these forms of commitment is associated with labour turnover and intentions to leave the organisation but suggest that a stronger relationship exists between affective commitment and a range of desirable employee outcomes which include: attendance, job performance, stress, health and work–non-work conflict (Meyer *et al.* 2002). Earlier studies also suggest that affective commitment is driven by work experience rather than the recruitment or selection of employees, and highlight the importance of perceived organisational support in this process (Meyer *et al.* 2002). Indeed, later in this chapter we illustrate the effects of commitment on business performance in Nationwide through its effects on employee turnover and customer commitment, but for now we focus on the determinants of commitment itself.

Social identity theory proposes that individuals view themselves as members of social categories (Turner 1985; Tajfel and Turner 1986; Hogg and Abrams 1988; Ashforth and Mael 1989). Within social identity theory, an individual's view of themself, their 'self-concept', is influenced by their membership of social organisations, including the organisation for which they work (Ashforth and Mael 1989; Dutton *et al.* 1994). Individuals attempt to establish or enhance their positive self-concept through the comparison of their characteristics and the groups to which they belong with other individuals and groups (Turner 1985; Tajfel and Turner 1986; Ashforth and Mael 1989). Favourable comparisons lead to an enhanced self-concept, unfavourable ones to reduced self-esteem. Perceptions of an organisation's identity, the beliefs held by a member of an organisation concerning the 'distinctive, central, and enduring attributes of the organisation' (Dutton *et al.* 1994: 233–4), may influence the strength of identification of an individual with an organisation. Hence, social identity theory hypothesises that individuals are happiest when they associate themselves with organisations that have positive reputations because it is association with those organisations that will enhance their self-concept (Tajfel and Turner 1986; Maignan and Ferrell 2001). Social identity theory suggests that 'individuals tend to choose activities congruent with salient aspects of their identities, and they support the institutions embodying those identities' (Ashforth and Mael 1989: 25). At the same time the 'individual is argued to vicariously partake in the successes and status of the group: indeed positive and negative inter-group comparisons have been found to affect a member's self-esteem accordingly' (Ashforth and Mael 1989: 22). For example, to the extent that CSR contributes positively to the reputation of the organisation, employees are likely to more strongly identify with the organisation (Peterson 2004) and have higher levels of self-esteem (Ashforth and Mael 1989).

Identifying the determinants of commitment in Nationwide

Here we describe the data and approach used to identify the determinants of employee commitment to Nationwide. The data are derived from Nationwide's own employee attitude survey. The survey has been administered for over a decade but the data analysed here were gathered in the 2002 fiscal year. The survey was distributed by company mail to all employees, and employees were encouraged to complete them during work time. The surveys were collected by post-paid envelopes that were pre-addressed to an independent research company who processed the survey responses. After eliminating observations with missing data, the survey provides a usable response rate of 62 per cent across the entire organisation. In order to restrict the analysis to a relatively homogeneous group of employees the sample in this chapter is composed of the 4,712 usable responses obtained from those employees who work in the retail branch network.

Table 8.1 presents descriptive statistics for the variables used here. The sample used for the regression analysis is representative of the population of Nationwide's

Table 8.1 Descriptive statistics for the sample of 4,712 employee responses from the retail branch network

	Mean	Std. Deviation	VIF
Organisational commitment	4.33	0.75	
Procedural justice	2.90	0.76	3.25
External CSR	4.43	0.71	1.38
Training	2.94	0.90	2.56
Job satisfaction	2.96	0.59	3.80
Leadership	3.20	0.66	2.45
Women	0.82	0.38	1.23
Ethnic minority	0.06	0.25	1.05
Part time	0.31	0.46	1.36
Low-level customer facing staff	0.67	0.47	
High-level customer facing staff	0.27	0.45	1.45
Non-customer facing staff	0.06	0.23	1.25
Aged less than 24 years	0.13	0.34	1.81
Aged 24–29 years	0.19	0.39	1.39
Aged 30–40 years	0.40	0.49	
Aged 41–50 years	0.20	0.40	1.21
Aged 51 or more years	0.08	0.28	1.13
Tenure less than 1 year	0.08	0.27	1.85
Tenure of 1–2 years	0.07	0.26	1.76
Tenure of 2–3 years	0.08	0.27	
Tenure of 3–4 years	0.08	0.27	1.86
Tenure of 5 or more years	0.69	0.46	3.60

employees in retail banking. Women comprise 83 per cent of the sample, though this proportion declines dramatically as we move away from the flexible, part-time jobs available at the lower end of the firm's job hierarchy. We see that 68 per cent are employed on a full time basis. Approximately 69 per cent have been with Nationwide for at least five years; though there is clear evidence that turnover is greater at the lower levels of the job hierarchy.

Some of the variables constructed from the employee attitude survey are simple demographic controls, while others are constructs built from groups of attitudinal questions. We turn now to a description of our organisational commitment variable and move on to describe the independent variables used in the analysis.

Dependent variable

The measurement of organisational commitment forms the basis of an extensive literature (e.g. Kacmar *et al.* 1999; Balfour and Wechsler 1996; Mowday *et al.* 1979). In this study we measured affective commitment using a three-item scale which draws on the questions developed by Balfour and Wechsler (1996). In each case the questions were placed in the context of the surveyed company and were assessed in the context of a five-point Likert scale. Typical statements included 'I am proud to say I work for Nationwide' and 'I would recommend a job at Nationwide to friends'. The construct has a Cronbach's alpha of 0.85. This implies a high degree of internal consistency in the responses to the individual questions. We used confirmatory factor analysis to examine the proposed construct, and the construct loads onto a single factor explaining 78 per cent of the variance. Consistent with the approach suggested in Hair *et al.* (1998: 119–20), we used normalised summated scores for our constructs instead of factor scores in order to facilitate interpretation, generalisability and transferability.

Independent variables

Following Tepper and Taylor (2003) we estimated procedural justice using a six-item scale which draws on earlier work by Moorman (1991). Respondents used a five-point Likert scale (1 = 'disagree' to 5 = 'agree') to indicate their level of agreement with a set of statements which were framed within the context of the survey company. Typical statements included 'The decisions management makes about employees are usually fair' and 'I believe Nationwide offers equality of opportunity to all employees'. The proposed construct is one-dimensional and displays a Cronbach's alpha of 0.87. Employee perceptions of external corporate social responsibility were measured using a single-item construct (External CSR). Employees were asked to respond on a five-point Likert scale (1 = 'disagree' to 5 = 'agree') to the statement 'Nationwide is a socially responsible member of the community'. Employee perceptions of training and development were investigated using a three-item construct (Training). Respondents were asked to express a level of agreement with these three statements on a Likert scale (1 = 'disagree' to 5 = 'agree'). Typical statements included 'There are sufficient opportunities to develop and improve my skills in my current job'. The proposed construct is one-dimensional and displays a Cronbach's alpha of 0.81.

Control variables

Our analysis also includes a series of control variables. These are variables that have been shown to have important links with commitment in previous studies. Job satisfaction is measured using a nine-facet scale (pay, promotion, supervision, fringe benefits, contingent rewards, operating conditions, co-workers, nature of work, communication) adapted from the Job Satisfaction Survey (JSS) as detailed by Spector (1997). Our measure contains 31 questions and typical questions included 'how satisfied are you with your current opportunities?' and 'how satisfied are you with your basic pay?'. In each case respondents were asked to respond on a five-point Likert scale. The construct has good internal reliability with a Cronbach's alpha of 0.93. Leadership is measured using a seven-item construct. Typical statements included 'senior management is doing a good job at leading the business forward' and 'Nationwide is well led'. Respondents expressed their agreement with these statements on a five-point Likert scale, and confirmatory factor analysis reveals that these questions load onto a single factor with an alpha of 0.91. Gender is coded as a dummy variable which takes the value of one for women (Women), and is otherwise equal to zero. We also used a dummy variable which is equal to one for all respondents from ethnic minorities (Ethnic Minority). A further dummy variable was created which is equal to one for all respondents who are not full-time employees (Part Time). There are ten different job levels represented in the survey and we used dummy variables to isolate three ranges of this hierarchy. We use these variables to control the different levels of commitment associated with different levels of the firm hierarchy. Our approach is similar to the one taken by Gibson and Barron (2003), but our approach is slightly more general as it does not impose any linear restrictions on the way different hierarchical levels influence commitment. Age and tenure are described by sets of dummy variables (Age, Tenure).

Results

We use linear regression analysis to estimate the relationship between the independent variables described above with affective commitment, while controlling for the effects of other variables. This section reports the results. Descriptive statistics are provided in Table 8.2. The correlation coefficients between the independent variables are generally low and the variance inflation factors do not exceed four suggesting that multi-collinearity is unlikely to prove a significant problem (Hair *et al.* 1998).

All of the hypothesised correlations are significantly different from zero and have the anticipated sign. The significance levels are not surprising given the sample size at our disposal.[2] The high degree of power available in our statistical tests also means that we should focus at least as much on coefficient magnitudes instead of simply examining significance levels. Table 8.2 demonstrates a strong bivariate correlation between affective commitment and procedural justice (0.69), and a weaker relationship between affective commitment and employee perceptions of external CSR (0.49).

The relationship between affective commitment and corporate social responsibility is estimated using OLS and the results are shown in Table 8.3. This shows the relationship between the three dimensions of corporate social responsibility and affective commitment within a model which estimates the direct effects of gender and includes the other independent variables. Since significance levels are likely to be relatively high in models with large sample sizes we present the standardised regression coefficients so that both the significance of the explanatory variables and their contribution to the explanatory power of the model can be explored.[3]

The overall explanatory power of the regression model is satisfactory within the context of a cross-section study; R-squared is 0.61 and the F statistic is highly significant. The results suggest that CSR contributes significantly to organisational commitment and provide substantial support for the hypothesised relationships.[4]

The results in Table 8.3 provide substantial support for a significant relationship between CSR and affective commitment. All three measures of CSR are significant ($p<0.01$) and the results provide substantial support for the hypothesised relationships. As anticipated a positive and significant relationship ($p<0.01$) was found between employee perceptions of external CSR and affective commitment;

supporting the view that employee identification with external CSR results in increased levels of affective commitment. We expected a positive relationship between commitment and employee perceptions of procedural justice since employees may be expected to identify with fair processes and procedures within the organisation. This hypothesis is supported by the positive and significant relationship between procedural justice and affective commitment ($p<0.01$). Training is positively and significantly related to affective commitment providing support for the view that employees will identify with organisations which provide training. Although all three aspects of perceived CSR are positively related to affective commitment the strength of this relationship differs significantly between types of CSR. Procedural justice has the highest standardised coefficient and the difference between procedural justice and the coefficients for training and external CSR is highly significant ($p<0.01$).

Taken together these results emphasise the importance of fairness and equity within organisations; indeed only job satisfaction contributes more to affective commitment than procedural justice and this difference is not significant ($p>0.10$). Within the set of CSR variables external CSR has the second highest standardised coefficient and the difference between external CSR and training is highly significant ($p<0.01$). Although external CSR is both discretionary and has at best an indirect benefit to employees, through social identity, while training has both a direct benefit to employees through corporate investment in the employees human capital and an indirect benefit through employee identification with a socially responsible organisation, external CSR is seen to have a significantly larger impact on affective commitment. This result emphasises the importance of external CSR and the contribution of social identity to organisational commitment. No significant relationship was found between gender and levels of affective commitment providing additional support for earlier fully specified models which find no evidence of a significant direct relationship between gender and affective commitment (Aranya *et al.* 1986; Russ and McNeilly 1995), though previous work has identified important gender differences in the connections between CSR perceptions and affective commitment in Nationwide (Brammer *et al.* 2007).

The results for the control variables are broadly consistent with earlier studies. Affective commitment levels increase with age and there is no evidence that tenure with the firm is an important determinant of commitment, except for junior members of the company (length of service less than one year). Part-time employees are no more or less committed to the organisation than their full-time counterparts. Job satisfaction and level within the organisation are positively related to affective commitment.

Service–value chain in the retail branch network

The determinants of commitment identified in the last section are interesting, and they can be clearly linked to the business strategy adopted by Nationwide. This is good news for Nationwide if the general connections between affective commitment and business performance identified in the literature apply in Nationwide. We

Table 8.2 Correlation coefficients

	(1)	(2)	(3)	(4)	(5)	(6)	(7)	(8)	(9)	(10)
1 Organisational commitment	1									
2 Procedural justice	0.693 ***	1.000								
3 External CSR	0.489 ***	0.449 ***	1.000							
4 Training	0.606 ***	0.652 ***	0.334 ***	1.000						
5 Job satisfaction	0.689 ***	0.776 ***	0.426 ***	0.771 ***	1.000					
6 Leadership	0.670 ***	0.730 ***	0.498 ***	0.566 ***	0.671 ***	1.000				
7 Women	-0.044 ***	-0.054 ***	-0.003	-0.046 ***	-0.033 **	-0.008	1.000			
8 Ethnic minority	-0.087 ***	-0.095 ***	-0.059 ***	-0.040 ***	-0.083 ***	-0.067 ***	-0.025 *	1.000		
9 Part time	-0.053 ***	-0.056 ***	-0.006	-0.095 ***	-0.041 ***	-0.044 ***	0.282 ***	-0.038 ***	1.000	
10 Low-level customer facing staff	-0.214 ***	-0.168 ***	-0.111 ***	-0.168 ***	-0.143 ***	-0.145 ***	0.337 ***	0.059 ***	0.338 ***	1.000
11 High-level customer facing staff	0.177 ***	0.132 ***	0.090 ***	0.146 ***	0.115 ***	0.120 ***	-0.222 ***	-0.044 ***	-0.284 ***	-0.874 ***
12 Non-customer facing staff	0.094 ***	0.087 ***	0.052 ***	0.059 ***	0.070 ***	0.065 ***	-0.256 ***	-0.034 **	-0.141 ***	-0.350 ***
13 Aged less than 24 years	-0.023	0.028 *	-0.058 ***	0.016	-0.002	0.012	-0.058 ***	0.054 ***	-0.164 ***	0.190 ***

	(1)	(2)	(3)	(4)	(5)	(6)	(7)	(8)	(9)	(10)
14 Aged 24–29 years	-0.037 **	-0.013	-0.030 **	0.000	-0.018	-0.027 *	-0.069 ***	0.063 ***	-0.190 ***	-0.016
15 Aged 30–40	0.033 **	0.010	0.030 **	-0.014	0.017	0.020	0.069 ***	-0.008	0.190 ***	-0.120 ***
16 Aged 41–50 years	0.014	-0.019	0.028 *	-0.003	-0.006	-0.006	0.020	-0.056 ***	0.057 ***	-0.030 **
17 Aged 51 or more years	0.001	-0.006	0.020	0.010	0.008	-0.003	0.018	-0.060 ***	0.048 ***	0.046 ***
18 Tenure less than 1 year	0.059 ***	0.083 ***	0.000	0.077 ***	0.061 ***	0.066 ***	-0.052 ***	0.107 ***	-0.093 ***	0.168 ***
19 Tenure of 1–2 years	-0.038 ***	-0.004	-0.042 ***	-0.004	-0.014	-0.012	-0.003	0.076 ***	-0.086 ***	0.155 ***
20 Tenure of 2–3 years	-0.023	-0.001	-0.031 **	-0.004	-0.026 *	-0.020	-0.002	0.049 ***	-0.094 ***	0.114 ***
21 Tenure of 3–4 years	-0.049 ***	-0.047 ***	-0.008	-0.047 ***	-0.054 ***	-0.052 ***	-0.018	0.039 ***	-0.062 ***	0.016
22 Tenure of 5 or more years	0.030 **	-0.017	0.046 ***	-0.012	0.020	0.012	0.044 ***	-0.156 ***	0.193 ***	-0.260 ***

* = Correlation is significant at the 0.10 level
** = Correlation is significant at the 0.05 level
*** = Correlation is significant at the 0.01 level

Table 8.3 Standardised coefficients from ordinary least squares regressions. T-statistics in parentheses. Dependent variable in all models is organisational commitment.

	Model 1
	Full sample
Sample size	4712
R-squared	0.6130
Variables related to hypotheses	
Procedural justice	0.2055 ***
	(12.3970)
External CSR	0.1429 ***
	(13.2210)
Training	0.1174 ***
	(7.9670)
Control variables	
Constant	0.0000 ***
	(19.4320)
Job satisfaction	0.2121 ***
	(11.8280)
Leadership	0.2246 ***
	(15.5860)
Women	0.0070
	(0.6840)
Ethnic minority	−0.0176 *
	(1.8640)
Part-time	0.0140
	(1.3030)
High-level customer facing staff	0.0838 ***
	(7.5510)
Non-customer facing staff	0.0487 ***
	(4.7320)
Aged less than 24 years	−0.0225 *
	(1.8180)
Aged 24–29 years	−0.0227 **
	(2.0940)
Aged 41–50 years	0.0066
	(0.6490)
Aged 51 or more years	−0.0021
	(0.2160)
Tenure less than 1 year	0.0190
	(1.5230)
Tenure of 1–2 years	−0.0103
	(0.8400)
Tenure of 3–4 years	−0.0103
	(0.8230)
Tenure of 5 or more years	−0.0256
	(1.4650)

* = significant at 0.10 level
** = significant at 0.05 level
*** = significant at 0.01 level

quantify the links between commitment and business performance in Nationwide by building a service–profit chain model of the retail branch network.

The retail network is organised into 34 areas each of which include between 14 and 25 branches. The areas are headed up by an area manager who in turn reports to one of three retail heads of operation dependent upon location. We can disaggregate all data to the branch/employee level (as appropriate) with the exception of the employee attitude data. Confidentiality restrictions imposed in the implementation of the employee attitude survey mean that although we have every employee response at our disposal we can only aggregate these data at the area level. HR data (e.g. turnover and absence) are collected for each branch and aggregated to an area level to match the granularity of the employee survey data. We have identical survey data on employee attitudes within each area for the four years from 2003 through 2006. This represents the limit on the time dimension of our data. This data structure gives us almost twice the time series variation available in Bartel (2004) and provides a good opportunity to understand the impact of employee commitment on turnover, customer satisfaction and business performance.

We begin our task with a description of our empirical approach and some measurement issues before presenting our results.

Quantifying the links between people and performance

Quantifying links between people and performance in this setting requires an integrated modelling approach to be successful. This can be done in several ways but for the purposes of this chapter we implement a three equation seemingly unrelated regression model. This allows us to model some of the interactions between employee commitment, turnover, customer satisfaction and business performance. The three equations can be summarised as follows:

$$N_{i,t} = \alpha_0 + \alpha_1 C_{i,t} + \alpha_2 C_{i,t-1} + \alpha_3 Z_{i,t} + \alpha_4 D_t + \alpha_5 N_{i,t-1} + \varepsilon_{i,t} \tag{8.1}$$

$$S_{i,t} = \beta_0 + \beta_1 N_{i,t} + \beta_2 N_{i,t-1} + \beta_3 D_t + \beta_4 D_i + \beta_5 S_{i,t-1} + \xi_{i,t} \tag{8.2}$$

$$P_{i,t} = \gamma_0 + \gamma_1 N_{i,t} + \gamma_2 N_{i,t-1} + \gamma_3 S_{i,t} + \gamma_4 S_{i,t-1} + \gamma_5 D_t + \gamma_6 D_i + \gamma_7 H_{i,t}$$
$$+ \gamma_8 P_{i,t-1} + \psi_{i,t} \tag{8.3}$$

These three equations exploit the time–series dimension of the available data to understand the dynamic relationships between employee attitudes, turnover and customer satisfaction in order to estimate their combined effects on business performance. Commitment is measured as described in the fourth section, and we represent the average level of organisational commitment in area i at time t as $C_{i,t}$. Employee turnover ($N_{i,t}$) is gathered from the personnel records of Nationwide, and it averages just above 10 per cent over the period (s.d. = 3.2%). Equation 8.1 shows our assumption that this turnover is determined by current and past employee commitment, as well as a series of control variables ($Z_{i,t}$) capturing demographic information at the area level,[5] year dummy variables (D_t) and lagged turnover. We include the lagged value as a control for time-invariant variables which may have been omitted from the model. Equation 8.2 similarly shows our assumption that customer satisfaction ($S_{i,t}$) depends on current and lagged values of employee turnover, while Equation 8.3 examines the combined effects of satisfaction and turnover on business performance ($\beta_{i,t}$). Consistent with our earlier description of the importance of the mortgage portfolio to the business strategy of Nationwide, we define business performance as the value of mortgages made in an area as a percentage of the mortgage target for that area in a particular year. Given this measure of performance we also include controls in this equation for average house prices ($H_{i,t}$).

The use of lags in our work allows some investigation of dynamic processes which have been unexamined in previous work on the HR–performance link in financial services organisations but the limited number of areas means that we have only 102 observations. These observations are built up from branch-level information, and as such still provide meaningful estimates of the effects of commitment on turnover, satisfaction and performance but the small number of observations limits the power of our statistical tests.

Table 8.4 presents the results of our regression analysis. The table reports coefficient estimates and significance levels for relevant variables in each equation. In examining employee turnover we can see that organisational commitment is inversely related to employee turnover, but only after a one-year delay. This is consistent with existing evidence on the impact of organisational commitment on intention to quit and turnover (Meyer *et al.* 2002).

Customer satisfaction is modelled as a function of turnover, and we see that turnover has immediate negative effects on customer satisfaction. This could happen because it takes time for employees to be replaced thus raising pressure on remaining staff to meet customer needs, or it could be the result of the loss of skills and knowledge built up through continuing employment.

Business performance is measured as the percentage of the mortgage target achieved by each area, and this is modelled as a function of both turnover and customer satisfaction. We can see that both of these items influence business performance in the predicted directions. We see a negative effect of employee turnover on business performance. This may be because of replacement costs, or again this may be the result of the loss of skills and knowledge built up through employment. Customer satisfaction has an immediate impact on business performance

These relationships are not only significant, but they are also managerially meaningful. To illustrate this we calculated the ultimate impact of a one standard deviation increase in organisational commitment on business performance. This represents a 4.2 per cent increase in commitment. This is a reasonable benchmark as in the data at our disposal, changes in excess of this magnitude occur at the area level 18.6 per cent of the time and such changes must be more likely at the branch level. Our model suggests that a 4.2 per cent increase in organisational commitment would lead to a fall in employee turnover of 1.30 points (a decline

Table 8.4 Output from three equations seemingly unrelated regression model. Data from 34 areas of Nationwide Building Society from 2003 to 2006. Construction of lags results in 102 useful observations from 2004 to 2006.

Dependent variable:	Employee turnover	Coefficient
	Average organisational commitment	−0.023
	Lagged average employee commitment	−9.276**
	Intercept	41.008**
	Lagged dependent variable	0.175*
	Employee demographics	Yes
	Year fixed effects	Yes
	R-squared	0.381
Dependent variable:	Customer satisfaction (3-items)	
	Employee turnover	−0.499**
	Lagged employee turnover	0.042
	Intercept	101.541**
	Lagged dependent variable	−0.177*
	Year fixed effects	Yes
	Area fixed effects	Yes
	R-squared	0.703
Dependent variable:	Mortgage completions vs. target	
	Employee turnover	0.206
	Lagged employee turnover	−0.383*
	Customer satisfaction	1.247**
	Lagged customer satisfaction	−0.725
	Intercept	27.911
	Percent change in house prices	0.691**
	Lagged dependent variable	0.217**
	Year fixed effects	Yes
	Area fixed effects	Yes
	R-squared	0.956

* = significant at the 95% level
** = significant at the 99% level

of 12.8 per cent). This change spurs a small, but significant, change in customer satisfaction (0.8 per cent) and a modest percentage change in mortgage performance (1.2 per cent).

These changes are small compared to the 6 per cent change in business performance associated with a one standard deviation improvement in commitment identified in Gelade and Young (2005), but we believe this is a reflection on the high level of commitment already achieved by Nationwide. In essence, we suspect there are diminishing returns to employee commitment. The relatively high levels of commitment in Nationwide, coupled with its associated high staff retention (average tenure is approximately 10 years), mean that Nationwide has already moved well along the curve. To assess this claim we have conducted simple polynomial tests for non-linearity and we can reject the null hypothesis of linearity at the 99 per cent level in all three equations.[6]

The resulting picture is one in which a change in commitment at time t generates changes in turnover and satisfaction at time $t + 1$. The change in customer satisfaction has an impact on business performance at $t + 1$, and the effect of turnover on business performance is felt at $t + 2$.

Conclusion

The results presented in this chapter apply the work of preceding chapters in the context of a particular organisation. Nationwide Building Society is a high values organisation, and its business model is set accordingly. The retail branch network is governed by a single set of HR practices and it provides an excellent environment in which to analyse the effects of HR practice using quantitative methods. This is because the various business units can be compared to each other, and any variations in employee attitudes that can be linked to HR can be attributed to the way this set of practices are implemented.

The history and current operations of Nationwide lead us to select mortgage performance as our key benchmark and the literature suggests that employee tenure is particularly important for the delivery of performance in financial services. The determinants of commitment in Nationwide are: job satisfaction, internal and external corporate social responsibility, and leadership. Commitment can then be seen to flow through employee turnover and customer service through to mortgage performance.

These relationships take time to manifest. A change in employee commitment this year will change customer satisfaction and turnover figures in the following year and continue to influence business performance a year after that. The lag structure we have identified is no doubt influenced by the short duration of our panel, but we believe it serves to illustrate the existence of a link between employee attitudes and business performance in Nationwide, as well as to illustrate that these relationships take time to work themselves through. Further work is warranted to expand on these results.

The non-linearity in the relationships we identify suggests that the existing strengths associated with the high-commitment position occupied by Nationwide create risks associated with any reductions in commitment. Put differently: the high-commitment position of Nationwide does create value but any gains from further improvements in commitment are probably small compared with the losses that would be expected were Nationwide to experience decreases in affective commitment.

The results for Nationwide are specific to Nationwide and they should not be regarded as directly applicable in all circumstances. Other companies in other industries with different business strategies may well find that other things matter. Still, this chapter illustrates how internal data can be used in conjunction with academic theory to move beyond the general evidence of a link between HR and performance and move towards the generation of a specific evidence base for the links between HR and performance in a particular context.

9 Implications for the development of theory and practice

This book has sought to draw on recent research and our own empirical data to investigate the links between HR practices and organisational performance. We began by reviewing the previous work in the field and then proposing our analytical model. In the second section we moved on to developing the model by examining culture, HR practices, the roles of line managers and employee attitudes. The third section then applied this model to help us understand the links between HR practices and performance for different occupations and in the professional knowledge worker and financial services sectors. Finally, in this section we consider the conclusions and implications of our findings. This chapter has three aims: (a) to provide a brief summary of the principal findings, (b) to consider the implications for future research and (c) to discuss the implications of our findings for practitioners.

Summary of main findings

We summarise our main findings by examining the strengths and weaknesses of previous research, the exposition of the model and then the application of the model.

Strengths and weaknesses of previous research

In Chapter 1 we noted that there has been extensive research in the field but the results in many ways are disappointing (Boselie *et al.* 2005; Lepak *et al.* 2006; Wall and Wood 2005; Wright *et al.* 2005). Much of the research has focused on very detailed aspects of the precise links between HR and organisational perform-ance. Although this approach has increased the validity and reliability of the

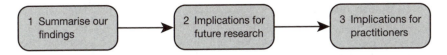

Figure 9.1 Structure of the chapter

research it has often produced results which are difficult to interpret especially for the practitioner. In some ways the search for methodological purity has robbed the research of wider accessibility.

The main weaknesses highlighted in the previous research in Chapter 1 were: the failure to distinguish between intended and experienced practices, the lack of an employee voice and the failure to take account of the wider context within which these practices took place. Moreover, there were problems with actually measuring performance, the need to account for changes over time and to consider the needs of different groups of employees. Underlying all this was the failure to develop adequate theory in the field – a problem first noted by Guest in 1997. We argued that until attention was given to this aspect of the research it would be difficult to make progress.

We subsequently followed what has been referred to as the 'analytical HRM' approach (Boxall *et al.* 2007b) and developed the Bath HR causal chain model drawing on the research of others in the field especially Appelbaum *et al.* (2000), Wright and Snell (1998) and Wright and Nishii (2004). This model has formed the framework for the whole book.

HR causal chain model

The second section devoted four chapters to an exposition of this model. We began by drawing attention to the need to study the organisational culture and values within which the HR practices exist. We used examples of Selfridges and Jaguar to examine the ways in which the values of an organisation can have a powerful influence on the impact of HR practices on employee attitudes and behaviour. In particular, we drew attention to the importance of a pervasive set of values which we referred to as the 'Big Idea'. These values were embedded in the organisation, connected to other activities such as HR practices, robust and enduring, widely shared and able to be measured and managed. We were able to show that organisational commitment was higher in organisations which were able to demonstrate the presence of a 'Big Idea'.

The second stage of the model was to consider the importance of the difference between intended and experienced HR practices. We began our discussion of this in Chapter 3 by summarising the research around the so-called 'best fit' and 'best practice' debates and concluded that much of this attention was actually misplaced. We argued that it was important not only to look at the intended practices, as documented for example in written statements, but also the way the practices were implemented and experienced by employees.

This led us to discuss the role of line managers in much more detail in Chapter 4 and in particular their role in bringing practices to life. We considered four aspects of their role: (a) implementation of practices which considered whether the practices were actually put into operation; (b) the actual enactment of practices especially the extent to which they did or did not follow the written practice statement of HR practices and the level of commitment and enthusiasm which they exhibited; (c) the leadership role which they demonstrated often comprising a whole series of small actions such as showing empathy for employees' personal circumstances which contributed to a strong interpersonal relationship; and (d) the controlling aspect of this leadership role which referred to the degree to which line managers engaged in close personal supervision or allowed employees to work more independently. We drew on practical examples from Selfridges to illustrate the latitude and freedom that line managers had when implementing practices and the impact these had on employee attitudes and behaviour.

The final stage of our exposition was in Chapter 5 which examined the impact of HR practices on employee attitudes and behaviour. In particular we looked in more detail at the influences on employees' motivation to exert discretionary effort. We paid particular attention to the implications of social exchange theory for the delivery on the psychological contract. We particularly highlighted employee attitudes reflecting relationships between employees and their organisations (organisational commitment and job satisfaction), employees and their leaders (e.g. LMX and POS), and employees and their co-workers (e.g. TMX and TMS). We drew on a detailed case from Tesco to show how the same HR practices could be implemented in different ways in different locations with traceable impacts on organisational performance.

Having completed the exposition of the model we then applied this to three specific contexts.

Applications of the model

The following three chapters made up the third section and allowed us to demonstrate the insights which the model could give by looking at the links between HR practices and performance for different occupational groups, professional knowledge workers and the financial services sector.

The occupational analysis carried out in Chapter 6 provided a number of valuable results relating to the claims made for the links between HR practices and performance. We found that there were some aspects of HR practices and job design which were associated with the commitment of employees in virtually all occupational groups – satisfaction with the work itself, satisfaction with the sense of achievement and social support from managers. We failed to find evidence to support the influence of practices such as career opportunities, training and job involvement. This provided support for the HR causal chain model, especially the need to distinguish between intended and experienced HR practices implemented by line managers. However, we found that there were also some practices which did not affect the commitment of all groups. For instance, the commitment of sales employees was not associated with support from line managers perhaps because of their independent working arrangements. However, there was a link between commitment and control over working time and job security. The lack of a link between pay satisfaction and commitment for these employees was especially interesting. There was a contrast here with professional workers whose commitment was associated with the ability to use their initiative and their control over their working hours. These findings have important implications for theoretical models of strategic HR and for practitioners which we discuss below.

Chapter 7 then looked at the links between HR practices and the commitment of one particular group, professional knowledge workers, in much more detail. After establishing the distinctive characteristics of these employees and their organisations the chapter examined the specific HR challenges which are faced. In particular, we found that the HR practices had to manage a series of potentially conflicting pulls on the identity of these professional knowledge workers from the organisation, the team, their clients and their profession.

The last chapter in this section, Chapter 8, looked at the links between HR practices and performance in Nationwide Building Society. We illustrated the connection between people and performance beginning with the initial values of the organisation (e.g. putting members first), looking at the way employee experiences of HR practices generated commitment to the organisation, and ultimately how employee commitment generated financial performance through its effects on employee turnover and customer satisfaction.

Having summarised our findings we can now consider their implications for theory and for practice.

Implications for theory and for future research

Reflecting on the last ten years of studies into the links between HR practices and organisational performance Boxall *et al.* (2007b: 2) noted that there are major challenges to be faced for both theory and practice. Indeed, Becker and Huselid (2006: 921) suggest that even though progress had been made, research in the field is at a 'crossroads'. This echoes the comments discussed in Chapter 1 regarding the theoretical weaknesses in the area and the links between this and the particular statistically based methodologies which have been adopted.

However, Boxall *et al.* (2007b: 2) believe that if these challenges can be overcome 'HRM is poised to assume a greater role in the theory of organisational effectiveness'. We believe that theoretical development in the field is needed before this contribution can be realised.

Perhaps the immediate implication for theory is the very definition of HRM itself (Purcell and Kinnie 2007). Boxall *et al.* (2007b: 7) have pointed to the dangers of adopting a very specific definition. 'The narrowness of perceiving HRM as solely what HR departments do (where they exist) or of perceiving HRM as only about one style of people management are enemies of the subject's relevance and intellectual vigour.'

In many ways the definition of HRM and its principal concerns reflect the types of organisations which exist at the time. Lepak and Snell (2007: 211) suggest that HRM has had to shift from an emphasis on managing jobs which reflected the maturation of the profession during large-scale manufacturing to one more concerned with the management of people and their knowledge. To put it another way, the HR activity has proved to be very adaptive to the organisational contingencies which are encountered (Tyson 1987). We argue that the definition of HRM needs to be modified to take account of the changing organisations which it is seeking to analyse. We need to consider the changes in the nature of environments, organisations, jobs and people if we are to improve our understanding of how HR contributes to the performance of the business.

We believe our clearest contribution is that we have placed the management of people (both line managers and workers) at the centre of our analysis. This effectively means moving away from the organisation as a unit of analysis, with all its attendant problems of making the link with performance, to the level of the employee and team. This change is necessary because organisations are increasingly relying on the knowledge and skill of their employees. These employees are frequently organised into teams of some kind and they often work across the boundaries of the organisations which employ them.

We argue that HRM has to develop an analytical framework which takes account of the kinds of findings we have identified. Once we place the management of people at the centre of our analysis there are three further implications which flow from this (as summarised in Table 9.1):

1   the focus on HR practices as experienced by employees draws attention to the role played by line managers;
2   the diversity of skills and knowledge within organisations means we must analyse the heterogeneity of HR practices which are needed to cater for these different groups;
3   if we focus on the employee we quickly realise that they have valuable relationships both inside and outside the organisation.

Table 9.1 Implications for future research and for practice

Theme		Implications for research	Implications for practitioners
Implementation of strategy is key	Implementation of strategy and practices by line managers is key leading to a gap between intended and experienced practices	Managers' accounts alone cannot be relied upon: need to collect data from employees and to study the role of line managers	Key role for line managers – how to close the intended-experienced practice gap
Heterogeneity of HR practices	Knowledge-based perspective highlights the heterogeneous groups within the organisation which need to be managed in different ways	Heterogeneity of HR practices needed within the organisation to develop various kinds of knowledge and skill	How to manage the needs of different groups within the organisation: dilemma between generic and dedicated HR practices
Cross-boundary HRM	Organisations operate outside the boundaries of the firm and interact with network members	Need to examine network-based constraints on strategic HR choice and the extension of HR practices outside the organisation	Managing strategic tensions within the network, balancing the interests of network members and of employees inside the organisation

These three themes are closely linked. Recent research has pointed to the importance of the implementation of strategy as a source of competitive advantage. This draws attention to the role of the line manager and creates the opportunities for the difference between intended and experienced practices. In most organisations this implementation of strategy relies heavily on the skills and knowledge of employees. Not all employees will have the same skills and knowledge; some will be central to the success of the firm whereas others will be more peripheral. However, the success of organisations is likely to depend increasingly on the ability to coordinate the efforts of these different sets of knowledge and skills. These variations in knowledge and skill sets are likely to be managed by heterogeneous rather than consistent HR practices. The knowledge and skills of workers are important both inside and outside the boundaries of the firm. This will involve a range of activities with different members of networks including clients, suppliers, temporary agencies, free-lancers and subcontractors. Thus we need to look outside the boundaries of the firm if we are to understand the influences of and the influences on the network members.

Role of line managers and the differences between intended and experienced HR practices

The role of line managers is central to the HR causal chain model. Their role, discussed extensively in Chapter 4, is increasingly to implement and 'bring to life' the HR practices. The key point here is that HR is not just the concern of specialists but also of line managers. This emphasis on implementation reflects recent changes within the strategy literature. As Barney (2001: 54) has noted 'the ability to implement strategies is, by itself, a resource that can be a source of competitive advantage'. Indeed, Becker and Huselid (2006: 903) see 'effective strategy implementation as the key mediating variable between HR architecture and firm performance'. Thus, rather than simply assuming that once designed HR practices are implemented as intended, this focus sees implementation as problematic (Wright and Snell 1998; Wright and Boswell 2002).

The actions of the line manager may introduce a potential for a gap between the intended and experienced practices. They may choose, for example, not to implement a particular practice as intended because they do not know about the practice or they disagree with it. They may then implement the practice in their own way or not implement it at all. The actual experience of employees of that practice may well differ from the experience intended by the designer of that practice and the implementer of that practice. For example the problem solving approach to performance appraisal intended by the designer may be experienced in quite a different way because of an authoritarian approach adopted by the line manager.

The emphasis on implementation and the role of the line manager has a number of important implications for future research. This means we can no longer rely on the accounts of, usually senior, managers of HR practices. Their version of events is likely to convey an optimistic view of what is intended rather than what is actually experienced. In addition to this we need to capture the views of employees, especially their perceptions of the number of HR practices and their actual experience of these practices. Indeed, it is increasingly being recognised that employees play a mediating role between HRM and organisational performance (Bowen and Ostroff 2004; Wright *et al.* 2005). This, of course, presents a formidable, but not insurmountable, methodological challenge. Clinton and Guest (2007) note some of these problems: long service employees may have limited knowledge of some contemporary practices (for example selection); their attitudes may have been affected, either positively or negatively, by the sheer act of being selected to respond; and there may be low inter-rater reliability which reflects actually differences in the ways various groups of employees are managed within the firm.

Recent research, however, has begun to collect data from employees. Wright *et al.* (2003, 2005) have drawn data from employees at the business unit level in a single organisation and they found (in the later study) that employee reports of HR practices were 'correlated strongly, positively and most significantly with the operational and financial measures observed later' (Wright *et al.* 2005: 432). Clinton and Guest (2007) found that although there was a poor correlation between managers' accounts of the number of HR practices and performance there was a better correlation between performance and employee accounts of the number of HR practices. The Tesco case in Chapter 5 provides some illustrations of this.

Second, we need to study the role of the line manager more carefully in the implementation of these practices. In particular we need to understand how and why they implement HR practices. Part of the answer to this may well lie in the way these line managers themselves are managed.

The focus on the role of line managers in implementing HR practices is linked to our second theme which is the heterogeneity of HR practices which we discussed in Chapter 6. The implementation of HR practices takes place at the level of the individual employee and the work group. These employees and work groups typically operate within business processes which are usually below the level of the organisation. Indeed, Becker and Huselid (2006: 903) argue that these 'business processes are a source, perhaps *the* source, of the value customers derive from a firm's products and services'. This follows Porter's argument (1996: 62) that 'strategic positioning means performing different activities from rivals or performing similar activities in different ways'.

These business processes may be based within departments (e.g. a finance department), project teams (for instance a team set up to devise a new job evaluation scheme) or account teams working for a particular external client. The outputs of these business processes are usually coordinated together at the organisational level. Thus, most people experience the organisation from the team or workgroup perspective. This, in turn, places importance on the contribution of different groups of employees within the organisation (Becker and Huselid 2006: 905).

Heterogeneity in HR strategy: adopting a knowledge-based perspective on HR

These different groups of people contribute to the output of the organisation based on their knowledge and skills (Grant 1996; Child and McGrath 2001). The emphasis therefore is increasingly on converting this human capital into products and services which have value in the marketplace – which we have referred to as intellectual capital. In particular, greater emphasis is placed on tacit rather than explicit knowledge which cannot be codified or standardised. This may involve exploiting existing knowledge or exploring new knowledge through creativity and innovation or a combination of the two. Lepak and Snell (2007: 223) have argued 'what differentiates successful firms from others may very well be how companies manage knowledge flows; that is how companies effectively leverage, integrate and create knowledge among individuals within and across employment modes'. This knowledge is likely to be increasingly specialist and heterogeneous. Successful organisations are likely to be those who can bring together quite different groups of employees to focus on a common task, for example, in a hospital where consultants, doctors, nurses, specialists and administrative staff work together to provide patient care.

If the key resource of organisations is knowledge and the most vital knowledge is tacit knowledge then it follows that the focus needs to be on managing the people who hold this knowledge. In particular, this poses questions about what are the appropriate HR practices for managing this human capital and especially the conversion of this human capital into intellectual capital (Kinnie *et al.* 2006). We need to consider what are the appropriate practices for managing both the stocks and flows of knowledge, for example, how does HR stimulate the sharing of knowledge internally and externally. Kang *et al.* (2007) identify the cooperative and entrepreneurial archetypes and the effective HR practices which are associated with these.

We can recall from our discussion in Chapter 6 that the HR architecture model (Lepak and Snell 1999) distinguishes between strategic value determined by the skill sets that employees have which enable the organisation to enact its strategies and the uniqueness which is the extent to which the knowledge and skills are firm specific. This model is essentially distinguishing between employees based on their knowledge and skills (Lepak and Snell 2007: 213).

Lepak and Snell (1999: 32) have noted that the strategic HRM literature has tended to emphasise the consistency of HR practices within the organisation. Moreover, failing to recognise the diversity that exists within firms 'results in a flawed analysis and interpretation of existing results'. Similarly, Becker and Huselid (2006: 904) note that 'not all employees, or employee skills, are inherently strategic, and employees with different roles in the value creation process ought to be managed differently'.

This means that a differentiated or heterogeneous approach to HR practices will be needed to meet the demands of different groups. For example, Rubery *et al.* (2004: 1200) argue that employees who have valuable and unique skills will be managed by high commitment practices following a resource-based view of strategy. Further support for this is provided by our findings in Chapter 6 where we saw that the commitment of different occupational groups was affected by different HR practices.

This has profound implications for future research because it means that we cannot assume that all employees will be managed in the same way within the firm. The HR practices applied, for example, to the largest occupational group may not be appropriate for other groups. Indeed, the success of an organisation may be dependent on its ability to manage and coordinate the contributions of different groups of employees. The research task of capturing the heterogeneity of HR practices within a firm is not an easy one. Wright and Boswell (2002: 265) also suggest shifting the unit of analysis to one which focuses on core or key groups within the organisation. The success of a firm may be influenced by its ability to tailor its HR practices to the needs of different groups of employees (Becker and Huselid 2006: 905).

This suggests ways in which research in this area might be developed. Our analysis looks at large employee groupings which are homogenous only in the broadest sense. More progress could be made if greater precision is introduced by looking at narrowly defined occupational groupings. These could be based on criteria derived from the human capital theory (Becker 1964) which might allow a series of 'occupational bundles' of HR practices to be identified. A form of this occupational bundling or configuration has already been noted by Purcell (1999) in the context of core and peripheral employees. Further progress might be made if the concept of HR architecture (Lepak and Snell 1999, 2007) discussed earlier is developed solely for internal groups of employees again based on the extent of their firm-specific knowledge and their value to the organisation (Gonzalez and Tacorante 2004).

Our advocacy of a knowledge-based perspective on HRM also provides a link to our final theme of the importance of cross-boundary working.

Cross-boundary human resource management

In many contemporary organisations knowledge-based working extends beyond the boundary of the organisation. As we have seen in Chapter 7, knowledge intensive organisations interact extensively with members of often extensive networks including clients, suppliers, partners and regulators. This has major consequences for the study of HRM as Marchington *et al.* (2005: 2) have argued, 'in the context of blurred boundaries and fragmented activities, the established, textbook, ideas of an organisation as a discrete entity and of the employment relationship as a clear cut contract for services becomes difficult to sustain'. In practice it is often unclear where one organisation ends and another begins, and staff are placed in multiple employment relationships where obligations as well as allegiances are negotiable rather than stable. Indeed, as Child and McGrath (2001: 1144) have noted the 'unfettered', without boundaries organisation 'brings us to one of the great unknowns with scholars' experiments with new forms: namely their effects on the employment relationship'.

This poses a challenge to existing assumptions that explanations for the links between HR practices and performance lie within the boundaries of the organisation. The emergence of the networked organisation and subcontracting is included in the HR architecture model (Lepak and Snell 1999). However, as Rubery *et al.* (2004: 1200) argue 'the focus on a stable protected core has been recognised as providing a rather static picture of interactions between organisations and their external environments' (Cappelli 1995; Ackroyd and Proctor 1998).

The existing models of analysis need to be developed for two reasons. First, they focus on managing employees who have valuable and unique skills using high commitment management leading to the development of an internal labour market. However, as Lepak and Snell, (2007: 211) have argued, 'the knowledge that companies rely on for competitive success not only resides in the minds of their employees but also in the minds of contractors, consultants and other external workers with whom they collaborate'. Second, the study of HR strategy has tended to assume that managers have freedom to choose, while we argue that there are important constraints in the network which must be considered.

As we have discussed in Chapter 7, the distinctive characteristics of professional service firms, especially their reliance on knowledge-based networks, present challenges to the existing ways of thinking about HRM. Current models of strategic HRM do not provide a sufficient basis for analysing the organisational and network characteristics which we have observed although there has been some research into aspects of the practices which we have discussed here. Rubery *et al.* (2004: 1220) believe there is a danger of networks 'being the black holes of HR analysis' and they suggest

> rather than treating such organisations as a special case we need to move towards a more general framework where internal and external influences on the management of HR are seen as mutually constituted, iterative and interactive. It is the interplay between these factors in a dynamic context that provide the basis for analysing HR policy in permeable organisations.

There are therefore two important aspects of cross-boundary HRM which need to be considered. First, we need to recognise that the success of many firms depends on a whole series of people, not all of whom are employees, a group sometimes referred to as the 'non-employed workforce' (Kersley *et al.* 2006: 103). Various groups of workers who are not employees can have a significant impact on the performance of the organisation including insourced and outsourced agency workers, subcontractors, freelance workers and partners. Although there has been some discussion of the issues surrounding the management of workers who are not employed, this has tended to be restricted to non-core employees such as IT subcontracting (Grimshaw and Miozzo 2006) and clerical agency staff (Purcell *et al.* 2004b). We also need to consider human capital which has high value and uniqueness but is not, for a variety of reasons, directly employed.

This existence of valuable human capital at the network level outside the boundaries of the firm throws up definitive tension for HR managers. They know that there are staff who are vital to the success of their business but whom they do not employ and hence have a limited ability to influence. We need to examine what kinds of HR practices are needed to create and develop this valuable external human capital (Swart *et al.* 2007; Kinnie *et al.* 2006). Therefore we need to adopt a much broader view of HRM – one that exists beyond the boundaries of the firm. We refer to these as 'inside out' HR practices.

Second, we need to pay much more attention to the network of constraints within which managers operate. Managers of HR are often strongly influenced by the actions of a series of outside parties – clients, suppliers of both goods and services, customers, partners and consultants (Swart and Kinnie 2003; Kinnie *et al.* 2006). These actions have both a direct and indirect influence on their HR strategy and structure and can be referred to as 'outside-in' influences. This throws up a second tension caused by these network characteristics. HR managers do not have complete freedom to manage their employees because they are influenced by the wishes of other important external bodies such as clients.

The discussion of these external influences on HR practices has been almost completely in the manufacturing sector and concerned with the relations between customers or clients and their suppliers (Sako 1992; Sinclair *et al.* 1996; Rainnie 1989; Kinnie *et al.* 1999; Dyer and Nobeoka 2000; Lamming 1993). Studies which have looked at the influence of clients (Rubery *et al.* 2002, 2004; Marchington *et al.* 2005; Kinnie *et al.* 2006) on internal HR practices in these kinds of networks have tended to examine the relatively direct interventions in recruitment and selection, and pay and performance management systems. Our discussion in Chapter 7 drew attention to the more subtle, intricate and finely grained influences concerning small differences between the high-level skills of professional staff. Whereas in a call centre, for example, a client may simply wish to be assured that the employees working on their account have the necessary customer service skills, the matching process in PSFs is much more delicate and precise. Here clients are looking for employees who can develop skills and knowledge which are finely tuned to their specific needs. They also want to ensure that their ways of working are compatible because of the importance placed on developing close interdependent relationships. The network structures especially the network relationships and dynamics are therefore much more client specific in PSFs compared with less knowledge-intensive firms.

Implications for practice

As we noted in the introduction to this book, HRM has been leading something of a 'double life'. While research has been seeking to demonstrate the vital contribution of HR to performance, HR practitioners have found they are increasingly under pressure to justify their positions. Caldwell (2003: 985) has noted that the HR function is faced by a series of pressures: the devolution of authority to strategic business units makes it more difficult to adopt a strategic approach; the HR activity itself is fragmented into a series of specialist activities such as recruitment, learning and reward; parts of the HR activity itself are faced with being outsourced, for example, training or recruitment of senior staff; line managers may take on more responsibilities which were formerly entrusted to HR itself, for example, the coaching of staff; and certain parts of the HR activity, for example the allocation of employee benefits, may be managed by the employees themselves using an online facility.

These changes have produced some intensive debates about the nature of HRM and its possible future developments among academics (Losey *et al.* 2005) and practitioners (CIPD 2007b). Much of this discussion and debate has been formed around typologies of the HR role (Tyson 1987; Schuler 1990; Storey 1992; Ulrich 1997). We do not believe that it is valuable to pursue this approach since it tends to move towards further refinement of existing models (Ulrich and Brockbank 2005) and does not actually provide insights into the key HR issues or contribute towards analytical HRM. We believe greater insights are provided if we place the employee at the centre of the analysis and examine the dilemmas and tensions which HR has to manage within complex organisations. Indeed, Boxall *et al.* (2007b: 63) have argued that 'it is useful to understand the goals of HRM as fundamentally about the management of strategic tensions'. The management of tensions has long been discussed within the HRM field (Legge 1978; Guest and King 2004) and we believe it provides key insights into the challenges facing HRM. We consider the tensions which are derived from the three main themes which we have identified.

Role of line managers: closing the intended–experienced HR practice gap

The importance attached to the line manager role and the associated gap between intended and experienced practices has a whole series of practical implications. First, although it is still important to pay close attention to the design of practices it is equally important to consider how these practices are actually implemented and experienced by employees. As Lepak *et al.* (2006: 919) have noted, 'designing an HR system is not the problem. The challenge is motivating line managers to implement these systems.' This points to the importance for managers of collecting data directly from employees, for example via surveys, in order to gain a more accurate, first-hand picture of what is actually happening. Are their carefully designed HR practices being implemented as intended?

Second, this may lead to the identification of a gap between the intended and experienced practices. This then prompts further attempts to try to understand why this gap exists. Is it, for example, because the line managers do not know what practices they are supposed to follow or that they lack the skills or willingness to implement them in the way that is intended? This in turn poses further questions about the extent of the knowledge and skills of line managers and their attitudes towards these practices.

Third, this then points to particular actions needed which might close the intended–experienced gap. This might involve training schemes for line managers to improve their knowledge of the relevant practices and their skill in implementing them. In addition, this might also involve training for the managers of the line managers.

Fourth, there are various implications for the role of the HR specialists. The changes we have discussed imply a modified role for specialists where they are principally involved in designing practices which are effective and appropriate. Their task is to support and encourage the line managers to implement the HR practices in the way which was intended.

Knowledge-based perspective and HR strategy heterogeneity

We have discussed the importance of human capital and especially the knowledge and skills of that capital in creating competitive advantage. Indeed, it has been argued (Quinn 1992) that knowledge is an important source of advantage for all organisations. This implies that managers need to adopt a knowledge-based HR strategy (Lepak and Snell 2007). This requires managers to analyse their organisations not in terms of the number of employees they have in particular departments and levels but to focus on the knowledge of their staff and how this knowledge flows through the organisation. In practice this involves identifying the types of knowledge that they need inside and outside the organisation in order to be successful and in particular highlight gaps and inadequacies which need to be addressed. Some organisations may rely heavily on stimulating creativity whereas others may rely more on accessing and using existing knowledge. Maister (2003: 21–30) and Lowendahl (2005: 118–50), for example, have drawn attention to the varying HR practices which will be needed for knowledge intensive firms that trade mostly on their expertise, their experience and their efficiency. The next step is to consider what role HR practices might play in stimulating the desired stocks and flows of knowledge and the associated attitudes and behaviours (Kinnie *et al.* 2006; Lepak and Snell 2007). This pays particular attention to the ways various HR practices stimulate and stymie the flow of knowledge within the organisation. For example, exhortations to share knowledge among staff may be strongly counteracted by performance management systems which do not reward this behaviour or even provide a disincentive to share knowledge because they are heavily based on individual performance. Similarly, organisations which genuinely want to share knowledge will include evidence of this as part of their selection processes.

This typological approach is too simple for many organisations in practice because, as we have discussed, many organisations will employ different groups of staff whose outputs need to be coordinated. Indeed, we can recall that the WERS 2004 survey found that the average workplace had four different occupational groups (Kersley *et al.* 2006: 23). Moreover, organisations may change over time, for example from being highly creative to a re-user of knowledge, so that the demands placed upon them will also change. This emphasis on the knowledge and skill of employees reveals that not all employees contribute in the same way to the performance of the organisation. This in turn prompts the question as to how these different groups should be managed.

Our discussion in Chapter 6 revealed that that there will be some HR practices which are associated with increasing the organisational commitment of all employees, while there are others which are linked only to particular groups. HR practices which increase the commitment of one group of employees within the organisation, for instance professionals' scope to use their initiative, will not have the same impact on sales workers. This points to the need for HR managers to identify the HR practices which are associated with increasing the commitment of particular groups of employees. In essence the task is to identify the generic and dedicated triggers of organisational commitment (Becker and Huselid 2006). Some firms may choose not to invest in certain groups of employees if they believe they are not central to the organisation and can be easily replaced (Lepak and Snell. 2002). However, this is a controversial area which has been widely debated in work on labour market segmentation and the flexible firm. The tailoring of HR policy based on these criteria has profound implications for HR strategy and policy.

This raises concerns about fairness of treatment across all groups of employees. HR managers are often under pressure to promote consistency of treatment of employees because of legal and equity concerns. However, our research shows that the commitment of different groups is linked to different HR practices. One possible solution is to adopt a two-tier approach to HR strategy as we discussed in Chapter 6. A minimum set of practices are applied to all employees which adhere to legal requirements and the standards of the employer. In addition to this the employer can develop a series of HR practices which are dedicated to the needs of particular employee groups.

Adopting this employee-centric knowledge-based view also highlights the tensions associated with managing people and managing knowledge (Swart and Kinnie 2004; Kinnie *et al.* 2006). As we discussed in Chapter 7, three kinds of tensions can be identified. First, firms know that they need to develop their staff in order to service the needs of their clients. However, at the same time, developing this skill may increase the attractiveness of their staff to other employers creating a potential problem of retaining those staff, a situation made worse because staff often work across organisational boundaries. Second, firms will seek to develop skills and knowledge which are specific to the firm and to particular clients, while employees are often more interested in developing transferable skills and knowledge in order to improve their employability. Third, employees will often have a high sense of ownership over their own knowledge and skills, because they themselves have invested heavily in these. At the same time the firm will be seeking to maximise the value they gain from this knowledge and these skills in order to service the needs of their clients. This often results in high salaries and benefits for knowledge workers.

Cross-boundary HRM: choice and constraint

Our discussion in Chapter 7 primarily concentrated on the particular issues faced by HR managers in professional service organisations. Perhaps the key implication here is related to the characteristics of the networks within which these firms operate. The importance of these networks has two practical implications for managers of HRM. Both mean that these managers find that they must operate across organisational boundaries. First, we have to recognise that the responsibilities of the HR manager are no longer simply confined to employees working within the boundaries of the organisation. Some employees will not be physically present on the employer's site and may, for instance, be based on a client's site for operational reasons. In other instances there will be people who are carrying out important work on the employer's site who are not employees. In short, HR managers have to be concerned with all the people who work for them whether or not they are employees who are present on their own site.

Second, many theories of strategic choice seem to assume that employers have freedom of choice over the HR practices which they adopt. We have seen that this is misleading because of the variety of constraints and influences which affect their decision-making processes. In addition to the constraints imposed by the state, with which we are familiar, we have seen in Chapter 7 the way in which external groups, most notably clients, can seek to influence the HR practices which are adopted. Managers of HR therefore need to assess the likely impact of these external parties on the design and implementation of their HR practices.

Three competing pulls on managers of HR can be recognised in these circumstances (Maister 2003). First, there are the pressures from the market for products or services and the actions of competitors within these markets. These are most clearly seen in the professional service organisations we discussed in Chapter 7 where individual clients often exercise considerable influence over not just the products and services of their supplying firm but also their HR practices. Managers of HR need to identify the potential impact of these important parties and consider the extent to which they need to tailor their HR practices to fit their needs. Second, there is the pull of the employment market. As we discussed in Chapter 7, employees often find that they have scarce skills and knowledge which give them power in the employment market. They will not be afraid to use this power to extract greater financial returns from their employer and improve their jobs. HR managers have to make careful judgements about their position within the employment market and the impact this will have on the retention of their staff. Third, there are the needs of the financial markets, or at least the needs to make a sufficient financial return on investments. Most organisations will have performance targets to meet and will devise a series of control mechanisms in order to achieve these.

Managers of HR can play a vital role in managing these potentially competing pressures. They need to satisfy the needs of their customers and clients and at the same time address the concerns of their employees while concurrently making a suitable financial return. In many ways HR managers are fortunate because they are in a unique position within the organisation to see the interactions between these three sets of pressures. However, the question remains as to whether HR managers and directors have sufficient influence within strategic decision-making in order to affect the way in which these pressures are managed (Guest and King 2004).

To sum up we have identified three major themes within this book and considered their implications for future research and for practitioners. These themes are derived from our basic argument that we need to place employees rather than HR practices at the centre of the analysis of people management. They concern the role of line managers and the differences between intended and experienced practices, the heterogeneity of HR practices linked to the knowledge of different groups of employees and the importance of managing HR across organisational boundaries. These themes represent the key challenges faced by both academics and managers when seeking to understand the links between HR practices and organisational performance.

Appendix
The research projects

Our research draws on a series of projects conducted between 1999 and 2007. The main projects were:

1   People and Performance project examining the links between HR and performance in 12 organisations – discussed in more detail below;
2   People and Performance in growing knowledge intensive firms (GKIFs) which examined the HR–performance links in six knowledge intensive firms;
3   Managing people and managing knowledge in professional service firms – a collaborative project with Cornell University focusing on the role of HR practices in the professional service sector (reported in more detail in Kinnie *et al.* (2006) and Swart *et al.* (2007));
4   More recently research has been conducted for the CIPD and the NHS examining the role of line managers.

The key features of the People and Performance and GKIFs projects upon which we principally draw are as follows:

1   We identified organisations that were either known for the quality of their human resource management or actively sought to improve the link between people management–performance. We worked closely with these organisations over a two- or three-year period during which they were part of an advisory council which met regularly to assess the progress of the research and to help in the identification of the key themes and ideas.
2   In each case we chose a unit of analysis as the focus for the case study. A unit was an identifiable area within the bigger business organisation which was small enough for us to be able to identify a sample of employees to be selected for interview and where this number of employees would constitute a reasonable proportion of the total number. This was also a unit where performance data would ideally be collected in order to attempt to show a direct connection between people and performance.
3   We used a detailed questionnaire in our face-to-face interviews with employees. These employees were normally front-line staff or direct production workers with a minimum of one year's service. We repeated these

interviews a year or so later. Where possible we interviewed the same people in the second year but given labour turnover, shift patterns and absence this was never complete. We conducted over 1,000 such interviews. On average each interview lasted 50 minutes. The purpose of the face-to-face interviews, rather than using a self-completion questionnaire, was to ensure both a high response rate (it was very rare to have a refusal to cooperate) and to enable us to explore understandings and explanations of why each person gave a particular answer to various attitudinal questions. This allowed us to collect a large number of verbatim quotations and find out why people felt motivated, had organisational commitment or found their job satisfying and helped us to understand why they thought certain aspects of the organisations' HR practices were positive or negative. This is a unique feature of our research allowing for both qualitative and quantitative analysis.

4   Some of the questions in the questionnaire were taken directly from the employee survey in the 1998 Workplace Employee Relations Survey (WERS 98). This allowed for comparisons and benchmarking both nationally and by occupation and sector.

5   Interviews were conducted with senior management to understand how the business operated at site or unit level, and in each case, where unions played an active part, also with local union leaders. Line managers responsible for the unit of analysis were interviewed using a semi-structured questionnaire designed to explore how people management practices were managed and implemented on a day-to-day basis in their area.

6   In these interviews with policy makers our concern was to understand the history and current circumstances of the business environment and its effect on HR practice. We also wished to explore, in detail, questions of organisational values and culture and the way these influenced HR and performance. These interviews allowed us to identify the key contextual variables and the historical path taken by each organisation.

7   Our approach to performance data was to ask the organisations to identify the performance measures which they considered the most important and where the link with people management was most likely to be observed. We sought to do this by collecting the performance in the unit of analysis and not at the firm level. We wished to explore the direct connection between the employee views, the line manager responses and performance within the unit. Even this proved very hard to achieve as in many cases the performance data were not available.

8   We fed back the results of the first round of research to each of the participating organisations, and to most in the second round. Our research thus took on attributes of action research where the research influences subsequent policy. In a number of cases we were aware of action taken following the first year's research feedback and were able to monitor its effects in the second round.

Notes

1 Understanding the link between people management and organisational performance

1 We discuss the limitations of this approach, especially the importance of contextual factors, (Guthrie 2001; Arthur 1994; Datta *et al.* 2005; Capelli and Neumark 2001; Way 2002) in Chapter 3.
2 This issue is discussed in more detail in Chapter 3.
3 This issue is discussed in more detail in Chapter 6.

2 Culture and values

1 The Workplace Employee Relations Survey (WERS) 1998 is based on large samples which are representative of the great majority of workplaces in Great Britain and involves interviews with managers, employee representatives and employees. The data used here are based on employee responses.

3 Intended HR practices

1 The practices and processes described here reflected those in place at the time of the research. The company has since changed its name.

4 Bringing practices to life: the vital role of front line managers

1 Cronbach's alpha for the construct consisting of these five questions is 0.8622, and as such we believe the combination of these variables into a single construct is reasonable.
2 Commitment is a combination of three questions, as is job satisfaction. Job discretion is a single question.
3 The low N of 40 precludes more sophisticated statistical analysis.

5 Employees' perceptions, attitudes and discretionary behaviour

1 While we were initially assured that there were meaningful performance differences between the stores we were not given any performance data until after the completion of the section manager interviews.

6 HR architecture and employment sub-systems: practices and perceptions

1 Precise details of the design and execution of this study are beyond the scope of this chapter, but readers are encouraged to consult Kersley *et al.* (2006) for details.

2 We measure affective commitment using the same three-item scale from the employee questionnaire that appeared in WERS 98. This captures affective commitment through questions asking employee respondents to express their degree of agreement with questions like, 'I am proud to tell people who I work for'. Evaluated on a five-point Likert scale anchored by 'strongly agree' and 'strongly disagree', this measure provides an internally reliable and externally valid measure of commitment. WERS 2004 (Kersley *et al.* 2006) includes no measures of continuance or normative commitment, but this limitation is not severe as the literature on commitment suggests that 'affective commitment is expected to have the strongest positive relation … to these desirable work behaviors' (Meyer *et al.* 2002: 21).

3 We regard the 99 per cent threshold as an appropriate level of confidence for statistical inferences based on representative samples of the size presented here. Table 6.1 also indicates those relationships that are significant at the 95 per cent level to aid interpretation of the results.

4 There are three other non-managerial occupational groups: the Personal Service group follows the common pattern in that commitment is associated with managerial support and satisfaction with the work itself. However, three further findings are worthy of comment. There is a strong association between commitment and the availability of homeworking perhaps because of the type of work involved. There are also weaker links with pay and teamworking. The findings for associated professionals and administrators have some similarities with many other groups in that managerial trust and satisfaction with work itself are important for their commitment. However, there are two other findings which are of interest. There is a strong association with a standardised induction programme and with job challenge. For administrators the distinctive finding is that satisfaction with work itself is not positively associated with their commitment, although the sense of achievement with work is strongly associated.

5 We could have used the full sample of employees which would have meant including responses from groups who did not make up the largest occupational group. This would have meant we were assuming that HR practices were applied to all employees irrespective of whether they were in the largest occupational group. Neither method is perfect, but we felt that the one used was the better of the two because we could be more confident that we were dealing with employee responses from the largest occupational group.

6 We are indebted to the WERS 2004 Information and Advice Service for providing clear guidance and sample code to facilitate the application of these methods.

7 Our employee-level controls include age, tenure, education, nationality, marital status, union membership, contract status, pay levels and family situation. Our workplace-level controls include industry, workplace size, the ownership structure of the firm, establishment age and a range of other variables that control for workforce composition.

7 People and performance in professional knowledge intensive organisations

1 We conceptualise knowledge-based outputs here as intellectual capital.

8 Analysing the links between people management and organisational performance: the case of Nationwide Building Society

1 The factual information relating to Nationwide was correct at the time the research was conducted.

2 DeGroot (1984: 450).

3 Heteroscedastic consistent estimates of the standard errors were generated using the procedure developed by White (1980).

4 The contribution of CSR to affective commitment was also investigated within a set of hierarchical models which excluded and then included the measures of internal and external CSR. In each case the increase in explanatory power was highly significant ($p<0.01$).

5 Demographics include proportions of employees who are women and minorities, as well as figures for average salary, average age and absence.

6 Although both our scale and the one employed by Gelade and Young (2005) purport to measure the same employee attitude, and although both do this using three questions scored on five-point Likert scales ranging from 'disagree' to 'agree', direct comparison of our measures of commitment is not strictly appropriate due to differences in the questions used. Still, we think it worth noting that Gelade and Young report an average commitment score that is 60 per cent of the maximum possible (3.4 on a scale measured from 1 to 5), while Nationwide reports an average score at 84 per cent of maximum (3.36 on a scale from zero to 4).

References

Ackroyd, S. and Proctor, S. (1998) 'British manufacturing organisation and workplace industrial relations: Some attributes of the new flexible firm', *British Journal of Industrial Relations*, 36(2): 163–183.

Adams, J. S. (1965) 'Inequality in social exchange', in L. Berkovitz (ed.), *Advances in Experimental Social Psychology, Vol 2*. New York: Academic Press.

Adler, P., Goldoftas, B. and Levine, D. (1999) 'Flexibility versus efficiency? A case study of model changeovers with Toyota production system', *Organisational Science*, 10(1): 43–68.

Afuah, A. (2000) 'How much do your competitors' capabilities matter in the face of technological change?' *Strategic Management Journal*, Special issue, 21: 387–404.

Albert, S. and Whetten, D. A. (1985) 'Organisational identity', in L. L. Cummings and B. M. Staw (eds), *Research in Organisational Behavior*, 7: Greenwich, CT: JAI Press.

Albert, S., Ashforth, B. and Dutton, J. (2000) 'Organisational identity and identification: charting new waters and building new bridges', *Academy of Management Review*, 25(1): 13–17.

Allen, M. R. and Wright, P. (2007) 'Strategic management and HRM', in P. Boxall, J. Purcell and P. Wright (eds), *The Oxford Handbook of Human Resource Management*, Oxford: Oxford University Press.

Allen, N. J. and Meyer, J. P. (1990) 'The measurement and antecedents of affective, continuance, and normative commitment to the organisation', *Journal of Occupational Psychology*, 63: 1–18.

Allen, N. J. and Grisaffe, D. B. (2001) 'Employee commitment to the organisation and customer reactions: mapping the linkages', *Human Resource Management Review*, 11: 209–236.

Alvesson, M. (1993) 'Organisation as rhetoric. Knowledge-intensive companies and the struggle with ambiguity', *Journal of Management Studies*, 30(6): 997–1015.

Alvesson, M. (1995) *Management of Knowledge Intensive Companies*, Berlin/New York: de Gruyter.

Alvesson, M. (2000) 'Social identity and the problem of loyalty in knowledge intensive companies', *Journal of Management Studies*, 37(8): 1101–1123.

Alvesson, M. (2001) 'Knowledge work: ambiguity, image and identity', *Human Relations*, 54(7): 863–886.

Alvesson, M. (2002) *Understanding Organisational Culture*, London: Sage.

Alvesson, M. and Willmott, H. (2002) 'Identity regulation as organisational control: producing the appropriate individual', *Journal of Management Studies*, 39(5): 619–644.

Amit, R. and Schoemaker, P. J. H. (1993) 'Strategic assets and organisational rent', *Strategic Management Journal* 14(1): 33–46.

Anderson, E. and Schmittlein, D. C. (1984) 'Integration of the sales force: an empirical examination', *Rand Journal of Economics*, 15(3): 385–395.

Appelbaum, E., Bailey, T. and Berg, P. (2000) *Manufacturing Advantage: Why High-Performance Systems Pay Off*. London: Economic Policy Institute: Cornell University Press.

Aranya, N., Kushnir, T. and Valency, A. (1986) 'Organisational commitment in a male-dominated profession', *Human Relations* 39: 433–448.

Argyris, C. (1960) *Understanding Organisational Behavior*, Homewood, IL: Dorsey Press.

Argyris, C. and Schon, D. A. (1974) *Theory into Practice*, San Francisco: Jossey-Bass.

Armstrong, P. and Goodman, J. (1979) 'Managerial and supervisory custom and practice', *Industrial Relations Journal*, 10(3): 12–24.

Arthur, J. (1992) 'The link between business strategy and industrial relations systems in American Steel Minimills', *Industrial and Labor Relations Review*, 45(3): 488–506.

Arthur, J. (1994) 'Effects of human resource systems on manufacturing performance and turnover', *Academy of Management Journal*, 37(3): 670–687.

Ashforth, B. E. and Mael, F. (1989) 'Social identity theory and the organisation', *Academy of Management Review*, 14: 20–39.

Atkinson, J. (1984) 'Manpower strategies for flexible organisations', *Personnel Management*, August: 28–31

Baird, L. and Meshoulam, L. (1988) 'Managing two fits of strategic human resource management', *Academy of Management Review*, 13(1): 116–128.

Balfour, D. L. and Wechsler, B. (1996) 'Organisational commitment: Antecedents and outcomes in public organisations', *Public Productivity and Management Review*, 29: 256–277.

Barnard, C. (1938). *The functions of the Executive*, Cambridge, MA: Harvard University Press.

Barney, J. (1991) 'Firm resources and sustained competitive advantage', *Journal of Management*, 17(1): 99–120.

Barney, J. B. (2001) 'Is the Resource-Based Theory a Useful Perspective for Strategic Management Research? Yes.' *Academy of Management Review* 26(1): 41–56.

Barney, J. and Wright, P. (1998) 'On becoming a strategic partner: the role of human resources in gaining competitive advantage', *Human Resource Management*, 37(1): 37–46.

Baron, R. and Kreps, D. (1999) *Strategic Human Resources: Frameworks for General Managers*, New York: Wiley.

Bartel, A. (2000) *Human Resource Management and Performance in the Service Sector: the Case of Bank Branches*. NBER Working Paper Series. Cambridge, MA: National Bureau of Economic Research.

Bartel, A. P. (2004) 'Human resource management and organisational performance: evidence from retail banking', *Industrial and Labor Relations Review*, 57: 181–204.

Bateman, T. S. and Strasser, S. (1984) 'A longitudinal analysis of the antecedents of organisational commitment', *Academy of Management Journal*, 27: 95–112.

Batt, R. and Moynihan, L. (2002) 'The viability of alternative call centre production models', *Human Resource Management Journal*, 12(4): 14–34.

Batt, R. and Valcour, P. M. (2003) 'Human resources practices as predictors of work–family outcomes and employee turnover', *Industrial Relations*, 42(2): 189–220.

Beaumont, P. B., Hunter, L. C. and Sinclair, D. (1996) 'Customer–supplier relations and the diffusion of employee relations changes', *Employee Relations*, 18(1): 9–19.

Beck, K. and Wilson, C. (2001) 'Have we studied, should we study, and can we study the development of commitment? Methodological issues and the developmental study of work-related commitment', *Human Resource Management Review*, 11: 257–278.

Becker, B. and Gerhart, B. (1996) 'The impact of human resource management on organisational performance: progress and practice', *Academy of Management Journal*, 39(4): 779–801.

Becker, B. and Huselid, M. (1996) 'Methodological issues in cross-sectional and panel estimates of the human resource–firm performance link', *Industrial Relations*, 35: 400–422.

Becker, B. and Huselid, M. (1999) 'Strategic human resource management in five leading firms', *Human Resource Management*, 38(4): 287–301.

Becker, B. and Huselid, M. (2006) 'Strategic human resource management: where do we go from here?' *Journal of Management*, 32(6): 898–925.

Becker, G. (1964) *Human Capital*, New York: Columbia University Press.

Becker, T., Billings, R., Eveleth, D. and Gilbert, N. (1996) 'Foci and bases of employee commitment: implications for job performance', *Academy of Management Journal*, 39(2): 464–482.

Beer, M., Spector, B., Lawrence, P., Quinn Mills, D. and Walton, R. (1985) *Human Resource Management: A General Manager's Perspective*, New York: Free Press.

Berg, P. (1999) 'The effects of high performance work practices on job satisfaction in the United States steel industry', *Relations Industrielles*, 54(1): 111–134.

Berg, P., Appelbaum, E., Bailey, T. and Kalleberg, A. (1996) 'The performance effects of modular production in the apparel industry', *Industrial Relations*, 35(3): 356–373.

Bettencourt, L. A., Gwinner, K. P. and Meuter, M. L. (2001) 'A comparison of attitude, personality, and knowledge predictors of service-oriented organisational citizenship behaviors,' *Journal of Applied Psychology*, 86(1): 29–41.

Blackler, F. (1995) 'Knowledge, knowledge work and organisations: an overview and interpretation', *Organisation Studies*, 16(6): 1021–1046.

Blau, P. (1964) *Exchange and Power in Social Life*, New York: Wiley.

Bontis, N. (1998) 'Intellectual capital: an exploratory study that develops measures and models', *Management Decision*, 36(2): 63–76.

Boselie, P., Dietz, G. and Boon C. (2005) 'Commonalities and contradictions in research on human resource management and performance', *Human Resource Management Journal*, 15(3): 67–94.

Bourdieu, P. and Wacquant, L. J. D. (1992) *An Invitation to Reflexive Sociology*, Chicago, IL: University of Chicago Press.

Bowen, D. and Ostroff, C. (2004) 'Understanding HRM–firm performance linkages: the role of the "strength" of the HRM system', *Academy of Management Review*, 29: 203–221.

Bowman, C. and Swart, J. (2007) 'Whose human capital? The challenge of value capture when capital is embedded', *Journal of Management Studies*, 44(4): 488–507.

Boxall, P. (1996) 'The strategic HRM debate and the resource-based view of the firm', *Human Resource Management Journal*, 6(3): 59–75.

Boxall, P. (1998) 'Achieving competitive advantage through human resource strategy: towards a theory of industry dynamics', *Human Resource Management Review*, 8(3): 265–288.

Boxall, P. (2003) 'HR strategy and competitive advantage in the service sector', *Human Resource Management Journal*, 13(3): 5–20.

Boxall, P. (2007) 'The Goals of HRM' in P. Boxall, J. Purcell and P. Wright (eds), *The Oxford Handbook of Human Resource Management*, Oxford: Oxford University Press.

Boxall, P. and Steeneveld, M. (1999) 'Human resource strategy and competitive advantage: a longitudinal study of engineering consultancies', *Journal of Management Studies*, 36(4): 443–463.

Boxall, P. and Purcell, J. (2003) *Strategy and Human Resource Management*, Basingstoke: Palgrave MacMillan.

Boxall, P. and Purcell, J. (2008) *Strategy and Human Resource Management*, 2nd edn Basingstoke: Palgrave Macmillan.

Boxall, P., Purcell, J. and Wright, P. (2007a) *The Oxford Handbook of Human Resource Management*, Oxford: Oxford University Press.

Boxall, P., Purcell, J. and Wright, P. (2007b) 'Human resource management: scope, analysis and significance', in P. Boxall, J. Purcell and P. Wright (eds), *The Oxford Handbook of Human Resource Management*, Oxford: Oxford University Press.

Brammer, S., Millington, A. and Rayton, B. A. (2007) 'The contribution of corporate social responsibility to organisational commitment,' *International Journal of Human Resource Management* 18(10): 1701–1719.

Braverman, H. (1974) *Labor and Monopoly Capital*, New York and London: Monthly Review Press.

Brewster, C., Gill, C. and Richbell, S. (1983) 'Industrial relations policy: a framework for analysis', in K. Thurley and S. Wood (eds), *Industrial Relations and Management Strategy*, Cambridge: Cambridge University Press.

Bromiley, P. and Papenhausen, C. (2003) 'Assumptions of rationality and equilibrium in strategy research: the limits of traditional economic analysis', *Strategic Organisation*, 1(4): 413–437.

Brown, A. D. and Starkey, K. (2000) 'Organisational identity and learning: a psychodynamic perspective', *Academy of Management Review*, 25(1): 102–120.

Brown, S. P. and Chin, W. W. (2004) 'Satisfying and retaining customers through independent service representatives', *Decision Sciences*, 35(3): 527–550.

Brown, W. (1972) 'A consideration of custom and practice', *British Journal of Industrial Relations*, 10(1): 42–61.

Brown, W. (1973) *Piecework Bargaining*, London: Heinemann.

Browne, J. (1973) *The Used Car Game*, Lexington: Lexington Books.

Brusoni, S., Prencipe, A. and Pavitt, K. (2001) Knowledge specialisation, organisational coupling and the boundaries of the firm: why do firms know more than they make? *Administrative Science Quarterly*, 46: 597–621.

Bryson, A., Charlwood, A. and Forth, J. (2006) 'Worker voice, managerial response and labour productivity: an empirical investigation', *Industrial Relations Journal*, 37(5): 438–455.

Burt, G. (1992) *Structural Holes*, Cambridge: Harvard University Press.

Caldwell, R. (2003) 'Changing roles for personnel managers', *Journal of Management Studies*, 40(4): 983–1004.

Cappelli, P. (1995) 'Rethinking employment', *British Journal of Industrial Relations* 33(4): 563–602.

Cappelli, P. (1999) *The New Deal at Work*, Boston: Harvard Business School Press.

Cappelli, P. and Neumark, D. (2001) 'Do "high performance" work practices improve establishment level outcomes?' *Industrial and Labor Relations Review*, 54(4): 737–776.

Carmichael, L. (1983) 'Firm-specific human capital and promotion ladders', *Bell Journal of Economics*, 14(1): 251–258.

Chartered Institute of Personnel and Development (2006) *The Changing HR Function: The Key Questions*, Chartered Institute of Personnel and Development: London.

Child, J. and Partridge, B. (1982) *The Lost Managers: Supervisors in Industry and Society.* Cambridge: Cambridge University Press.

Child, J and McGrath, R. G. (2001) 'Organisations unfettered: organisational form in an information-intensive economy', *Academy of Management Journal*, 44(6): 1135–1148.

CIPD (2006) *Reward Management Survey*, London: Chartered Institute of Personnel and Development.

CIPD (2007a) *Learning and Development 2007 Survey*, London: Chartered Institute of Personnel and Development.

CIPD (2007b) *CIPD HR Survey: the Changing HR Function*, London: Chartered Institute of Personnel and Development.

CIPD (2007c) *Latest Trends in Learning, Training and Development*, London: Chartered Institute of Personnel and Development.

Clinton, M. and Guest, D. (2007) 'Can employees fill the "black box" between HRM–performance? Examining a mediating model using both employer and employee reports', Paper presented at the Dutch HRM network Conference, Tilburg, The Netherlands.

Coase, Ronald (1937) 'The nature of the firm', *Economica*, 4: 386–405.

Cohen-Charash, Y. and Spector, P. E. (2001) 'The role of justice in organisations: a meta-analysis' *Organisational Behavior and Human Decision Processes* 86(2): 278–321.

Coleman, J. S. (1990) *Foundations of Social Theory*. Cambridge: Mass., HUP.

Collins, H. (1993) 'The Structure of Knowledge', *Social Research*, 60: 95–116.

Collinson, D. L., Knights, D. and Collinson, M. (1990) *Managing to Discriminate*, London: Routledge.

Colquitt, Jason A. (2001) 'On the dimensionality of organisational justice: a construct validation of a measure,' *Journal of Applied Psychology*, 86(3): 386–400.

Combs, J., Yongmei, L., Hall, A. and Ketchen, D. (2006) 'How much do high performance work practices matter? A meta-analysis of their effects on organisational performance', *Personnel Psychology*, 59: 501–528.

Coyle-Shapiro, J. and Kessler, I. (2000) 'Consequences of the psychological contract for the employment relationship: a large scale survey', *Journal of Management Studies* 37(7): 903–930.

Coyle-Shapiro, J., Kessler, I. and Coleman, J. S. (1988) 'Social capital in the creation of human capital', *American Journal of Sociology*, 94: S94–S120.

Coyle-Shapiro, J., Kessler, I. and Purcell, J. (2004) 'Exploring organisationally directed citizenship behaviour: reciprocity or "it's my job"', *Journal of Management Studies*, 41(1): 85–105.

Cunningham, I. and Hyman, J. (1995) 'Transforming the HRM vision into reality: the role of line managers in implementing change,' *Employee Relations*, 17(8): 5–20.

Cunningham, I. and Hyman, J. (1999) 'Devolving human resource responsibilities to the line: beginning of the end or a new beginning for personnel?' *Personnel Review*, 28(1/2): 9–27.

Currivan, D. B. (1999) 'The causal order of job satisfaction and organisational commitment in models of employee turnover', *Human Resource Management Review*, 9(4): 495–524.

Curry, J. P., Wakefield, D. S., Price, J. L. and Mueller C. W. (1986) 'On the causal ordering of job satisfaction and organisational commitment', *Academy of Management Journal*, 29: 847–858.

Datta, D. K., Guthrie, J. P. and Wright, P. M. (2005) 'Human resource management and labor productivity: does industry matter?' *Academy of Management Journal*, 48: 135–145.

Davenport, T. (1999) *Human Capital*, San Francisco: Jossey-Bass.

Davis-Blake, Alison and Uzzi, Brian (1993) 'Determinants of employment externalisation: the case of temporary workers and independent contractors', *Administrative Science Quarterly*, 38(2): 195–223.

De Ruyter, K. and Wetzels, M. (2000) 'Determinants of a relational exchange orientation in the marketing manufacturing interface – an empirical investigation', *Journal of Management Studies*, 37(2): 257–276.

De Saá-Pérez, Petra and García-Falcón, Juan Manuel (2002) 'A resource-based view of human resource management and organisational capabilities development' *International Journal of Human Resource Management* 13(1): 123–140.

Deal, T. E. and Kennedy, A. A. (1982) *Corporate Cultures*. Cambridge: Perseus Books.

Deery, S. J. and Iverson, R. (2005) 'Labor management co-operation: antecedents and organisational performance', *Industrial and Labor Relations Review*, 58(4): 588–610.

Deetz, S. (1995) *Transforming Communication, Transforming Business: Building Responsive and Responsible Workplaces*, Cresskill, NJ: Hampton Press.

DeGroot, M. H. (1984) *Probability and Statistics*, 2nd edn, Reading, MA: Addison-Wesley.

Delbridge, R. (2007) 'HRM and contemporary manufacturing' in P. Boxall, J. Purcell and P. Wright, (eds), *The Oxford Handbook of Human Resource Management*, Oxford: Oxford University Press.

Delery, J. (1998) 'Issues of fit in strategic human resource management: implications for research', *Human Resource Management Review*, 8(3): 289–309.

Delery, J. and Doty, D. (1996) 'Modes of theorising in strategic human resource management: tests of universalistic, contingency and configurational performance predictions', *Academy of Management Journal*, 39(4): 802–835.

Delery, J. and Shaw, J. (2001) 'The strategic management of people in work organisations: review, synthesis and extension', *Research in Personnel and Human Resources Management*, 20: 165–197.

DeLong, T. J. and Nanda, A. (2003) *Professional Services: Text and Cases*, New York: McGraw Hill.

Dougherty, T. W., Bluedorn A. C. and Keon T. L. (1985) 'Precursors of employee turnover: A multiple-sample causal analysis', *Journal of Occupational Behaviour*, 6, 259–271.

Dowling, B. and Richardson, R. (1997) 'Evaluating performance related pay for managers in the national Health Service', *International Journal of Human Resource Management*, 8(3) 348–366.

Dutton, J. E., Dukerich, J. M. and Harquail, C. V. (1994) 'Organisational images and member identification', *Administrative Science Quarterly*, 39: 239–263.

Dyer, J. H. and Nobeoka, K. (2000) 'Creating and managing a high-performance knowledge-sharing network: the Toyota case', *Strategic Management Journal*, 21: 345–367.

Dyer, L. and Reeves, T. (1995) 'Human resource strategies and firm performance: what do we know and where do we need to go?' *International Journal of Human Resource Management*, 6(3): 656–670.

Edwards, P. and Wright M. (2001) 'High involvement work systems and performance outcomes: the strength of variable, contingent and context bound relationships', *International Journal of Human Resource Management*, 12(4): 568–585.

Eisenberger, R., Huntington, R., Hutchison, S. and Sowa, D. (1986) 'Perceived organisational support', *Journal of Applied Psychology*, 71(3): 500–507.

Eisenberger, R., Jones, J. R., Aselage, J. and Sucharski, I. L. (2004) 'Perceived organisational support', in J. Coyle-Shapiro, L. M. Shore, M. S. Taylor and L. E. Tetrick (eds),

The Employment Relationship: Examining Psychological and Contextual Perspectives, Oxford: Oxford University Press.

Eisenberger, R., Stinglhamber, F., Vandenberghe, C., Sucharski, I. and Rhoades, L. (2002) 'Perceived supervisor support: contributions to perceived organisational support and employee retention', *Journal of Applied Psychology*, 87: 565–573.

Empson, L. (2001) 'Fear of exploitation and fear of contamination: impediments to knowledge transfer in mergers between professional services firms', *Human Relations*, 54(7): 839–862.

Empson, L. (2004) 'Organisational identity change: Managerial regulation and member identification in an accounting firm acquisition', *Accounting Organisations and Society*, 29: 145–176.

Empson, L. (2007) 'Surviving and thriving in a changing world: the special nature of partnership', in L. Empson (ed.), *Managing the Modern Law Firm: New Challenges and New Perspectives*, Oxford: Oxford University Press.

Epitropaki, O. and Martin, R. (2005) 'From ideal to real: A longitudinal study of implicit leadership theories, leader–member exchanges and employee outcomes', *Journal of Applied Psychology*, 90: 659–676.

Farkas, A. and Tetric, L. (1989) 'A three-wave longitudinal analysis of the causal ordering of satisfaction and commitment in turnover decisions', *Journal of Applied Psychology*, 74: 855–868.

Fenton O'Creevy, M. (2001) 'Employee involvement and the middle manager: saboteur or scapegoat?' *Human Resource Management Journal*, 11(2): 24–40.

Fombrun, C., Tichy, N. and Devanna, M. (1984) *Strategic Human Resource Management*, New York: Wiley.

Foulkes, F. K. (1980) *Personnel Policies in Large Non-union Companies*, Englewood Cliffs, NJ: Prentice Hall.

Fox, A. (1974) *Beyond Contract: Work, Power and Trust Relations*. London: Faber.

Frenkel, S. and Sanders, K. (2007) 'Explaining variations in co-worker assistance in organisations', *Organisation Studies*, 28(6): 797–823.

Frenkel, S., Korczynski, M., Shire, K. and Tam, M. (1999) *On the Front Line: Work Organisation in the Service Economy*, Ithaca, NY: ILR/Cornell University Press.

Fulmer, I., Gerhart, B. and Scott, K. (2003) 'Are the 100 best better? An empirical investigation of the relationship between being a "great place to work" and firm performance', *Personnel Psychology*, 56: 965–993.

Gaertner, S. (1999) 'Structural determinants of job satisfaction and organisational commitment in turnover models', *Human Resource Management Review*, 9(4): 479–493.

Gardner, H., Morris, T. and Anand, N. (2007) 'Developing new practices: recipes for success', in L. Empson (ed.), *Managing the Modern Law Firm: New Challenges and New Perspectives*, Oxford: Oxford University Press.

Gargiulo, M. and Benassi, M. (2000) Trapped in your own net? Network cohesion, structural holes, and the adaptation of social capital. *Organisation Science*, 11(2): 183–196.

Gelade, G. and Ivery, M. (2003) 'The impact of human resource management and work climate on organisational performance', *Personnel Psychology*, 56: 383–404.

Gelade, G. and Young, S. (2005) 'Test of a service profit chain model in the retail banking sector', *Journal of Occupational and Organisational Psychology*, 78: 1–22.

Gennard, J. and Kelly, J. (1997) 'The unimportance of labels: the diffusion of the personnel/HRM function', *Industrial Relations Journal*, 28(1): 27–42.

Gerhart, B. (2005) 'Human resources and business performance: findings, unanswered questions and an alternative approach', *Management Revue*, 16(2): 174–185.

Gerhart, B. and Milkovich, G. T. (1990) 'Organisational differences in managerial compensation and financial performance', *Academy of Management Journal*, 33: 663–691.

Gerhart, B., Wright, P., McMahan, G. and Scott, S. (2000) 'Measurement error in research on human resources and firm performance: how much error is there and does it influence effect size estimates?' *Personnel Psychology*, 5: 803–834.

Gerstner, C. R. and Day, D. V. (1997) 'Meta-analytic review of leader–member exchange theory: Correlates and construct issues', *Journal of Applied Psychology*, 82: 827–844.

Ghoshal, S. and Bartlett, C. A. (1995) 'Changing the role of top management: beyond structure to process', *Harvard Business Review*, January–February: 86–96.

Ghoshal, S. and Bartlett, C. A. (1997) *The Individualised Corporation: A Fundamentally New Approach to Management*: New York: Harper Business.

Gibson, D. E. and Barron, L. A. (2003) 'Exploring the impact of role models on older employees', *Career Development International*, 8(4): 198–209.

Godard, J. (2004) 'A critical assessment of the high performance paradigm', *British Journal of Industrial Relations*, 42(2): 349–378.

Golding, N. (2004) 'Strategic human resource management', in I. Beardwell, L. Holden and T. Claydon (eds), *Human Resource Management*, Harlow: Pearson.

Gonzalez, S. and Tacorante, D. (2004) 'A new approach to the best practices debate: are best practices applied to all employees in the same way?' *International Journal of Human Resource Management*, 15(1): 56–75.

Gordon, G. and DiTomaso, N. (1992) 'Predicting corporate performance from organisational climate', *Journal of Management Studies*, 26(6): 783–798.

Gospel, H. F. (1992) *Markets, Firms and the Management of Labour in Modern Britain*, Cambridge: Cambridge University Press.

Gouldner, A. (1960) 'The norm of reciprocity: a preliminary statement', *American Sociological Review*, 25: 161–178.

Goyder, M. (1998) *Living Tomorrow's Company*, Aldershot: Gower.

Granovetter, M. (1973) 'The strength of weak ties', *American Journal of Sociology*, 78: 1360–1380.

Granovetter, M. (1985) 'Economic action and social structure: the problem of embeddedness', *American Journal of Sociology*, 91(3): 481–510.

Grant, D. (1999) 'HRM, rhetoric and the psychological contract: a case of "easier said than done"', *International Journal of Human Resource Management*, 10(2) 327–350.

Grant, R. (1996) 'Towards a knowledge-based view of the firm', *Strategic Management Journal*, 17: 109–122.

Gratton, L. (2000) *Living Strategy: Putting People at the Heart of Corporate Performance*, Hemel Hempstead: Prentice Hall.

Gratton, L., Hope-Hailey, V., Stiles, P. and Truss, C. (1999) *Strategic Human Resource Management: Corporate Rhetoric and Human Reality*, Oxford: Oxford University Press.

Greene, W. H. (2003) *Econometric Analysis*, 5th edn, Upper Saddle River, NJ: Pearson Education.

Greenwood, R. (2007) 'The defining professionalism? The impact of management change', in L. Empson (ed.), *Managing the Modern Law Firm: New Challenges and New Perspectives*, Oxford: Oxford University Press.

Greenwood, R. and Suddaby, R. (eds), (2006) *Professional Service Firms Research in the Sociology of Organisations*, Oxford: JAI Press.

Greenwood, R., Suddaby, R. and McDougald, M. (2006) 'Introduction', in R. Greenwood, and Suddaby, R. (eds), (2006) *Professional Service Firms Research in the Sociology of Organisations*, Oxford: JAI Press.

Grimshaw, D. and Miozzo, M. (2006) 'Institutional effects on the IT outsourcing market: analysing clients, suppliers and staff transfers in Germany and the UK', *Organisation Studies*, 27(9): 1229–1259.

Grimshaw, D. and Rubery, J. (2007) 'Economics and HRM', in P. Boxall, J. Purcell, and P. Wright (eds), *The Oxford Handbook of Human Resource Management*, Oxford: Oxford University Press.

Grimshaw, D., Ward, K., Rubery, J. and Beynon, H. (2001) 'Organisation and the transformation of the internal labour market', *Work, Employment and Society*, 15(1): 25–54.

Grimshaw, D., Marchington, M., Rubery J. and Willmott H. (2005) 'Introduction: fragmenting work across organisational boundaries' in M. Marchington, D. Grimshaw, J. Rubery and H. Willmott (eds), *Fragmenting Work*, Oxford: Oxford University Press.

Guest, D. (1987) 'Human resource management and industrial relations', *Journal of Management Studies*, 24(5): 503–521.

Guest, D. (1997) 'Human resource management and performance: a review and research agenda', *International Journal of Human Resource Management*, 8(3): 263–276.

Guest, D. (1998) 'Is the psychological contract worth taking seriously?' *Journal of Organisational Behavior*, 19: 649–664.

Guest, D. (2001) 'Human resource management: when reality confronts theory', *International Journal of Human Resource Management*, 12, 1092–1106.

Guest, D. (2007) 'Human resource management and the worker: towards a new psychological contract?' in P. Boxall, J. Purcell, and P. Wright (eds), *The Oxford Handbook of Human Resource Management*, Oxford: Oxford University Press.

Guest, D. and Conway, N. (2002) *The State of the Psychological Contract*, London: CIPD.

Guest, D. and King, Z. (2002) 'HR and the bottom line', *People Management*, 27: September, 29–34.

Guest, D. and Conway, N. (2004) *Employee well-being and the psychological contract: a report for the CIPD*, London: CIPD.

Guest, D. and King, Z. (2004) 'Power, innovation and problem solving: the personnel managers' three steps to heaven?', *Journal of Management Studies*, 41(3): 401–423.

Guest, D., Michie, J., Conway, N. and Sheehan, M. (2003) 'Human resource management and corporate performance in the UK', *British Journal of Industrial Relations*, 41(2): 291–314.

Gulati, R. (1995) 'Does familiarity breed trust? The implications of repeated ties for contractual choices', *Academy of Management Journal*, 35: 85–112.

Gulati, R., Nohria, N. and Zaheer, A. (2000) 'Strategic networks', *Strategic Management Journal*, 21: 203–215.

Guthrie, J. (2001) 'High-involvement work practices, turnover and productivity: evidence from New Zealand', *Academy of Management Journal*, 44(1) 180–190.

Hair, J. F., Anderson, R. E., Tatham, R. L. and Black, W. C. (1998) *Multivariate Data Analysis*, 5th edn, New Jersey: Prentice-Hall.

Hales, C. (2005) 'Rooted in supervision, branching into management: continuity and change in the role of first-line manager', *Journal of Management Studies*, 42(3): 471–506.

Hamel, G. and Prahalad, C. (1994) *Competing for the future*, Boston, MA: Harvard Business School Press.

Hannah, D. and Iverson, R. (2004) 'Employment relationships in context: implications for policy and practice', in J. Coyle-Shapiro, L. Shore, S. Taylor and L. Tetrick (eds), *The employment relationship: examining psychological and contextual perspectives*, Oxford: Oxford University Press, pp. 332–350.

Harris, L. (2001) 'Rewarding employee performance: line managers' values, beliefs and perspectives', *International Journal of Human Resource Management*, 12(7): 1182–1192.

Harter, J., Schmidt, F. and Haynes, T. (2002) 'Business unit level relationships between employee satisfaction, employee engagement and business outcomes: a meta analysis', *Journal of Applied Psychology*, 87(2): 268–279.

Hashimoto, M. (1979). 'Bonus payments, on-the-job training and lifetime employment in Japan', *Journal of Political Economy*, 87: 1086–1104.

Hashimoto, M. and Yu, Ben T. (1980). 'Specific capital, employment contracts, and wage rigidity', *Bell Journal of Economics*, 11(2): 536–549.

Hatch, M. J. and Schultz, M. (2002) 'The dynamics of organisational identity', *Human Relations*, 55(8): 989–1017.

Heinz, J. P. and Laumann, E. O. (1978) 'The legal profession: client interests, professional roles, and social hierarchies', *Michigan Law Review*, 76: 1111–1142.

Hendry, C. (1995) *Human Resource Management. A Strategic Approach to Employment*, London: Butterworth Heinemann.

Hesketh, A. and Fleetwood, S. (2006) 'Beyond measuring the human resources–organisational performance link: applying critical realist meta-theory', *Organisation*, 13(5) 677–700.

Heskett, J. L., Jones, T. O., Loveman, G. W., Sasser, W. E. Jr and Schlesinger, L. A. (1994) 'Putting the service-profit chain to work', *Harvard Business Review*, March/April: 164–174.

Hitt, M. A., Bierman, L., Shimizu, K. and Kochhar, R. (2001) 'Direct and moderating effects of human capital on strategy and performance in professional service firms: a resource based perspective', *Academy of Management Journal*, 44(1): 13–28.

Hodson, R. and Sullivan, T. (1995) *The Social Organisation of Work*, Washington: Wadsworth.

Hoffman, B. J., Blair, C. A., Meriac, J. P. and Woehr, D. J. (2007) 'Expanding the Criterion Domain? A quantitative review of the OCB literature', *Journal of Applied psychology*, 92(2): 555–566.

Hofstede, G., Neuijen, B., Ohayv, D. D. and Sanders, G. (1990) 'Measuring organisational cultures: a qualitative and quantitative study across twenty cases', *Administrative Science Quarterly*, 35: 286–316.

Hogg, M. A. and Abrams, D. (1988) *Social Identifications: A Social Psychology of Intergroup Relations and Group Processes*, London: Routledge.

Hogg, M. A. and Terry, D. J. (2000) 'Social identity and self-categorization processes in organisational contexts', *Academy of Management Review*, 25(1): 121–140.

Hui, C., Law, K. S. and Chen, Z. X. (1999) 'A structural equation model of the effects of negative affectivity, leader–member exchange, and perceived job mobility on in-role and extra-role performance: a Chinese case', *Organisational Behavior and Human Decision Processes* 77: 3–21.

Huselid, M. (1995) 'The impact of human resource management practices on turnover, productivity and corporate financial performance', *Academy of Management Journal*, 38(3): 635–672.

Huselid, M. and Becker, B. E. (2000) 'Comment on "Measurement error in research on human resources and firm performance: how much error is there and how does it influence effect size estimates?" by Gerhart, Wright, McMahan and Snell', *Personnel Psychology*, 53(4): 835–854.

Hutchinson, S. and Wood, S. (1995) *Personnel and the Line: Developing the New Relationship*, London: Chartered Institute of Personnel and Development.

Hutchinson, S. and Purcell, J. (2003) *Bringing Policies to Life: the Vital Role of Front Line Managers*, London: Chartered Institute of Personnel and Development.

Hutchinson,S. and Purcell, J. (2007) *The Role of Line Managers in People Management*, London: Chartered Institute of Personnel and Development.

Hutchinson, S., Kinnie, N., Purcell, J., Collinson, M., Scarborough, H. and Terry, M. (1998) *Getting Fit, Staying Fit: Developing Lean and Responsive Ways of Working*, IPD.

Ibarra, H. (1999) 'Provisional selves: experimenting with image and identity in professional adaptation' *Administrative Science Quarterly*, 44: 764–791.

Jackson, S. and Schuler, R. (1995) 'Understanding human resource management in the context of organisations and their environments', *Annual Review of Psychology*, 46: 237–264.

Jacoby, S. (2005) *The Embedded Corporation: Corporate Governance and Employment Relations in Japan and the United States*, Princeton, NJ: Princeton University Press.

James, W. (1950) *The Principles of Psychology*, New York: Dover.

Janis, I. L. (1982) *Groupthink: Psychological Decisions of Policy Decisions And Fiascos*, Boston, MA: Houghton Mifflin.

Judge, T., Thoresen, C., Bono, J. and Patton, G. (2001) 'The job satisfaction–job performance relationship: a qualitative and quantitative review', *Psychological Bulletin*, 127: 376–407.

Kabanoff, B., Waldersee, R. and Cohen, M. (1995) 'Espoused values and organisational change themes', *Academy of Management Journal* 38(4): 1075–1104.

Kacmar, K. M., Carlson, D. S. and Bryner, R. A. (1999) 'Antecedents and consequences of organisational commitment: a comparison of two scales', *Educational Psychology Measures*, 59: 976–994.

Kalleberg, A. L. (1977) 'Work values and job rewards: A theory of job satisfaction', *American Sociological Review*, 42: 124–143.

Kalleberg, A. L. and Moody, J. W. (1994) 'Human resource management and organisational performance', *American Behavioral Scientist*, 37(7): 948–962.

Kamdar, D. and Dyne, L. V. (2007) 'The joint effects of personality and workplace social exchange relationships in predicting task performance and citizenship performance', *Journal of Applied Psychology*, 92(5): 1286–1298.

Kamdar, D., McAllister D. J. and Turban, D. B. (2006) 'All in a day's work: how follower individual differences and justice perceptions predict OCB role definitions and behavior', *Journal of Applied Psychology*, 91(4): 841–855.

Kang, S. C., Morris, S. and Snell, S. (2007) 'Managing intellectual and capital architectures: HRM and bilateral learning in law firms', *Academy of Management Journal*.

Kaplan, R. and Norton, D. (1996) *The Balanced Scorecard: Translating Strategy into Action*, Boston, MA: Harvard Business School Press.

Karamanos, A. (2003) 'Complexity, identity and the value of knowledge-intensive exchanges', *Journal of Management Studies*, 40(7): 1871–1890.

Katz, D. (1964) 'The motivational basis of organisational behaviour', *Behavioral Science*, 9: 131–146.

Kaufman, B. E. (2007) 'The development of HRM in historical and international perspective', in P. Boxall, J. Purcell and P. Wright (eds), *The Oxford Handbook of Human Resource Management*, Oxford: Oxford University Press.

Keenoy, T. (1997) 'Review article: HRMism and the languages of representation', *Journal of Management Studies*, 34(5): 825–841.

Kelley, R. E. (1985) *The Gold Collar Worker: Harnessing the Brain Power of the New Workforce*, Reading, MA: Addison-Wesley.

Kersley, B, Alpin, C., Forth, J., Bryson, A., Bewley, H., Dix, G. and Oxenbridge S. (2006) *Inside the Workplace: Findings from the 2004 Workplace Employment Relations Survey*, London: Department of Trade and Industry.

Kidd, J. and Smewing, C. (2001) 'The role of supervisor in career and organisational commitment' *European Journal of Work and Organisational Psychology*, 10(1): 25–40.

King, Z. (2003) 'New or traditional careers? A study of UK graduates' preferences', *Human Resource Management Journal*, 13(1): 5–26.

Kinnie, N. and Parsons, J., (2004) 'Managing client, employee and customer relations: constrained strategic choices in the management of human resources in a commercial call centre', in S. Deery and N. Kinnie, *Call Centres and Human Resource Management*, Basingstoke: Palgrave Macmillan.

Kinnie, N., Purcell, J. and Hutchinson, S. (2000) 'Managing the employment relationship in telephone call centres' in K. Purcell, *Changing Boundaries in Employment*, Bristol: Bristol Academic Press.

Kinnie, N., Purcell, J. and Adams, M. (forthcoming) 'Explaining employees' experience of work in outsourced call centres: the influence of clients, owners and temporary work agencies', *Journal of Industrial Relations*.

Kinnie, N., Purcell, J., Hutchinson, S., Rayton, B. and Swart, J. (2005) 'Satisfaction with HR practices and commitment to the organisation: why one size does not fit all', *Human Resource Management Journal*, 15(4): 9–29.

Kinnie, N., Swart, J., Snell, S., Morris, S. and Kang, Sung-Choon (2006) 'Managing people and knowledge in professional service firms', London: Chartered Institute of Personnel and Development.

Kinnie, N., Purcell, J., Hutchinson, S., Terry, M., Collinson, M. and Scarbrough, H. (1999) 'Employment relations in SMEs: market driven or customer shaped?' *Employee Relations*, 22(3): 218–235.

Koch, M. and McGrath, R. (1996) 'Improving labor productivity: human resource policies do matter', *Strategic Management Journal*, 17: 335–354.

Kochan, T. and Barocci, T. A. (1985) *Human Resource Management and Industrial Relations: Text, Readings and Cases*, Boston: Little Brown.

Korczynski, M. (2002) *Human Resource Management in Service Work*, Basingstoke: Palgrave.

Korsgaard, M. A., Schweiger, D. M. and Sapienza, H. J. (1995) 'Building commitment, attachment and trust in strategic decision making teams: the role of procedural justice', *Academy of Management Journal*, 38(1): 60–84.

Lam, A. (2005) 'Work roles and careers of R&D scientists in networked organisations', *Industrial Relations*, 44(2): 242–275.

Lam, A. (2007) 'Transnational learning and knowledge transfer: a comparative analysis of Japanese and US MNCs' overseas R&D laboratories', in C. Smith, B. McSweeney and R. Fitzgerald (eds), *Remaking Management Practices: Beyond Global and National Approaches*, Cambridge: Cambridge University Press.

Lamming, R. (1993) *Beyond Partnership*, Hemel Hempstead: Prentice Hall.

Lance, C. E. (1991) 'Evaluation of a structural model relating job satisfaction, organisational commitment, and precursors to voluntary turnover', *Multivariate Behavioral Research*, 26: 137–162.

Larsen, H. H. and Brewster, C. (2003) 'Line management responsibility for HRM: what is happening in Europe?' Employee Relations, 25(3): 228–244.

Latham, G. P. and Wexley, K. N. (1981) *Increasing Productivity through Performance Appraisal*, Reading, MA: Addison-Wesley.

Lawler, E. E. (1992) 'The ultimate advantage: creating the high-involvement organisation', San Francisco, CA: Jossey-Bass.

Lazear, E. (1996) 'Performance pay and productivity', NBER working paper 5672, Cambridge, MA.

Leana, C. R. and van Buren, H. J. (1999) 'Organisational social capital and employment practices', *Academy of Management Review*, 24(3): 538–555.

Legge, K. (1978) *Power, Innovation and Problem Solving in Personnel Management*, London: McGraw-Hill.

Legge, K. (1995) *Human Resource Management: Rhetorics and Realities*, Basingstoke: Macmillan.

Legge, K. (2001) 'Silver bullet or spent round? Assessing the meaning of the high commitment management/performance relationship,' in J. Storey (ed.), *Human Resource Management: A Critical Text*, 2nd edn, London: Thompson.

Legge, K. (2005) *Human Resource Management: Rhetorics and Realities*, 2nd edn, Basingstoke: Palgrave Macmillan.

Lepak, D. and Snell, S. A. (1999) 'The human resource architecture: toward a theory of human capital allocation and development', *Academy of Management Review*, 24(1): 31–48.

Lepak, D. and Snell, S. (2002) 'Examining the human resource architecture: the relationships among human capital, employment and human resource configurations', *Journal of Management*, 28(4): 517–543.

Lepak, D. and Snell, S. (2007) 'Employment sub-systems and the HR architecture' in P. Boxall, J. Purcell and P. Wright (eds), *The Oxford Handbook of Human Resource Management*, Oxford: Oxford University Press.

Lepak, D., Takeucki, R. and Snell, S. A. (2003) 'Employment flexibility and firm performance: examining the interaction effects of employment mode, environmental dynamism and technological intensity', *Journal of Management*, 29: 681–703.

Lepak, D., Liao, H., Chung, Y. and Harden, E. E. (2006) 'A conceptual review of human resource management systems in strategic human resource management research', *Personnel and Human Resource Management*, 25: 217–271.

LePine, J. A., Erez, A. and Johnson, D. E. (2002) 'The nature and dimensionality of organisational citizenship behavior: a critical review and meta-analysis', *Journal of Applied Psychology*, 87(1): 52–65.

Lerner, M. J. (1980) *The Belief in a Just World: a Fundamental Delusion*, New York: Plenum Press.

Levinson, H. (1965) 'Reciprocation: The relationship between man and organisation', *Administrative Science Quarterly*, 9(4): 370–390.

Liden, R. Bauer, T. and Erdogan, B. (2004) 'The role of leader member exchange in the dynamic relationship between employer and employee: implications for employee socialization, leaders and organisations', in J. Coyle-Shapiro, L. Shore, S. Taylor and L. Tetrick (eds), *The Employment Relationship: Examining Psychological and Contextual Perspectives*, Oxford: Oxford University Press.

Lincoln, J. R. and Kalleberg, A. L. (1990) *Culture, Control and Commitment: A study of Work Organisation And Work Orientations in the United States and Japan*, Cambridge: Cambridge University Press.

Lincoln, J. R. and Kalleberg, A. L. (1996) 'Commitment, quits and work organisation: A study of U.S. and Japanese plants', *Industrial and Labor Relations Review*, 50: 738–760.

Liu, W., Lepak, D. P., Takeuchi, R. and Sims, H. P. (2003) 'Matching leadership styles with employment modes: strategic human resource management perspective', *Human Resource Management Review*, 12: 127–152.

Locke, E. A. (1976) 'The nature and causes of job satisfaction', in M. D. Dunnette (ed.), *Handbook of Industrial and Organisational Psychology*, Chicago: Rand-McNally.

Losey, M., Meisinger, S. R. and Ulrich, D. (2005) 'Conclusion: reality, impact and professionalism', *Human Resource Management*, 44(2): 201–206.

Lowendahl, B. (2005) *Strategic Management in Professional Service Firms*, 3rd edn, Copenhagen: Copenhagen Business School.

Lund, D. B. (2003) 'Organisational culture and job satisfaction', *Journal of Business and Industrial Marketing*, 18(3): 219–236.

McConville, T. and Holden, L. (1999) 'The filling in the sandwich: HRM and middle managers in the health sector.' *Personnel Review*, 28(5/6): 406–424.

MacDuffie, J. P. (1995) 'Human Resource bundles and manufacturing performance: organisational logic and flexible production systems in the world auto industry', *Industrial and Labor Relations Review*, 48(2): 197–221.

McGovern, P., Gratton, L., Hope-Hailey, V., Stiles, P. and Truss, C. (1997) 'Human resource management on the line?' *Human Resource Management Journal*, 7(4):12–29.

McGregor, D. (1960) *The Human Side of Enterprise*, New York: McGraw-Hill

McNabb, R. and Whitfield, K. (1997) 'Unions, flexibility, teamworking and financial performance', *Organisation Studies*, 18(5): 821–838.

Maddern, H., Maull, R., Smart, A. and Baker, P. (2007) 'Customer satisfaction and service quality in UK financial services' *International Journal of Operations and Production Management* 27(9): 998–1019.

Mael, F. A. and Ashforth, B. E. (1995) 'Loyal from day one: biodata, organisational identification and turnover among newcomers', *Personnel Psychology*, 48: 309–333.

Maignan, I. and Ferrell, O. C. (2001) 'Corporate citizenship as a marketing instrument' *European Journal of Marketing*, 35: 457–484.

Maister, D. (1993) *Managing the Professional Services Firm*, New York: Free Press.

Maister, D. (2003) *Managing the Professional Service Firm*, London: Simon and Schuster.

Marchington, M. (2001) 'Employee Involvement at work', in J. Storey (ed.), *Human Resource Management: A critical text*, 2nd edn, London: Thomson.

Marchington, M. and Grugulis, I. (2000) 'Best practice human resource management: perfect opportunity or dangerous illusion?', *International Journal of Human Resource Management*, 11(6): 1104–1124.

Marchington, M. and Wilkinson, A. (2002) *People Management and Development: Human Resource Management at Work*, London: Chartered Institute of Personnel and Development.

Marchington, M. Grimshaw, D., Rubery, J. and Willmott, H. (eds) (2005) *Fragmenting Work*, Oxford: Oxford University Press.

Marsden, D. (1999) *A Theory of Employment Systems*, Oxford: Oxford University Press.

Masten, S. (1988) 'A Legal Basis for the Firm', *Journal of Law, Economics and Organisation*, 4(1): 181–198.

Mathieu, J. E. (1991) 'A cross-level nonrecursive model of the antecedents of organisational commitment and satisfaction', *Journal of Applied Psychology*, 76: 607–618.

Maxwell, G. A. and Watson, S. (2006) 'Perspectives on line managers in HRM: Hilton International's UK hotels', *The International Journal of Human Resource Management*, 17(6): 1152–1170.

May, T. Y., Korczynski, M. and Frenkel, S. J. (2002) 'Organisational and occupational commitment: knowledge workers in large organisations', *Journal of Management Studies*, 39(6): 775–801.

Meyer, J. P. and Herscovitch, L. (2001) 'Commitment in the workplace: toward a general model', *Human Resource Management Review*, 11: 299–326.

Meyer, J. P., Stanley, D. J., Herscovitch, L. and Topolnytsky, L. (2002) 'Affective, continuance, and normative commitment to the organisation: a meta-analysis of antecedents, correlates, and consequences', *Journal of Vocational Behavior*, 61: 20–52.

Miles, R. and Snow, C. C. (1978) *Organisational Strategy, Structure and Process*, New York: McGraw-Hill.

Miles, R. and C. Snow (1984) 'Designing strategic human resources systems', *Organisational Dynamics*, Summer: 36–52.

Milgrom, P. (1988) 'Employment contracts, influence activities, and efficient organisation', *Journal of Political Economy*, 96: 42–60.

Mintzberg, H. (1998) 'Covert leadership: notes on managing professionals', *Harvard Business Review*, November–December: 140–147.

Moorman, R. H. (1991) 'Relationship between organisational justice and organisational citizenship behaviours: do fairness perceptions influence employee citizenship?' *Journal of Applied Psychology*, 76: 845–855.

Morris, T. (2000) 'Promotion policies and knowledge bases in the professional services firm', in M. Peiperl, M. Arthur, R. Goffee and T. Morris (eds), *Career Frontiers*: Oxford: Oxford University Press, pp. 138–152.

Mowday, R. T., Steers, R. M. and Porter, L. W. (1979) 'The measurement of organisational commitment', *Journal of Vocational Behavior*, 14: 224–247.

Mowday, R. T., Steers, R. M. and Porter, L. W. (1982) *Employee–Organisation Linkages: The Psychology of Commitment, Absenteeism, and Turnover*, New York: Academic Press.

Mueller, F. (1996) 'Human resources as strategic assets: an evolutionary resourced-based theory', *Journal of Management Studies*, 33(6): 757–785.

Mueller, C. W., Wallace, J. E. and Price, J. L. (1992) 'Employee commitment: resolving some issues', *Work and Occupations*, 19: 211–236.

Nahapiet, J. and Ghoshal, S. (1998) 'Social capital, intellectual capital and the organisation advantage' *Academy of Management Review*, 23(2): 242–266.

Nalbantian, H. R. and Szostak A. (2004) 'How Fleet Bank fought employee flight,' *Harvard Business Review*, 116–125.

Newman, K. (2001) 'SERVQUAL: a critical assessment of service quality measurement in a high street retail bank', *International Journal of Bank Marketing*, 19(3): 126–139.

Nonaka, I. and Takeuchi, H. (1995) *The Knowledge Creating Company: How Japanese Companies Create the Dynamics of Innovation*. New York: Oxford University Press.

Oliver, A. L. and Ebers, M. (1998) 'Networking network studies: an analysis of conceptual configurations in the study of inter-organisational relationships', *Organisation Studies*, 19(4): 594–583.

Oliver, C. (1997) 'Sustainable competitive advantage: combining institutional and resource-based views', *Strategic Management Journal*, 18(9): 697–713.

O'Reilly, C. and Caldwell, D. (1980) 'Job choice: the impact of intrinsic and extrinsic factors on subsequent satisfaction and commitment', *Journal of Applied Psychology*, 65: 559–565.

O'Reilly, C. and Caldwell, D. (1981) 'The commitment and job tenure of new employees: Some evidence of postdecisional justification', *Administrative Science Quarterly*, 26: 597–616.

O'Reilly, C. and Chatman, J. (1996) 'Culture as social control: corporations, culture and commitment', *Research in Organisational Behaviour*, 18: 157–200.

O'Reilly, C. A., Chatman, J. and Caldwell, D. F. (1991) 'People and organisational culture: A profile comparison approach to assessing person–organisation fit', *Academy of Management Journal*, 34(3): 487–516.

Organ, D. W. (1988) *Organisational Citizenship Behaviour: The Good Soldier Syndrome*, Lexington, MA: Lexington Books.

Organ, D. W., Podsakoff, P. M. and MacKenzie, S. B. (2006) *Organisational Citizenship Behavior: Its Nature, Antecedents, and Consequences*, London: Sage.

Orlikowski, W. J. (2002) 'Knowing in practice: Enacting a collective capability in distributed organising', *Organisation Science*, 13(3): 249–273.

Osterman, P. (1987) 'The choice of employment systems in internal labor markets', *Industrial Relations*, 26: 46–67.

Osterman, P. and Burton, M. D. (2005) 'Ports and ladders: the nature and relevance of internal labor markets in a changing world', in P. Tolbert and R. Batt (eds), *Oxford Handbook on Work and Organisation*. Oxford: Oxford University Press.

Ostroff, C. (1992) 'The relationship between satisfaction, attitudes and performance: an organisational level analysis', *Journal of Applied Psychology*, 77: 963–974.

Ostroff, C. and Bowen, D. (2000) 'Moving HR to a higher level: HR practices and organisational effectiveness', in K. Klein and S. Kozlowski (eds), *Multilevel Theory, Research and Methods in Organisations: Foundations, Extensions and New Directions*, San Francisco: Jossey-Bass.

Paauwe, J. (2004) *HRM–performance. Achieving Long Term Viability*, Oxford: Oxford University Press.

Paauwe, J. (2007) 'HRM–performance: in search of balance', Inaugural address, Tilburg University: Tilburg.

Parasuraman, A., Zeithmal, V. A. and Berry, L. L. (1985) 'A conceptual model of service quality and its implications for future research', *Journal of Marketing*, 49: 41–50.

Park, S. H. (1996) 'Managing an interorganisational network: a framework of the institutional mechanism for network control', *Organisation Studies*, 17(5): 795–824.

Pass, S. (2006) *The HR Function Today's Challenges, Tomorrow's Direction*, CIPD: London.

Patterson, M., West, M., Lawthom, R. and Nickell, S. (1997) *Impact of People Management Practices on Business Performance*, London: Institute of Personnel and Development.

Paul, A. and Anantharaman, R. (2003) 'Impact of people management on organisational performance: analysis of a causal model', *International Journal of Human Resource Management*, 14(7): 1246–1266.

Pennings, J. M., Lee, K. and Van Witteloostuijn, A. (1998) 'Human capital, social capital and firm dissolution', *Academy of Management Journal*, 41(4): 425–440.

Peteraf, M. A. (1993) 'The cornerstones of competitive advantage: a resource-based view', *Strategic Management Journal*, 14: 179–192.

Peters, T. and Waterman, R. (1982) *In Search of Excellence*, New York: Harper and Rowe.

Peterson, D. K. (2004) 'The relations between perceptions of corporate citizenship and organisational commitment', *Business and Society*, 43: 296–319.

Pfeffer, J. (1994) *Competitive Advantage Through People*, Boston, MA: Harvard Business School Press.

Pfeffer, J. (1998) *The Human Equation: Building Profits by Putting People First*, Boston, MA: Harvard Business School Press.

Pinfield, L. T. and Berner, M. F. (1994) 'Employment systems: toward a coherent conceptualization of internal labor markets', *Research in Personnel and Human Resources Management*, 12: 41–78.

Podsakoff, P. M., MacKenzie, S. B., Moorman, R. H. and Fetter, R. (1990) 'Transformational leader behaviors and their effects on followers' trust in leader, satisfaction, and organisational citizenship behaviors', *Leadership Quarterly*, 1: 107–142.

Podsakoff, P. M., MacKenzie, S. B., Paine J. B. and Bachrach, D. G. (2000) 'Organisational citizenship behavior: a critical review of the theoretical and empirical literature and suggestions for future research', *Journal of Management*, 26(3): 513–563.

Polanyi, M. (1966) *The Tacit Dimension*, London: Routledge and Kegan Paul.

Porter, L. W., Steers, R. M. and Mowday, R. T. (1974) 'Organisational commitment, job satisfaction and turnover among psychiatric technicians', *Journal of Applied Psychology*, 59(5): 603–609.

Porter, M. (1980) *Competitive Strategy Techniques for Analysing Industries and Competitors*, New York: Free Press.

Porter, M. (1996) 'What is strategy?' *Harvard Business Review*, November–December: 61–78.

Powell, W. (1990) 'Neither market nor hierarchy: Network forms of organisation', *Research in Organisational Behaviour*, 12: 295–336.

Powell, W. W., Koput, K. W. and Smith-Doerr, L. (1996) 'Interorganisational collaboration and the locus of innovation: networks of learning in biotechnology', *Administrative Science Quarterly*, 41: 116–145.

Pratt, M. G. and Foreman, P. O. (2000) 'Classifying managerial responses to multiple organisational identities', *Academy of Management Review*, 25(1): 18–42.

Price, J. L. (1997) *Handbook of Organisational Measurement*, Bradford, UK: MCB University Press.

Priem, R. L. and Butler, J. E. (2001) 'Is the resource-based theory a useful perspective for strategic management research?' *Academy of Management Review*, 26(1): 22–40.

Purcell, J. (1987) 'Mapping management styles in employee relations.' *Journal of Management Studies*, 24: 533–548.

Purcell, J. (1999) 'The search for "best practice" and "best fit": chimera or cul-de-sac?', *Human Resource Management Journal*, 9(3): 26–41.

Purcell, J. and Hutchinson, S. (2007a) 'Front-line managers as agents in the HRM–performance causal chain: theory, analysis and evidence', *Human Resource Management Journal*, 17(1): 3–20.

Purcell, J. and Hutchinson, S. (2007b) *Rewarding Work: the Vital Role of Line Managers*, London: CIPD.

Purcell, J. and Kinnie, N. (2007) 'Human resource management and business performance', in P. Boxall, J. Purcell and P. Wright (eds), *The Oxford Handbook of Human Resource Management*, Oxford: Oxford University Press.

Purcell, J., Purcell, K. and Tailby, S. (2004b) 'Temporary work agencies: here today, gone tomorrow?', *British Journal of Industrial Relations*, 42(4): 705–725.

Purcell, J., Kinnie, N., Hutchinson, S., Rayton, B. and Swart, J. (2003) *Understanding the People and Performance Link: Unlocking the Black Box*, London: Chartered Institute of Personnel and Development.

Purcell, J., Kinnie, N., Hutchinson, S., Swart, J. and Rayton, B. (2004a) *Vision and Values: Culture and Values as Sources of Competitive Advantage*, London: CIPD.

Quinn, J. B. (1992) *Intelligent Enterprise*, New York: Free Press.

Rainnie, A. (1989) *Industrial Relations in Small Firms*, London: Routledge.

Ramsey, H., Scholarios, D. and Harley, B. (2000) 'Employees and high performance work systems: testing inside the black box', *British Journal of Industrial Relations*, 38(4): 501–531.

Rayton, B. (2006) 'Examining the interconnection of job satisfaction and organisational commitment: an application of the bivariate probit model', *International Journal of Human Resource Management*, 17(1): 139–154.

Rayton, B. (forthcoming) 'Transaction cost economics, labor economics and human resource management', in P. G. Klein and M. E. Sykuta (eds), *The Elgar Companion to Transaction Cost Economics*.

Reagans, R. and Zuckerman, E. W. (2001) 'Networks, diversity and productivity: the social capital of corporate R&D teams', *Organisation Science*, 12(4): 502–517.

Redman, T. and Snape, E. (2005) 'Unpacking commitment: multiple loyalties and employee behaviour', *Journal of Management Studies*, 42(2): 301–328.

Reed, M. I. (1996) 'Expert power and control in later modernity: an empirical review and theoretical synthesis', *Organisation Studies*, 17(4): 573–597.

Reich, R. (1991) *The Work of Nations: Preparing Ourselves for 21st Century Capitalism*, London: Simon and Schuster.

Renwick, D. (2003) 'Line manager involvement in HRM: an inside view', *Employee Relations*, 35(3): 262–280.

Rhoades, L. and Eisenberger, R. (2002) 'Perceived organisational support: a review of the literature', *Journal of Applied Psychology*, 87(4): 698–714.

Riketta, M. and Landerer, A. (2005) 'Does perceived threat to organisational status moderate the relationship between commitment and work behaviour?' *International Journal of Management*, 22(2): 193–200.

Ring, P. S. and Van de Ven, A. H. (1994) 'Developmental processes of cooperative interorganisational relationships', *Academy of Management Review*, 19(1): 90–118.

Robinson, S. (1996) 'Trust and the breach of the psychological contract', *Administrative Science Quarterly*, 41(4): 574–599.

Rousseau, D. (1990) 'New hire perceptions of their own and their employer's obligations', *Journal of Organisational Behavior*, 11: 389–400.

Rousseau, D. (1995) *Psychological Contracts in Organisations*, Thousand Oaks, CA: Sage.

Rousseau, D., Sitkin, S., Burt, R. and Camerer, C. (1998) 'Not so different after all: A cross-discipline view of trust', *Academy of Management Review*, 23: 393–404.

Rubery, J., Earnshaw, J., Marchington, M., Cooke, F. L. and Vincent, S. (2002) 'Changing organisational forms and the employment relationship', *Journal of Management Studies*, 39(5): 645–672.

Rubery, J., Carroll, M., Cooke, F. L., Grugulis, I. and Earnshaw, J. (2004) 'Human resource management and the permeable organisation: the case of the multi-client call centre', *Journal of Management Studies*, 41(7): 1199–1222.

Rucci, A. J., Kern, S. P. and Quinn, R. T. (1998) 'The employee–customer–profit chain at Sears', *Harvard Business Review* 76(1): 82–97.

Rumelt, R. (1987) 'Theory, strategy and entrepreneurship', in Teece, D. (ed.), *The Competitive Challenge*, New York: Harper and Row.

Russ, F. A. and McNeilly, K. M. (1995) 'Links among satisfaction, commitment and turnover intentions: the moderating effect of experience, gender and performance', *Journal of Business Research*, 34(1): 57–65.

Ryan, A-M., Schmit, M. and Johnson, R. (1999) 'Attitudes and effectiveness: examining relations at an organisational level', *Personnel Psychology*, 49: 853–882.

Ryle, G. (1949) *The Concept of Mind*, London: Hutchinson.

Sako, M. (1992) *Prices, Quality and Trust: Inter-organisational Relations in Britain and Japan*, Cambridge: Cambridge University Press.

Scarbrough, H. (1999) 'Knowledge as work: conflicts in the management of knowledge workers', *Technology Analysis and Strategic Management*, 11(1): 5–16.

Scarbrough, H. (2000) 'The HR implications of supply chain relationships', *Human Resource Management Journal*, 10(1): 5–18.

Schein, E. (1978) *Career Dynamics Matching Individual and Organisational Needs*, Reading, MA: Addison-Wesley.

Schein, E. (1985) *Organisational Culture and Leadership*, San Francisco: Jossey-Bass.

Schein, E. (1996) 'Culture: the missing concept in organisation studies', *Administrative Science Quarterly*, 41(2): 229–240.

Schuler, R. (1990) 'Repositioning the HR function: transformation or demise?' *Academy of Management Executive*, 4(3): 49–60.

Schuler, R. and Jackson, S. (1987) 'Linking competitive strategies and human resource management practices', *Academy of Management Executive*, 1(3): 207–229.

Scott, S., and Lane, V. (2000) 'A stakeholder approach to organisational identity', *Academy of Management Review*, 25(1): 43–63.

Shaw, M. E. (1981) *Group Dynamics: The Psychology Of Small Group Behavior.* New York: McGraw-Hill.

Sherer, P. D. (1995) 'Leveraging human assets in law firms: human capital structures and organisational capabilities', *Industrial and Labor Relations Review*, 48(4): 671–691.

Sheridan, J. E. (1992) 'Organisational culture and employee retention', *Academy of Management Journal*, 35(5): 1036–1056.

Simon, H., (1951) 'A formal theory of the employment relationship', *Econometrica*, 19(3): 293–305.

Sinclair, D., Hunter, L. and Beaumont, P. (1996) 'Models of customer–supplier relations', *Journal of General Management*, 22(2): 56–75.

Sinclair, R. R., Tucker, J. S., Cullen, J. C. and Wright, C. (2005) 'Performance differences among four organisational commitment profiles', *Journal of Applied Psychology*, 90(6): 1280–1287.

Sisson, K. (1993) 'In search of HRM', *British Journal of Industrial Relations*, 31: 201–210.

Skinner, W. (1981) 'Big hat, no cattle: managing human resources', *Harvard Business Review*, September–October: 106–114.

Smith, C. A., Organ, D. W. and Near, J. P. (1983) 'Organisational citizenship behavior: its nature and antecedents', *Journal of Applied Psychology*, 68(4): 653–663.

Smith, K. G., Collins, C. J. and Clark, K. D. (2005) 'Existing knowledge, knowledge creation capability and the rate of new product introduction in high technology forms', *Academy of Management Journal*, 48(2): 346–357.

Snell, S. A., Youndt, M. A. and Wright, P. M. (1996) 'Establishing framework for research in strategic human resource management: Merging resource theory and organisational learning', in G. R. Ferris (ed.), *Research in Personnel and Human Resource Management:* 61–90. Greenwich, CT: JAI Press.

Sobrero, M. and Schrader, S. (1998) 'Structuring inter-firm relationships: a meta-analytical approach', *Organisation Studies*, 19(4): 585–615.

Spector, P. E. (1997) *Job satisfaction: Application, assessment, cause, and consequences*, Thousand Oaks, CA: Sage Publications.

Starbuck, W. (1992) 'Learning by knowledge-intensive firms', *Journal of Management Studies*, 29(6): 713–740.

Staw, B. M. (1980) 'Rationality and justification in organisational life', in L. L. Cummings and B. M. Staw (eds), *Research in organisational behavior*, 2: 45–80. Greenwich, CT: JAI Press.

Storey, J. (1992) *Developments in the Management of Human Resources*, Oxford: Blackwell.

Storey, J. (1995) *Human Resource Management: A Critical Text*, London: Routledge.

Swart, J. (2006) 'Intellectual capital: disentangling an enigmatic concept', *Journal of Intellectual Capital*, 7(2): 136–159.

Swart, J. (2007) 'HRM and knowledge workers' in P. Boxall, J. Purcell, and P. Wright, (eds), *The Oxford Handbook of Human Resource Management*, Oxford: Oxford University Press.

Swart, J. and Kinnie, N. (2003) 'Knowledge-intensive firms: the influence of the client on HR systems', *Human Resource Management Journal*, 13(3): 37–55.

Swart, J. and Kinnie, N. (2004) *Managing the Careers of Professional Knowledge Workers*, London: CIPD.

Swart, J. and Powell, J. (2004) 'Homogeneity and heterogeneity of knowledge structures' Work in progress.

Swart, J. and Kinnie, N. (2007) 'Simultaneity of learning orientations within a marketing agency', *Management Learning*, 38(3): 337–357.

Swart, J., Kinnie, N. and Purcell, J. (2003) *People and Performance in Knowledge Intensive Firms*, London: CIPD.

Swart, J., Kinnie, N. and Rabinowitz, J. (2007) *Managing Across Boundaries*, London: Chartered Institute of Personnel and Development.

Tajfel, H. and Turner, J. C. (1986) 'The social identity theory of intergroup behaviour', in S. Worchel and W. G. Austin (eds), *Psychology of Intergroup Relations*, 2nd edn, Chicago: Nelson-Hall, pp. 7–24.

Tallman, S., Jenkins, M., Henry, N. and Pinch, S. (2004) 'Knowledge, clusters, and competitive advantage', *Academy of Management Review*, 29(2): 258–271.

Teachman, J. D., Paasch, K. and Carver, K. (1997) 'Social capital and the generation of human capital', *Social Forces*, 75(4): 1343–1359.

Tekleab, A. and Taylor, M. (2003) 'Aren't there two parties in the employment relationship? Antecedents and consequences of organisation–employee agreement on contract obligations and violations', *Journal of Organisational Behavior*, 24: 585–608.

Tepper, B. J. and Taylor, E. C. (2003) 'Relationships among supervisors and subordinates, procedural justice perceptions and organisational citizenship behaviours', *Academy of Management Journal*, 46(1): 97–105.

Terpstra, D. E. and Rozelle, E. J. (1993) 'The relationship of staffing practices to organisational level measures of performance', *Personnel Psychology*, 46: 27–48.

Terry, M. (1977) 'The inevitable growth of informality', *British Journal of Industrial Relations*, 15(1): 76–90.

Thompson, M. (2000) *Final Report: the Bottom Line Benefits of Strategic Human Resource Management*. The UK Aerospace People Management Audit, Oxford: Oxford University Press.

Thurley, K. and Wirdenius, H. (1973) *Supervision: A Re-appraisal*. London: Heinemann.

Truss, K. (2001) 'Complexities and controversies in linking HRM with organisational outcomes', *Journal of Management Studies*, 38(8): 1121–1149.

Tsoukas, H. (1996). 'The firm as a distributed knowledge system: a constructionist approach', *Strategic Management Journal*, 17: 11–25.

Turner, J. C. (1985) 'Social categorisation and the self-concept: Social cognitive theory of group behavior', in E. E. Lawler (ed.), *Advances in group processes*, Greenwich, CT: JAI, pp. 77–122.

Tyson, S. (1987) 'The Management of the Personnel Function', *Journal of Management Studies*, 24(5): 523–532.

Uhl-Bien M, Graen, G. B. (1998) 'Individual self-management: analysis of professionals' self-managing activities in functional and cross functional work teams', *Academy of Management Journal*, 41(1): 340–350.

Uhl-Bien, M. and Maslyn, J. (2003) 'Reciprocity in manager–subordinate relationships: components, configurations and outcomes', *Journal of Management*, 29(4): 511–532.

Uhl-Bien, M., Graen, G. and Scandura, L. (2000) 'Indicators of leader–member exchange (LMX) for strategic human resource management systems', *Research in Personnel and Human Resource Management*, 18: 137–185.

Ulrich, D. (1995) 'Shared services: from vogue to value', *Human Resource Planning*, 18(3): 12–23.

Ulrich, D. (1997) *Human Resource Champions*, Boston, MA: Harvard Business School Press.

Ulrich, D. and Brockbank, W. (2005) *The HR Value Proposition*, Boston MA: Harvard Business School Press.

Uzzi, B. (1996) 'The sources and consequences of embeddedness for economic performance of organisations: the network effect', *American Sociological Review*, 64: 674–698.

Uzzi, B., Lancaster, R. and Dunlap, S. (2007) 'Weighing the worth of social ties: the embeddedness and the price of legal services in the large law firm market', in L. Empson (ed.), *Managing the Modern Law Firm: New Challenges and New Perspectives*, Oxford: Oxford University Press.

Valcour, P. M. and Snell, S. A. (2002) 'The boundaryless career and work force flexibility: developing human and social capital for organisational and individual advantage', Annual Meeting of the Academy of Management, Denver, CO.

Van Deth, J. F. (2003) 'Measuring social capital: orthodoxies and continuing controversies', *International Journal of Social Research Methodology*, 6(1): 79–92.

Vandenberg, R. J. and Lance, C. E. (1992) 'Examining the causal order of job satisfaction and organisational commitment', *Journal of Management*, 18: 153–167.

Veblen, T. (1924) *The Theory of the Leisure Class: An Economic Study of Institutions*. New York.

Verburg, R. M. (1998) 'Human resource management: optimale HRM-praktijken en configuraties', Amsterdam: Vrije universiteit Amsterdam.

Von Glinow, M. A. (1988) *New Professionals: Managing Today's High Technology Employees*, Boston: Addison-Wesley.

Vroom, V. (1964) *Work and Motivation*, Chichester: John Wiley and Sons Ltd.

Wacjman, J. (2000) 'Feminism freeing industrial relations in Britain', *British Journal of Industrial Relations*, 38(2): 183–202.

Wall, T. and Wood, S. (2005) 'The romance of HRM and business performance, and the case for big science', *Human Relations*, 58(4): 29–62.

Wallace, J. E. (1995) 'Corporatist control and organisational commitment among professionals: the case of lawyers working in law firms', *Social Forces*, 73: 811–840.

Walton, R. E. (1985) 'From control to commitment in the workplace', *Harvard Business Review*, 63: March–April: 76–84.

Way, S. (2002) 'High performance work systems and intermediate indicators of firm performance within the US small business sector', *Journal of Management*, 28(6): 765–785.

Wenger, E. (2000) Communities of practice and social learning systems. *Organisation*, 7(2): 225–246.

Wernerfelt, B. (1984) 'A resource-based view of the firm', *Strategic Management Journal*, 5(2): 171–180.

West, M. A., Borrill, C., Dawson, J., Scully, J., Carter, M., Anelay, S., Patterson, M. and Waring, J. (2002) 'The link between the management of employees and patient mortality in acute hospitals', *International Journal of Human Resource Management*, 13(8): 1299–1310.

Westphal, J. D., Seidel, M. L. and Stewart, K. J. (2001) 'Second-order imitation: uncovering latent effects of board network ties', *Administrative Science Quarterly*, 46: 717–747.

White, H. (1980) 'A heteroscedasticity-consistent covariance matrix estimator and a direct test for heteroscedasticity', *Econometrica*, 48: 817–838.

Whitener, E. M. (2001) 'Do "high commitment" human resource practices affect employee commitment? A cross-level analysis using hierarchical linear modelling' *Journal of Management*, 27: 515–535.

Whittaker, S. and Marchington, M. (2003) 'Devolving HR responsibility to the line: threat, opportunity or partnership?' *Employee Relations*, 36(3): 245–261.

Williams, L. J. and Anderson, S. E. (1991) 'Job satisfaction and organisational commitment as predictors of organisational citizenship and in-role behaviors', *Journal of Management*, 17(3): 601–617.

Williamson, O. E. (1979) 'Transaction cost economics: the governance of contractual relations', *Journal of Law and Economics*, 22: 233–261.

Williamson, O. E. 1985. *The Economic Institutions of Capitalism*, New York: Free Press.

Williamson, O. E., Watcher, M. L. and Harris, J. E. (1975) 'Understanding the employment relation: the analysis of idiosyncratic exchange', *Bell Journal of Economics*, 6: 250–278.

Witt, L. A. (1991) 'Exchange ideology as a moderator of job attitudes–organisational citizenship behaviors relationships', *Journal of Applied Social Psychology*, 16: 1490–1502.

Wood, S. (1999) 'Human resource management and performance', *International Journal of Management Reviews*, 1(4): 367–413.

Wood, S. and Albanese, P. (1995) 'Can we speak of high commitment management on the shop floor?', *Journal of Management Studies*, 33(1): 53–77.

Wood, S. and De Menezes, L. (1998) 'High commitment management in the UK: evidence from the Workplace Industrial Relations Survey, and Employers' Manpower and Skills Practices Survey', *Human Relations*, 51(4): 485–515.

Wright, P. and Snell, S. (1998) 'Toward a unifying framework for exploring fit and flexibility in strategic human resource management', *Academy of Management Review*, 23(4): 756–772.

Wright, P. and Gardner, T. M. (2000) *Theoretical and Empirical Challenges in Studying the HR practice–Firm Performance Relationship*. Paper for the European Institute for Advanced Studies in Management.

Wright, P. and Boswell, W. (2002) 'Desegregating HRM: a review and synthesis of micro and macro human resource management research', *Journal of Management*, 28(3): 247–276.

Wright, P. and Gardner, T. (2004) 'The human resource–firm performance relationship: methodological and theoretical challenges', in D. Holman, T. Wall, C. Clegg, P. Sparrow and A. Howard (eds), *The New Workplace: A Guide to the Human Impact of Modern Work Practices*. London: John Wiley.

Wright, P. and Nishii, L. (2004) 'Strategic HRM and organisational behaviour: integrating multiple level analysis', Paper presented at the international seminar on HRM: What next? Erasmus Universiteit, Rotterdam.

Wright, P., McMahan, G. and McWilliams, A. (1994) 'Human resources and sustained competitive advantage: a resource-based perspective', *International Journal of Human Resource Management*, 5(2): 301–326.

Wright, P., Gardner, T. and Moynihan, L. M. (2003) 'The impact of HR practices on the performance of business units', *Human Resource Management Journal*, 13(3): 21–36.

Wright, P., Gardner, T., Moynihan, L. M. and Allen, M. (2005) 'The HR–performance relationship: examining causal direction', *Personnel Psychology*, 58(2): 409–446.

Yoon, M. H., Seo, J. H. and Yoon, T. S. (2004) 'Effects of contact employee supports on critical employee responses and customer service evaluation', *Journal of Services Marketing*, 18(5): 395–412.

Youndt, M., Snell, S., Dean, J. and Lepak, D. (1996) 'Human resource management, manufacturing strategy and firm performance', *Academy of Management Journal*, 39(4): 836–866.

Zuboff, S. (1988) *In the Age of the Smart Machine: The Future of Work and Power*, New York: Basic Books.

Index

ROUTLEDGE INTERNATIONAL HANDBOOKS

This outstanding new series provides a cutting-edge overview of classic research, current research and future trends in the social sciences, humanities and STM.

- each handbook draws together up to 60 newly commissioned chapters to provide a comprehensive overview of a sub-discipline
- the international team of contributors to each handbook have been specially chosen for their expertise and knowledge of each field
- each handbook is introduced and contextualised by leading figures in the field, lending coherence and authority to each volume.

Routledge International Handbooks aim to address new developments, while at the same time providing an authoritative guide to theory and method, the key sub-disciplines and the primary debates of today.

If you would like more information on our ongoing handbooks publishing programme, please contact us.

The Routledge Reference Team
Tel: +44 (0) 20 7017 6169
reference@routledge.co.uk

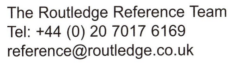

Routledge
Taylor & Francis Group

www.routledge.com/reference

Routledge
Taylor & Francis Group

Business History

Celebrating 50 years

Listed in the ISI Social Science Citation Index
(Business; History of Social Sciences)

New for 2008: Manuscript Central online submission system

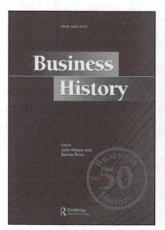

EDITORS:

John Wilson, *University of Central Lancashire, UK*
Steven Toms, *University of York, UK*

Business History is an international journal concerned with the long-run evolution and contemporary operation of business systems and enterprises. Its primary purpose is to make available the findings of advanced research, empirical and conceptual, into matters of global significance, such as corporate organization and growth, multinational enterprise, business efficiency, entrepreneurship, technological change, finance, marketing, human resource management, professionalization and business culture.

The journal has won a reputation for academic excellence and has a wide readership amongst management specialists, economists and other social scientists and economic, social, labour and business historians.

SUBSCRIPTION RATES
2008 - *Volume 50 (6 issues per year)*
Print ISSN 0007-6791
Online ISSN 1743-7938
Institutional rate (print and online): US$826; £486; €661
Institutional rate (online access only): US$784; £461; €627
Personal rate (print only): US$166; £111; €133

informaworld™

A world of specialist information for the academic, professional and business communities. To find out more go to: **www.informaworld.com**

eupdates
Taylor & Francis Group

Register your email address at **www.informaworld.com/eupdates** to receive information on books, journals and other news within your areas of interest.

For further information, please contact Routledge Customer Services at either of the following:
T&F Informa UK Ltd, Sheepen Place, Colchester, Essex, CO3 3LP, UK
Tel: +44 (0) 20 7017 5544 Fax: 44 (0) 20 7017 5198
Email: tf.enquiries@informa.com
Taylor & Francis Inc, 325 Chestnut Street, 8th Floor, Philadelphia, PA 19106, USA
Tel: +1 800 354 1420 (toll-free calls from within the US)
or +1 215 625 8900 (calls from overseas) Fax: +1 215 625 2940
Email: customerservice@taylorandfrancis.com

When ordering, please quote: XF25601A

View an online sample issue at:
www.informaworld.com/BusinessHistory

Accounting, Business & Financial History

An International and Comparative Review

EDITORS:
John Richard Edwards, *Cardiff Business School, UK*
Trevor Boyns, *Cardiff Business School, UK*

Accounting, Business & Financial History is a major journal which covers the areas of accounting history, business history and financial history. As well as providing a valuable international forum for investigating these areas, it aims to explore:

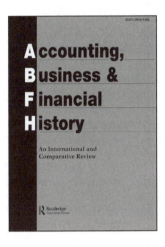

- the inter-relationship between accounting practices, financial markets and economic development.
- the influence of accounting on business decision-making.
- the environmental and social influences on the business and financial world.

The special features of ***Accounting, Business and Financial History*** include:

- an on-going record and analysis of past developments in business and finance history.
- explanations for present structures and practices.
- a platform for solving current problems and predicting future developments.

SUBSCRIPTION RATES
2008- *Volume* 18 (*3 issues per year*)
Print ISSN 0958-5206
Online ISSN 1466-4275
Institutional rate (print and online): US$548; £332; €438
Institutional rate (online access only): US$520; £315; €416
Personal rate (print only): US$188; £111; €150

informaworld

A world of specialist information for the academic, professional and business communities. To find out more go to: **www.informaworld.com**

@updates
Taylor & Francis Group

Register your email address at **www.informaworld.com/eupdates** to receive information on books, journals and other news within your areas of interest.

For further information please visit www.informaworld.com/abf or contact Routledge Customer Services at either:
T&F Informa UK Ltd, Sheepen Place, Colchester, Essex, CO3 3LP, UK
Tel: +44 (0) 20 7017 5544 Fax: +44 (0) 20 7017 5198
Email: tf.enquiries@informa.com
Taylor & Francis Inc, 325 Chestnut Street, 8th Floor, Philadelphia, PA 19106, USA
Tel: +1 800 354 1420 (toll-free calls from within the US)
or +1 215 625 8900 (calls from overseas) Fax: +1 215 625 2940
Email: customerservice@taylorandfrancis.com

When ordering, please quote: XF23201A

View an online sample issue at:
www.informaworld.com/abf

eBooks

eBooks – at www.eBookstore.tandf.co.uk

A library at your fingertips!

eBooks are electronic versions of printed books. You can store them on your PC/laptop or browse them online.

They have advantages for anyone needing rapid access to a wide variety of published, copyright information.

eBooks can help your research by enabling you to bookmark chapters, annotate text and use instant searches to find specific words or phrases. Several eBook files would fit on even a small laptop or PDA.

NEW: Save money by eSubscribing: cheap, online access to any eBook for as long as you need it.

Annual subscription packages

We now offer special low-cost bulk subscriptions to packages of eBooks in certain subject areas. These are available to libraries or to individuals.

For more information please contact webmaster.ebooks@tandf.co.uk

We're continually developing the eBook concept, so keep up to date by visiting the website.

www.eBookstore.tandf.co.uk